The Rise of Western Rationalism

The Rise of
Western Rationalism

Max Weber's Developmental History

Wolfgang Schluchter

Translated, with an introduction, by

Guenther Roth

UNIVERSITY OF CALIFORNIA PRESS

Berkeley · Los Angeles · London

University of California Press
Berkeley and Los Angeles, California
University of California Press, Ltd.
London, England
First published in 1979 by
Verlag J.C.B. Mohr (Paul Siebeck)
© 1981 by The Regents of the University of California
First Paperback Printing 1985
ISBN 0-520-05464-4
Printed in the United States of America

1 2 3 4 5 6 7 8 9

Library of Congress Cataloging in Publication Data

Schluchter, Wolfgang, 1938–

The rise of Western rationalism.

Translation of: Die Entwicklung des
okzidentalen Rationalismus
1. Weber, Max, 1864–1920. 2. History—Philosophy.
3. Rationalism. 4. Historical sociology. 5. Religion
and sociology. 6. Political science—Philosophy.
I. Title.
B3361.Z7S3413   301   81-2763
                          AACR2

"The realm of values is dominated by insoluble conflict, hence by the necessity for continuous compromises. Nobody can definitively decide how the compromises should be made, unless it be a 'revealed' religion." Max Weber in a letter to Robert Wilbrandt, April 2, 1913. Cited by W. J. Mommsen, *Max Weber und die deutsche Politik. 1890-1920.*

CONTENTS

PREFACE

This study does not intend to interpret all of Max Weber's work, but it is a systematic analysis with a methodological and a substantive aspect. Methodologically, I am concerned with Weber's relationship to evolutionism and neo-evolutionism, substantively with the problem of historical rationalization. A systematic perspective must not arbitrarily isolate Weber's major writings from one another. Methodology and substantive sociology must be considered together; the same holds for the sociologies of religion, law, domination and economy from both "parts" of *Economy and Society* and for the studies on the economic ethics of the world religions. The present analysis builds upon and elaborates my previous effort, in *Max Weber's Vision of History*, to explicate Weber's limited evolutionary program and his theory of rationalization on the basis of the sociology of religion alone.

I have benefitted from many discussions and suggestions, which I have not always been able to document. I would like to single out the conference on Weber's theory of rationalization at the University of Constance in 1977 (published by Constans Seyfarth and Walter Sprondel, eds., *Max Weber und das Problem des gesellschaftlichen Handelns*, Stuttgart: Enke, 1981) and the seminar on Weber's value theory and theory of history that I conducted with Dieter Henrich at the University of Heidelberg in 1977. I would also like to mention a discussion with Jürgen Habermas and his staff at the Max Planck Institute at Starnberg in 1978. I have greatly profited from Habermas' forthcoming study on action rationality and system rationality, which I read as a manuscript. Finally, I recall the many conversations I had with Guenther Roth during the writing of the manuscript in the summer of 1978.

Brigitte Schluchter supported the writing of the book in many ways, and I would like to thank her especially.

Heidelberg   Wolfgang Schluchter

Translator's note

Weber's works have been translated since the nineteen twenties. The diversity of the many translators and of their orientations and aims has greatly influenced the translations. It is a fact of scholarly life that a given translation cannot serve all purposes of interpretation equally well. Whenever possible, I have given the English references to Schluchter's many quotations from Weber. However, because of his particular analytical interest and his focus on Weber's "developmental history" I have found myself compelled to retranslate many passages in order to render them more adequately for his purposes. This includes some of my own previous translations. It would have been too cumbersome to indicate the retranslation in the citations. Let the reader be forewarned.

In this English version the introduction and the conclusion have been shortened. The German term *Gesellschaftsgeschichte*, borrowed from the "new social history" in Germany as a label for Weber's approach, has been abandoned by the author and replaced by *Entwicklungsgeschichte*, Weber's own term. It can be accurately and literally rendered as "developmental history."

Professor Caroline W. Bynum and Karen Wayenberg again helped edit the English version. Kai Martin and Barbara Foster efficiently did the difficult work of typing the translation into a word processor.

ABBREVIATIONS

AJ

    Ancient Judaism. Trans. and eds. Hans H. Gerth and Don Martindale. Glencoe: Free Press, 1952. A translation of Part III of "Die Wirtschaftsethik der Weltreligionen," first published in *Archiv für Sozialwissenschaft und Sozialpolitik*, 1917-19; reprinted, with a posthumously published study, "Die Pharisäer," as vol. III of *Gesammelte Aufsätze zur Religionssoziologie.* Tübingen: Mohr, 1920-21.

"Author's Introduction"

    Introduction to vol. I of *Gesammelte Aufsätze zur Religionssoziologie,* trans. Talcott Parsons, in *The Protestant Ethic and the Spirit of Capitalism* (see below), pp. 13-31. (Note that this text is not part of *The Protestant Ethic.*)

ASR

    American Sociological Review.

China

    The Religion of China. Confucianism and Taoism. Trans. and eds. Hans H. Gerth. New edition, with an introduction by C. K. Yang. New York: Macmillan, 1964 (1st ed. Free Press, 1951). A translation of "Konfuzianismus und Taoismus." Part I of "Die Wirtschaftsethik der Weltreligionen," first published in *Archiv für Sozialwissenschaft*, 1915, extensively revised in vol. I of *Gesammelte Aufsätze zur Religionssoziologie.*

ES

    Economy and Society. Eds. Guenther Roth and Claus Wittich; trans. E. Fischoff et al. New York: Bedminster Press, 1968; reissued Berkeley and Los Angeles: University of California Press, 1978. Based on the fourth edition of *Wirtschaft und Gesellschaft* (Tübingen: Mohr, 1956), ed. Johannes Winckelmann. First published in 1921-22.

    Note: All numbers in parenthesis are page references to *Economy and Society.*

India

The Religion of India. Trans. and eds. Hans H. Gerth and Don Martindale. New York: Free Press, 1958. A translation of "Hinduismus und Buddhismus." Part II of "Die Wirtschaftsethik der Weltreligionen," first published in *Archiv für Sozialwissenschaft*, 1916-17, vol. II of *Gesammelte Aufsätze zur Religionssoziologie*.

"Introduction"

"The Social Psychology of the World Religions," *From Max Weber*. Eds. and trans. H. H. Gerth and C. W. Mills. New York: Oxford University Press, 1958, pp. 267-301. A translation of "Einleitung" to "Die Wirtschaftsethik der Weltreligionen," first published in *Archiv für Sozialwissenschaft*, 1915, reprinted in revised form in vol. I of *Gesammelte Aufsätze zur Religionssoziologie*.

PE

The Protestant Ethic and the Spirit of Capitalism. Trans. Talcott Parsons. New York: Scribner, 1958 (first published in 1930). A translation of "Die protestantische Ethik und der Geist des Kapitalismus," *Archiv für Sozialwissenschaft*, 1904-5; reprinted in revised form in vol. I of *Gesammelte Aufsätze zur Religionssoziologie*.

PE II

Die protestantische Ethik II. Kritiken und Antikritiken. Ed. Johannes Winckelmann. Gütersloh: Siebenstern, 1978.

"Objectivity"

"Objectivity in Social Science and Social Policy," *The Methodology of the Social Sciences*. Eds. and trans. Edward A. Shils and Henry A. Finch. Glencoe: Free Press, 1949. A translation of "Die 'Objektivität' sozialwissenschaftlicher und sozialpolitischer Erkenntnis," *Archiv für Sozialwissenschaft*, 1904, reprinted in *Gesammelte Aufsätze zur Wissenschaftslehre* (1922); 2nd rev. ed. by Johannes Winckelmann (Tübingen: Mohr, 1951), pp. 146-214.

"Politics"

"Politics as a Vocation," *From Max Weber*, pp. 77-128. A translation of "Politik als Beruf," *Gesammelte politische Schriften* (1921); 3rd rev. ed. by Johannes Winckelmann (Tübingen: Mohr, 1971), pp. 505-560.

"Science"

"Science as a Vocation," *From Max Weber*, pp. 129-156. A translation of "Wissenschaft als Beruf," *Gesammelte Aufsätze zur Wissenschaftslehre*, pp. 566-597.

"Theory"

"Religious Rejections of the World and Their Directions," *From Max Weber*, pp. 323-362. A translation of "Zwischenbetrachtung: Theorie der Stufen und Richtungen religiöser Weltablehnung," *Archiv für Sozialwissenschaft*, 1915; reprinted in revised form in vol. I of *Gesammelte Aufsätze zur Religionssoziologie*, pp. 536-573.

INTRODUCTION

by Guenther Roth

For Max Weber the "rationalism of world mastery" was the product of a long ethical, religious and institutional development paralleling the "disenchantment" of the world.[1] For us today the course of Western rationalism remains a programmatic as well as historical topic, a matter of theoretical and normative analysis as well as of historical research. Every new generation must come to terms with the legacies and dynamics of Western rationalism, which have brought about a global "world history," the inescapable interdependence of all parts of the world and its irreversible dependence on scientific and technological world mastery. The tremendous costs and dangers of this dependence are clear to most of us. The temptations of cultural pessimism, reconciling us to the "decline of the West," are much greater today than they were in Oswald Spengler and Max Weber's days. If we want to avoid an "ethic of world adjustment," an attitude of accepting the world "as it is," we must reaffirm our historical identity and keep our future conceptually open for some measure of progress. In this regard scholarship is an inherently affirmative activism that is sustained by its own rationalist ethos of intellectual mastery of the world, although it takes place at a great remove from instrumental action in the political and economic spheres. Scholarship subordinates both uplifting speculation and paralyzing despair to the hard work of rethinking our path and situation.

Wolfgang Schluchter's reconstruction of Max Weber's vision of the rise of Western rationalism is a systematic as well as developmental analysis, not an historical narrative, paraphrase or direct normative prescription. It proceeds from the major transformation in contemporary social theory, the evolutionary reconstruction of its two dominant persuasions, structural functionalism and historical materialism, and it ends by making Weber's approach an "upgraded" alternative to both. Schluchter places Weber's sociology as a developmental his-

---

1. See Schluchter, "The Dialectical Development of the Rationalism of World Mastery: Religion and Science," in Roth and Schluchter, *Max Weber's Vision of History: Ethics and Methods* (Berkeley: University of California Press, 1979), pp. 45-59.

tory of the West next to the major neo-evolutionary approaches of the nineteen seventies, the functionalist evolutionism of Talcott Parsons and his most important successor, Niklas Luhmann, as well as the logical evolutionism of Jürgen Habermas, the leading proponent of critical theory. At the same time he rejects the recent reinterpretation by the philosopher and sociologist of culture, Friedrich H. Tenbruck, who claims that Weber must be placed squarely in the camp of evolutionism because he discovered the autonomous logic and historical primacy of religious ideas in shaping Western rationalism.[2]

The renascence of evolutionary theories has been important for empirical and normative social theory—the study of the is and the ought. Let us remember that sociology originated as an evolutionary theory of progress, which inextricably fused empirical and normative components. From Comte to Durkheim and Hobhouse sociology combined empirical and normative theory under the guise of a positive science of society. By contrast, the Marxist science of society suppressed the normative component with the laws of the stages of production, but retained the postulate of the unity of theory and practice through the belief in historical inevitability. Historical evolution, then, was either primarily or 'ultimately' an advance on the cognitive and evaluative levels—as for Comte and Durkheim—or on the material and technological level—as for Marx and the Marxists of Durkheim and Weber's time. The proper understanding of historical evolution was meant to help the actors promote progress. More than half a century ago American social science turned away from the older evolutionary tradition and toward a purely empiricist view of social theory. This stance is still the reigning dispensation today. Through a series of intellectual transmissions and transformations American social science also assimilated Max Weber's position, which on epistemological and historical grounds rejects the explicit fusion of empirical and normative theory in evolutionism and Hegelianism and its unacknowledged fusion in Marxism. Since the nineteen sixties empiricist social theory has been under heavy attack, as champions of normative and critical theory have pressed their claims on a broad front.[3]

When Talcott Parsons published *The Structure of Social Action* in 1937, asking rhetorically "Who now reads Spencer?," he adhered to the division between the normative and the empirical approach. But when he spent the last years of his life on the resurrection and "modernization" of the theory of social evolution, he could not maintain a strict separation. It is inherent in cognitive and

---

2. See Friedrich H. Tenbruck, "The Problem of Thematic Unity in the Works of Max Weber," *British J. of Sociology*, 31 (1980): 313-51; slightly abridged version of "Das Werk Max Webers," *Kölner Zeitschrift für Soziologie*, 27 (1975): 663-702.

3. See Richard J. Bernstein, *The Restructuring of Social and Political Theory* (New York: Harcourt, 1976). See also Jeffrey C. Alexander's critique of Bernstein in "Looking for Theory: 'Facts' and 'Values' as the Intellectual Legacy of the 1970s," *Theory and Society* 10 (1981): 279-292.

evaluative theories of evolution that they imply normative prescription. In addition, Parsons was fully convinced of the evolutionary superiority of modern Western society. His solution to current problems was "more of the same," more differentiation, adaptive upgrading, value generalization and inclusion.[4] Indicative of Parsons' affirmative stance toward Western rationalism is, for instance, his long essay on Christianity in the *Encyclopedia of the Social Sciences*, that infrequently consulted monumental self-portrayal of the social sciences. On balance, Parsons remained more retrospective than prospective, but Niklas Luhmann, the dominant figure in functionalism today, has gone further.[5] He has championed—in Habermas' phrase—a radicalized functionalism, which resolutely severs the link between historical causation and evolution and denies any relationship between the historical and evolutionary levels of analysis. He has introduced the notion of historical contingency to signify that evolutionary processes determine or select themselves. At the end of this line of reasoning lies an extreme 'liberal' version of a modern society that has, so to speak, complete self-control. Luhmann anticipates a functionalist world society in which nation states and their legal and bureaucratic components are overcome. In fact, he considers the political and legal development of the nation-state an evolutionary error. The normative implications of Luhmann's radical functionalism are clear: sociology, as an evolutionary theory, is supposed to become the operative self-awareness of a completely functionalized society, the flexibility of which makes it superior to all earlier societies. Sociology no longer needs history, unless it be for the sake of limiting the arbitrariness of statements of functionalist equivalence. This minimal utility of history has been criticized by Habermas.[6]

4. See statements like the following: "From a comparative and evolutionary perspective, the more privileged societies of the later twentieth century have successfully institutionalized the liberal values of a century ago. . . . The trend has been one of reduction in conspicuous consumption among elite groups. Though not much has happened for a generation, the future trend will be toward greater equality . . . The United States has led the change, but its features will spread through all modern societies . . . The new societal community, conceived as an integrative institution, must operate at a level different from those familiar in our intellectual traditions; it must go beyond command of political power and wealth and of the factors that generate them to value commitments and mechanisms of influence." Talcott Parsons, *The Evolution of Societies* (Englewood Cliffs: Prentice-Hall, 1977), pp. 208ff.

5. Cf. Niklas Luhmann, "Evolution und Geschichte," in *Soziologische Aufklärung 2: Aufsätze zur Theorie der Gesellschaft* (Opladen: Westdeutscher Verlag, 1975), pp. 150-169. For an overview of Luhmann's functionalist and evolutionist theory of society, see Gianfranco Poggi's introduction to Luhmann, *Trust--Power* (London: Wiley, 1979), pp. vii-xix.

6. For Habermas' critique of Luhmann, see "History and Evolution," *Telos*, 39 (1979): 5-44, esp. 26. This essay is a chapter from Habermas, *Zur Rekonstruktion des historischen Materialismus* (Frankfurt: Suhrkamp, 1976). For a previous discussion between the two theorists, see Jürgen Habermas and Niklas Luhmann, *Theorie der Gesellschaft oder Sozialtechnologie?* (Frankfurt: Suhrkamp, 1971).

In contrast to Luhmann, Habermas has more uses for history; he also is unwilling to give up on the causal explanation of the transition from one evolutionary stage to another. He believes that the rationalist and universalist tradition of Marxism remains our most valuable heritage, but argues that historical materialism can be relevant for the future only if it is 'reconstructed' in terms of a cognitive learning theory, which is derived from the developmental psychology of Jean Piaget and Lawrence Kohlberg through the parallelism of ontogenesis and phylogenesis.[7] Analysis must move from the level of the mode of production to the higher level of abstract organizational principles, which constitute an evolutionary sequence. History appears as a collective learning process. Modern societies can survive only if the effectiveness of learning is advanced by reflexive principles. Habermas puts his trust in the possibility of a universal speech ethic, which will make possible rational consensus. In this sense his critical theory is explicitly normative. It has transformed 'scientific socialism' from an empirical ('positivist') theory into a normative ('critical') theory, which provides us with the formal principles for reorganizing society.

Schluchter does not believe that the vast torso of Weber's work, as it lies before us, can directly contribute to the current debates in social theory, unless it is thoroughly reinterpreted. He responds to the neo-evolutionary trends with a comprehensive reconstruction of Weber's sociology—a reconstruction similar in depth to Habermas' reconstruction of historical materialism. Weber's work appears to Schluchter fragmentary not so much because of biographical accidents but because Weber allowed himself too high a degree of discretion in the selection of levels of aggregation and units of analysis. In particular, he did not clearly distinguish the structural from the developmental perspective. Therefore, Schluchter draws on Parsons to identify Weber's implicitly functionalist line of reasoning, insisting that Weber too must deal with the four functions of meaning, protection, want satisfaction and socialization and analyze the four corresponding partial orders: the cultural, political, economic and 'natural' (or 'educational') order. He clarifies the levels of social action and of social order with the help of David Lockwood's distinction between social integration and system integration. He utilizes Luhmann's sequence of segmental, stratified and functional differentiation and his distinction between levels of interaction, organization and society, thus regarding Weber's research program as a multi-level analysis. He relates Habermas' distinction between the general action structures and the core structures of a society to Weber's familiar one between the ordinary and the extraordinary aspects of social life. Crucial for Schluchter is Habermas' notion of 'organizational principles,' highly abstract regulations that describe a society's range of possibilities. An organizational principle consists of

---

7. See Jürgen Habermas, *Communication and the Evolution of Society*, tr. Thomas McCarthy (Boston: Beacon Press, 1979), chs. 3 and 4. These are two more chapters from *Zur Rekonstruktion des historischen Materialismus, op. cit.*

"regulations so abstract that in the social formation which it determines a number of functionally equivalent modes of production are possible."[8] Schluchter argues, however, that this relationship holds not only for the mode of production but also for the modes of domination and the ways in which a society fulfills the functions of meaning and socialization. He adapts Habermas to distinguish between basic configurations of social order and historical variants, a distinction on the level of world views as well as their institutionalization. This allows him to interpret Weber's sociology of domination, for example, in terms of developmental sequences of overarching configurations and subordinate variants. The basic configurations provide the range of possibilities, the variants are the historical articulations. For Schluchter developmental history identifies and explains specific historical sequences in terms of basic social configurations and historical variants. Weber himself does not clearly draw this distinction, but he frequently speaks of "developmental" and "universal" history—a fact downplayed by the extant translations.[9]

Working out the developmental dimension of Weber's sociologies of religion, law and domination is a major task and constitutes the bulk of Schluchter's analysis. Never before has this been done in such a systematic fashion: the sociology of religion yields stages of ethical development: magical 'ethic,' law ethic, ethic of conviction (or of good intentions), and ethic of responsibility. The sociology of law, much neglected in the literature, provides stages of legal norms and principles paralleling the ethical ones, and the sociology of domination, which has so often been studied in isolation, is methodically related to the developmental schemes of the other two sociologies. Schluchter also identifies the developmental aspects of charisma, rejecting the cyclical interpretation of Weber in terms of charismatic innovation and traditionalist or bureaucratic

8. *Op. cit.*, p. 153.

9. The adjective *entwicklungsgeschichtlich* cannot be translated smoothly as "developmental-historical" and therefore appears in English as "historical" or "developmental." Frequently Weber's compound nouns also do not appear in the translations. In *Economy and Society* and "The Economic Ethics of the World Religions" Weber speaks of developmental history, developmental process, developmental conditions, developmental tendencies and developmental stages. For instance, he refers to the developmental history of the modern state, China and the early Christian church. It seems that for Weber every world view and institution has a developmental history—the record of its structural changes and transformations.

The adjective *universalgeschichtlich* is also difficult to translate. Usually it is not identical with "world-historical." In the terminology of Weber's time "universal history" contrasts with specialized history. It refers to a synthetic effort to portray and analyze the history of an historical era or cultural area. Thus, Weber calls Eduard Meyer a universal historian of antiquity and Ernst Troeltsch a universal historian of Christianity. In the course of the writing of *Economy and Society* Weber began to call his developmental analysis "my sociology." On November 6, 1913, he wrote to his publisher about analytical innovations in his handbook: "This is also true of my 'sociology'—that's what my part is becoming, although I could never call it by that name."

routinization and explaining in what manner the "charisma of reason" is the end product of charismatic development.[10]

Although most of Schluchter's analysis deals with Weber's empirical social theory—the framework of sequential typologies constitutive of developmental history—his elaboration also has normative implications. As in the case of the other three theorists, the prescriptive sphere is entered when the evolutionary or developmental scheme reaches modernity, of which the present is a 'moving part.' When we change, in Hermann Lübbe's terms, from historical subjects into historical actors in the present, retrospection must be supplemented by formal prescription.[11] For Schluchter, the ethic of responsibility is a new basic configuration in its own right, not just another variant of the older ethic of conviction. As such it is not just a historical phenomenon originating in the 18th century, but remains the normative challenge of our times. Whereas Weber's distinction between the ethic of conviction and the ethic of responsibility was rudimentary and ambiguous, Schluchter has elaborated and integrated it into a theory of ethical development.

Schluchter's normative interests emerged already, and more explicitly, in his earlier essay on "Value-Neutrality and the Ethic of Responsibility," which was a stepping stone for his developmental reconstruction of Weber's sociology in the present work.[12] In both works his strategy has been to argue with Weber and against him and to extract the normative implications in the face of Weber's own insistence on separating fact and value, the empirical and the normative sciences. Schluchter's interest in the complex relationship between empirical and normative theory goes back to his study of a major constitutional theorist of the Weimar period, the socialist Hermann Heller, who tried to integrate again normative and positive legal theory, which had been sundered by Weber's friend Georg Jellinek in his famous *General Theory of the State* of 1900.[13] It was Weber who carried Jellinek's separation to its logical conclusion with his sociology of domination as the study of the empirical validity of legitimating beliefs and the consequences of institutionalization. Weber credited Jellinek with clarifying for him "the blurred tasks of sociology" with his notion of the "social theory of the state." Sociology was to deal with empirical validity, in contrast with the normative sciences.[14] Of course, for Schluchter too this separa-

10. Cf. my discussion in "The Charisma of Reason and the Impact of Marxism," Roth and Schluchter, *op. cit.*, pp. 132ff.

11. Cf. Hermann Lübbe, *Geschichtsbegriff und Geschichtsinteresse: Analytik und Pragmatik der Historie* (Basel: Schwabe, 1977), p. 169.

12. See ch. II of Roth and Schluchter, *op. cit.*; the essay was first published in 1971.

13. See Schluchter, *Entscheidung für den sozialen Rechtsstaat: Hermann Heller und die staatstheoretische Diskussion in der Weimarer Republik* (Cologne: Kiepenheuer, 1968); Georg Jellinek, *Allgemeine Staatslehre* (Bad Homburg: Gehlen, 1966), third ed.

14. See my essay on "The Genesis of the Typological Approach," in Reinhard Bendix and Roth, *Scholarship and Partisanship* (Berkeley: University of California Press, 1971), esp. pp. 260ff.

tion is constitutive of modernity. The normative challenge lies exactly in how to demonstrate that the ethic of responsibility in politics and the postulate of freedom from practical value-judgment in science are the ethically and institutionally appropriate positions for contemporary society and define the adequate relationship between politics and science. However, Schluchter limits his argument to the level of developmental history and does not attempt a philosophical foundation of the ethic of responsibility. In this respect, he differs from Habermas, who believes that he can integrate a developmental theory of cognition with a philosophical justification of critical theory.

For Weber, sociology was concerned not only with the empirical validity of beliefs, in contrast to the normative sciences (law, ethics, aesthetics); it was also concerned with generalizations rather than particularities, in contrast to history. In his well-known formulation, sociology deals with the construction of type concepts and searches for general uniformities within the stream of events, in contrast to "history, which aims at the causal analysis and causal attribution of individual actions, structures and personalities that have cultural significance." Sociology, however, remains in some respects Clio's handmaiden: it "proceeds especially according to considerations of the service it can render through its concept formation to the causal attribution of culturally significant phenomena."[15]

In an essay, which is one of Schluchter's reference points, I tried to identify three levels of historical analysis in Weber's diverse writings: configurational, developmental and situational. The first is the level of socio-historical models or typologies and thus of 'historical sociology.' The second is the level of secular theories, the description of the course of particular phenomena and the explanation of their genesis and consequences.[16] Here we find Weber's studies "On the History of the Medieval Trading Companies" (1889) and "The Protestant Ethic and the Spirit of Capitalism" (1904/5). On the third level Weber comes closest to the historical events and the historical actors—witness some of his writings on Imperial Germany and Imperial Russia.[17] The purpose of my statement was to suggest "practical" applications of Weber's historical sociology, for instance, how concepts such as patrimonialism and charismatic community

15. *ES*, p. 19.
16. See "Socio-historical Model and Secular Theory," Roth and Schluchter, *op. cit.*, pp. 124ff. My usage of the term 'developmental' for the level of secular theory does not fit Schluchter's usage. For him Weber's developmental history refers to the whole history of the West. Therefore, I should like to add to my previous statement that Weber's developmental history can be viewed as a configurational enterprise, insofar as it involved a sequence of typologies; it can also be viewed as one vast secular theory, insofar as it views Western rationalism as one historical case. However, there are many temporally limited secular theories in Weber's writings, which I had in mind. The secular theories of the Protestant ethic or of the rise of Marxism encompass several decades and several generations.
17. Cf. "Epilogue," *op. cit.*, pp. 195-206.

can be applied to contemporary phenomena around the world. This pragmatic interest is appropriate for sociologists, who live mostly by the study of the present. However, sociologists eager to mine Weber's work like a quarry in search of 'usable' concepts and hypotheses and historians eager to immerse themselves in particular cases can easily misperceive his intentions. Schluchter has now gone back to the fact that Weber's sociology is first of all a developmental theory of the West, an attempt to make sense out of thousands of years of history. *Economy and Society, The Agrarian Sociology of Ancient Civilizations* and the volumes on "The Economic Ethics of the World Religions" are long-range analyses spanning millennia and arise out of the evolutionary and typological tradition of economic history, constitutional theory and comparative religion.[18] These works are not primarily genetic explanations. Their concerns are quite different from much of the current "new history" that operates on the level of secular theories—witness the Marxist narrative histories of Perry Anderson and Immanuel Wallerstein.[19] Today the proper partner for Weber's developmental history is indeed neo-evolutionary theory because both deal with historical development as a whole, divisible into the progression of a small number of stages or phases.

18. See *The Agrarian Sociology of Ancient Civilizations*, tr. R. I. Frank (London: New Left Books, 1976). The English title of this massive 1909 study is as awkward as the German, literally translated as "The Agrarian Conditions of Antiquity." The title, which hides a developmental history of economy and polity in antiquity, was retained from a first very brief version in the *Handwörterbuch der Staatswissenschaften* of 1897.

19. Anderson and Wallerstein's focus on secular theory is indicated by the very titles of their books, which refer to "passages," "lineages," "origins" and "consolidation." See Perry Anderson, *Passages from Antiquity to Feudalism* and *Lineages of the Absolutist State* (London: New Left Books, 1974) and Immanuel Wallerstein, *The Modern World System I. Capitalist Agriculture and the Origins of the European World-Economy in the Sixteenth Century* and *The Modern World System II. Mercantilism and the Consolidation of the European World-Economy, 1600-1750* (New York: Academic Press, 1974 and 1980). Significantly, Anderson has use only for Weber's secular theories, not for his developmental history. He admires his "historical theory" of antiquity, which involves a controversial explanation of the rise and fall of the slave economy and of the capitalist exploitation of the conquered areas; but he believes that "after his pioneering early work on Antiquity . . . the notorious weaknesses of the notion of 'ideal-types' characteristic of his later work" (i.e., *Economy and Society*) left Weber bereft of "any historical theory proper," especially about the Middle Ages and modern history (*Lineages*, p. 410). Wallerstein, too, uses Weber only on the level of economic history. Using a terminology differing from mine, Randall Collins recently attempted a reconstruction of Weber's secular theory of capitalism and concluded that "it is the most comprehensive general theory of the origins of capitalism that is yet available. It continues to stand up well in comparison with recent theories, including Wallerstein's historical theory of the capitalist world-system. . . .Weber's model continues to offer a more sophisticated basis for a theory of capitalism than any of the rival theories of today." "Weber's Last Theory of Capitalism: A Systematization," *ASR*, 45 (1980): 926.

Like evolutionary theories, developmental history is a historical synthesis in its own right and conceptualized above *l'histoire événementielle*. It is a structural approach of a particular kind and cannot be directly applied to the causal explanation of specific historical events.[20] It is true that Weber was ultimately interested in a causal explanation of the uniqueness of modern Western rationalism, and Schluchter therefore properly devotes his last chapter to Weber's treatment of the Reformation in "The Protestant Ethic and the Spirit of Capitalism" and in his later developmental studies. In German Schluchter's chapter is titled "The Historical Problem of Explanation: The Role of the Reformation in the Transition to Modernity." It is important to understand clearly the nature of Weber's historical explanation. Causal attributions are made on the basis of ideal-typical comparisons and a mental experiment that assumes the logic of objective possibility. The explanations are couched in terms of "factors" influencing one another or operating next to one another. "The Protestant Ethic and the Spirit of Capitalism" puts the two phenomena indicated by the title in a time sequence and links them through a causal hypothesis. This was a specific historical problem on the level of secular theory; Weber spoke of "an essay in cultural history." His logic of explanation, however, remained the same on the level of socio-historical model or configuration as on that of secular theory. He thought in terms of an array of causal factors on the structural level, not in terms of concrete historical relationships on the action level—their study requires in each case highly detailed research. Significantly, Weber did not choose to follow up "The Protestant Ethic and the Spirit of Capitalism" with a study of specific generational sequences among religious, economic and political groups to reinforce his case for the causal significance of ascetic Protestantism for the spirit of capitalism and of depersonalization;[21] nor did he try to relate closely the various "material" and "spiritual" factors. Instead of moving toward the history of events, Weber enlarged the scope of developmental history on the basis of intercivilizational comparisons. In this perspective ascetic Protestantism reveals its uniqueness by comparison with the other forms of Christianity and other world religions. It appears as a singular blend of theocentrism, asceticism, this-world-

20. See my essay on "Duration and Rationalization: Fernand Braudel and Max Weber," *Max Weber's Vision of History, op. cit.*, pp. 166-93.

21. This has been attempted, in different ways, by Little and Marshall. See David Little, *Religion, Order, and Law: A Study in Pre-Revolutionary England* (New York: Harper, 1969) and Gordon Marshall, *Presbyteries and Profits: Calvinism and the Development of Capitalism in Scotland, 1560-1707* (Oxford: Clarendon Press, 1980). If Little and Marshall undertake a secular analysis, Steven Ozment presents a situational analysis of the Reformation. See Steven E. Ozment, *The Reformation in the Cities: The Appeal of Protestantism to Sixteenth-Century Germany and Switzerland* (New Haven: Yale University Press, 1975). In Ozment's close-up view the introduction of the Reformation appears as a matter of many small steps, gradually changing theological positions and the balance of power.

liness, good works and virtuosity. Following Weber, Schluchter argues that "only this combination creates the religious motivation for world mastery." Thus, ascetic Protestantism is said to produce a certain kind of motivation and therefore of causal efficacy. Conversely, its absence in China and India "explains," among other factors, the failure of these civilizations to develop anything approaching modern Western rationalism. This is an explanation on the level of "logics." Motivation appears as an attribute of a factor having an inner logic, not of real people.

As a critic of the organicist and functionalist analogies of his time, Weber insisted that only actors act in history and championed a methodological individualism. In any given historical situation people act on the basis of world views as well as of material and ideal interests, but in developmental history the logic behind the world views and institutions appears as the rationale of action. We do not ever see people act, neither 'great men' nor 'the masses,' and historical figures usually appear merely as typological illustrations.

In the balance of Weber's writings, then, typological and developmental constructs are dominant. This quality of his work has little to do with its unfinished and programmatic character but much with the intellectual tradition and the literary genre in which it was located. Although Weber created his developmental history as a critique of the evolutionary theories of his time, we must remember that *Economy and Society* builds on the theories of economic development proposed by the economic historians Karl Bücher, Gustav von Schmoller and Gustav Schönberg. *Economy and Society* owes its existence to Weber's decision to replace the latter's three-volume edition of the *Handbook of Political Economy* with a multi-volume edition.[22] For these three institutional economists theory meant basically typological stages; the causal analysis of the transition was left to the historical specialist. As a representative of the older evolutionary tradition, Bücher had a notion of 'necessary causality'—the economic stages were necessary sequences, if only in western and central Europe. The historical transitions, which could take hundreds of years, were a problem of a different kind of causality. There was a 'lawlike' causality as far as the sequence of stages was concerned, but the actual transition depended on contingent causes, the study of which was up to the historical specialist: "The construction of such 'economic stages' is from the point of method indispensable. It is indeed only in this way that economic theory can turn to account the results of the investigations of economic history. But these stages of development are not to be confused with the time periods of the historian. The historian must not forget to relate in any period everything important that occurred in it, while for his stages the theorist need notice only the normal, simply ignoring the accidental. In the

22. Cf. Gustav Schönberg, ed., *Handbuch der politischen Oekonomie* (Tübingen: Laupp, 1882), 3 vols., third ed. 1890/1. See esp. vol. 1 (1890), pp. 27-46: "The Economic Stages in the History of the Economy."

course of the gradual transformation which all economic phenomena and institutions undergo and which often encompasses centuries, it is inevitable that development is faster in some regions than in others. For the historian such abnormal phenomena can appear particularly important. However, the theorist is only concerned with the main phases of the total development. The so-called transitional periods, in which all phenomena are in a state of flux, must be disregarded. The theorist deals only with developmental stages and their laws of development."[23]

Weber rejected the notion of 'necessary' and 'lawlike' causality in favor of historical contingency, the paradox of consequences and the method of causal attribution; and he also pushed aside Bücher's simple typology. Moreover, he objected to the very free mixing of moral evaluation and exhortation and of empirical statement in the economic literature. But insofar as its treatment was empirical, he followed up the analysis of ethical and religious issues. He also advanced beyond the exposition of public administration in these handbooks and textbooks and formulated his model of bureaucracy.[24] A comparison shows not only Weber's evaluative self-restraint but also his superiority in systematic and substantive regards. *Economy and Society* offered a "complete theory and exposition" *(Theorie und Darstellung)* as a statement of the general historical relationships between economic and social organization and of the general developmental direction of changes ('rationalization'). Weber transformed the genre of economic stage theory and economic history not only through his alternative conception of causality but also through the manner in which he systematically analyzed the spheres of religion, law, domination and economy as well as their relationships. He was fully aware of his innovation. On December 30, 1913, he wrote to his publisher, Paul Siebeck: "Since Bücher's treatment of the 'developmental stages' is totally inadequate, I have worked out a complete theory and exposition that relates the major social groups to the economy: from the family and household to the enterprise, the kin group, ethnic community, religion (comprising all religions of the world: a sociology of salvation doctrines

23. Carl Bücher, *Industrial Evolution* (New York: Holt, 1907), p. 85f. First published in 1893. For Schmoller's priority claims, dating back to 1884, with regard to the theory of economic stages, see his *Grundriss der allgemeinen Volkswirtschaftslehre* (Leipzig: Duncker and Humblot, 1923), II, p. 765. Schmoller also laid claim to having pioneered the linkage of economic and administrative history.

24. Contrary to a widespread misunderstanding, Weber did not simply invent the ideal type of bureaucracy. He systematized features familiar in the field of public administration. See, e.g., the sections by Georg Meyer, "Basic Concepts, Nature and Tasks of Public Administration" (pp. 791ff.) and "The Organization of Internal Administration" (pp. 823ff.) in Schönberg, *op. cit.*, vol III (1891). See also Lorenz von Stein, *Handbuch der Verwaltungslehre* (Stuttgart: Cotta, 1888), 3rd rev. ed., pp. 38-68; Max von Heckel, "Besoldung und Besoldungspolitik," *Handwörterbuch der Staatswissenschaften*, 3rd ed. (1909). Gustav Schmoller, "Der deutsche Beamtenstaat vom 16. bis 18. Jahrhundert," *Umrisse und Untersuchungen* (Leipzig: Duncker, 1898), pp. 289-313.

and of the religious ethics—what Troeltsch did, but now for all religions, if much briefer), finally a comprehensive sociological theory of state and domination. I can claim that nothing of the kind has ever been written, not even as a precursor."[25]

Friedrich Tenbruck considers it inconceivable that Weber should have poured his major intellectual energies into the production of handbook articles and has therefore sought the core of his discoveries in the essays on the economic ethics of the world religions, but these were intended, after all, as supplements to *Economy and Society*. The fact remains that *The Agrarian Sociology of Ancient Civilizations*, which includes Weber's theory of ancient capitalism, appeared in the famous third edition of the *Handwörterbuch der Staatswissenschaften* and that *Economy and Society* was conceived as part of the *Handbook of Political Economy*, which was published under the final title *Outline of Social Economics*. The handbook article, not the research monograph, was the literary vehicle for Weber's most substantive writings. It pointed him in the direction of theoretical and historical synthesis, and he fully met the challenge. Insofar as the external form threatened to be a constraint, his intellectual originality and inventiveness made him break through it and produce the unwieldly, hard-to-read "articles" on which much of his fame rests.

It is the purpose of handbook articles to integrate a given state of knowledge, not to narrate history, decide specific historical issues or elaborate a theory. Readers approach a handbook with their own questions and interests and carry its suggestions in different directions. This is what Schluchter has done in the context of the renascence of evolutionary theory. It would be a mistake to conclude from the German names of some of the theorists addressed—Habermas, Luhmann and Tenbruck—that the issues involved are mostly "querelles d'Allemand" in the literal or proverbial sense. American social theory, especially structural functionalism, had considerable impact in West Germany after the Second World War, and in the seventies critical theory, especially the work of

25. In the quotation Weber refers to a manuscript that Bücher submitted to him as editor of the *Outline of Social Economics*. In his preface Schluchter warns against arbitrarily isolating Weber's major works from one another and pleads for viewing together both "parts" of *ES* and the supplementary studies on the economic ethics of the world religions. Recently our knowledge of the origins of *ES* and of its tortuous course of composition and assembly has improved, since the correspondence between Weber and his publisher, Paul Siebeck, was made available by the publishing firm of C. B. Mohr to the editors and staff of the projected *Max Weber Gesamtausgabe*, the complete edition of Weber's writings and speeches. A preliminary impression from this correspondence, which Schluchter cites at various points, is that Weber may in the end not have intended *ES* to stand the way it appears to us today. In my view, it is fortunate that both "parts," the older and the younger manuscript, have come down to us. However, on the basis of the correspondence, the established view becomes dubious that Weber intended to put a set of definitions in the younger Part I before the more descriptive exposition of the older Part II. See my essay "Abschied oder Wiedersehen?," *Kölner Zeitschrift für Soziologie*, 31 (1979): 318-27.

Jürgen Habermas, was given much attention in the United States. Presently more of the writings of Niklas Luhmann are becoming available in English.[26] Despite some continuing national traditions, there is a viable transatlantic universe of discourse. Habermas, Luhmann and Schluchter are important participants in it and draw equally on American and European literature. By looking back to Weber and forward to unresolved issues, Schluchter offers an agenda for the advance of social theory in the nineteen eighties.

26. See Niklas Luhmann, *The Differentiation of Society*, tr. Stephen Holmes and Charles Larmore (New York: Columbia University Press, 1981).

I

INTRODUCTION

The study of social development is guided mainly by two perspectives, the evolutionary and the comparative.[1] Under the first perspective history is interpreted with the help of a theory of stages. As a rule, stage theories assume that a higher stage emerges from a lower one and 'preserves' its achievements. Therefore, evolutionary theorists speak of one social development, which appears to them necessary, continuous and cumulative. They differ in terms of the developmental dimensions they select, the units they view as carriers of development, the number of stages they perceive and the directional criteria they emphasize. Other differences depend on whether they separate structural development from the history of events and whether they advance retrospective or also prospective claims. Evolutionary theories in this sense are found today especially in Marxism, diachronic functionalism and a sociological version of genetic structuralism.[2]

1. I distinguish between personnel change, social change and social development. Personnel change takes place when the top personnel in a social structure is replaced without any structural repercussions. Examples are palace revolts and coups d'état. Social change occurs when a social order is transformed into another but still operates under the same basic social configuration. For example, patrimonialism may change into sultanism or feudalism. Social development occurs when a basic configuration of social order changes. The major instance is the transition from tradition to modernity. Thus, I distinguish between basic social configurations and their historical variants in order to identify the systematic location of developmental questions in sociology. In my view, developmental history deals with the change of basic social configurations.

2. Cf. Urs Jaeggi and Axel Honneth, eds., *Theorien des historischen Materialismus* (Frankfurt: Suhrkamp, 1977), esp. Part I. On the methodology of a functionalist theory of evolution, see Niklas Luhmann, "Evolution und Geschichte," in *Soziologische Aufklärung* 2 (Opladen: Westdeutscher Verlag, 1975), pp. 150-69; "Differentiation of Society," *The Canadian J. of Sociology*, 2 (1977): 29-54; "Generalized Media and the Problem of Contingency," in J. Loubser et al., eds., *Explorations in General Theory in Social Science:* Essays in Honor of Talcott Parsons (New York: Free Press, 1976), II, pp. 507-532; *Trust—Power*, with an introduction by Gianfranco Poggi (London: Wiley, 1979). Talcott Parsons' writings from the 1960s are also pertinent: "Evolutionary Universals in Society," *ASR*, 29 (1964): 339—57; *Societies. Evolutionary and Comparative Perspectives* (Englewood Cliffs,

From the comparative viewpoint history is interpreted with the help of a theory of alternatives. As a rule, typical cases are contrasted. Therefore, comparativists speak of several social developments, which are relatively independent of one another. They also believe that no scientific statement can be made about the relative value of these cases. Comparativists differ in terms of the cases they choose and the criteria they apply. Theories of alternatives are today found especially among representatives of so-called historical sociology.[3]

There are considerable tensions between the evolutionary and the comparative perspective. These arise not only from substantive and methodological divergences but also from differences about the very purpose of sociology. From the perspective of evolutionary theory historical sociology ultimately leads to a sociological historism that dissolves sociology conceptually into type atomism and substantively into an arbitrary number of descriptions. From the perspective of historical sociology evolutionary theories ultimately reveal themselves as philosophies of history.[4] Today evolutionary theory tends to be anti-historical, historical sociology to be anti-evolutionary.

N. J.: Prentice-Hall, 1966); *The System of Modern Societies* (Englewood Cliffs, N. J.: Prentice-Hall, 1971). On the sociological version of genetic structuralism, see Jürgen Habermas, *Communication and the Evolution of Society*, tr. Thomas McCarthy (Boston: Beacon Press, 1979); "History and Evolution," *Telos*, 39 (1979): 5-44 (a reply to Luhmann's "Evolution und Geschichte," *op. cit.*). Klaus Eder, *Die Entstehung staatlich organisierter Gesellschaften* (Frankfurt: Suhrkamp, 1976); Jaeggi and Honneth, *op. cit.*, Part IV.

3. See esp. Ernst Schulin, ed., *Universalgeschichte* (Cologne: Kiepenheuer, 1974) and his introduction to the volume. Major studies that replace general evolutionary theory with the comparative analysis of historical structures are found in different traditions, from Tocqueville to Hintze, from Marc Bloch to Barrington Moore. They include the analysis of "great transformations." See also the writings of Reinhard Bendix, *Nation-Building and Citizenship* (New York: Wiley, 1964, rpt. Berkeley: U. of California Press, 1977) and *Kings or People: Power and the Mandate to Rule* (Berkeley: U. of California Press, 1978).

4. The "classic" critique of the various versions of historical teleology and objectivism remains Karl R. Popper, *The Poverty of Historicism* (London: Routledge and Kegan Paul, 1954) and the *The Open Society and Its Enemies* (London: Routledge and Kegan Paul, 1945). Popper's more recent work shows that his critique does not deny the rationale of evolutionary theory. See *Objective Knowledge: An Evolutionary Approach* (New York: Oxford, 1972).

Reinhard Bendix was one of the first critics of the reemergence of evolutionary theory in the works of such writers as Clark Kerr and Talcott Parsons in the late fifties and early sixties ("neo-evolutionism"). See *Nation-Building and Citizenship*, *op.cit.*, p. 10; "The Comparative Analysis of Historical Change," in Bendix and Roth, *Scholarship and Partisanship: Essays on Max Weber* (Berkeley: U. of California Press, 1971), chapter XI. Although Bendix belongs to the most severe critics of the evolutionary approach, which he traces from Marx to Daniel Lerner in the field of modernization theory, he leaves no doubt that "studies of social change are not possible without a 'before-and-after' model of the social structure in question." See *Embattled Reason* (New York: Oxford University Press, 1970), p. 280; on the methodology of comparative research see esp. pp. 175ff. and 250ff.

Max Weber is usually depicted as founder of an historical sociology that rejects evolutionism and the philosophy of history. His introduction to the *Collected Essays in the Sociology of Religion* supports this interpretation. There he argues that he wants to compare the world religions in their individuality and to refrain from arranging them in a sequence: "In no respect can one simply integrate various world religions into a chain of types, each of them signifying a new 'stage.' All the great religions are historical individualities of a highly complex nature; taken together, they exhaust only a few of the possible combinations that could conceivably be formed from the very numerous individual factors to be considered in such historical combinations."[5] In his studies on the methodology of *Kulturwissenschaft* as historical social science Weber is emphatically critical of an approach toward the relation between theory and history which he considers untenable but which all too frequently appears in the analysis of social development. Not only many evolutionists but also historians tend "to interpret the sequence of types which results from the chosen criteria . . . as a lawfully determined historical sequence." Thus, the logical ordering of concepts is conflated with, or mistaken for, "the empirical phenomena in time and space and their causal relationship" in such a way that these constructs appear even as "real (that is, metaphysical) 'forces,' 'tendencies,' etc."[6] Of course, Weber too resorts to developmental constructs in his sociology and emphasizes time and again their heuristic importance. But they have only instrumental value for him. They are means "for achieving, in a methodical way, the valid identification of the real causes of an historical event from among those possible according to the state of our knowledge."[7] No doubt, directional criteria play also a crucial role in Weber's developmental constructs. With regard to ancient Judaism and its cultural significance for Western modernity we can ask: "1. Were certain Judaic conceptions more or less archaic ('primitive') compared to the stages we find in the development of other religions? 2. Were they more or less intellectualized and rationalized (in the sense of eliminating magical notions)? 3. Were they more or less systematized? or 4. more or less sublimated in the direction of an ethic of conviction" than is true of other conceptions in their immediate or farther historical environment?[8]

However, whatever directional criteria we may select, they will at best lead, in Ernest Nagel's terminology, to characterizing, not to appraising value judgments.[9] If we rank, for instance, the Mosaic conception of God and the ethic of the Decalogue in terms of "higher" and "lower" stages, we cannot draw any conclusion about their higher or lower overall developmental potential or about their superiority or inferiority compared to other conceptions. Developmental constructs of this kind serve the typological identification of this conception of

    5. "Introduction," p. 292.   6. "Objectivity," p. 103.   7. *Op. cit.*, p. 102.
    8. *AJ*, p. 426.
    9. Ernest Nagel, "The Value-Oriented Bias of Social Inquiry," *The Structure of Science* (New York: Harcourt, 1961), p. 492f.

divinity and ethics within a comparative perspective. Therefore, the criteria employed do not point to a developmental path that must or should be taken by every religion or society. Weber's work can be viewed as the gigantic effort to refute the basic assumptions of every kind of evolutionism. Reinhard Bendix, Guenther Roth and Johannes Winckelmann have emphasized this point with good reason.[10] Winckelmann has even gone one step further. He has labeled Weber's sociology a "structural phenomenology of world history."[11] However, this interpretation has not gone unchallenged. Friedrich H. Tenbruck, among others, has championed a different view.[12] He uncovers in Weber's writings an evolutionary perspective, especially in his sociology of religion. According to Tenbruck, Weber was concerned not merely with identifying a "process of rationalization that permeates all of European history" but with discovering a general "rationale" of development, which he located in the autonomous logic of religious world views, in their inherent drive toward rationalization.[13] It is true that as an historical force this logic always remained precarious, but in the long run it prevailed over other historical forces, at least in the West. This, then, appears as the key to Western rationalization, which Weber divided into a phase of religious disenchantment and a phase of modernization based on science, economy and politics.

This interpretation has a number of intriguing aspects. First, it maintains at least implicitly that Weber advanced not only a theory of the genesis and development of modern Western culture but also a theory of the genesis and development of all culture. Second, it claims—and this can be demonstrated textually—that Weber reified the ideal-typical procedure at least insofar as the

10. Cf. Reinhard Bendix, *Max Weber: An Intellectual Portrait* (Berkeley: U. of California Press, 1977); Bendix and Roth, *op. cit.*, esp. Chapters IV, VI, XI, XIII; Roth, "Introduction" to *Economy and Society* (Berkeley: U. of California Press, 1978), XXXV; Johannes Winckelmann, "Max Weber—das soziologische Werk," *Kölner Zeitschrift für Soziologie*, 17 (1965): 743-90.; "Max Webers Verständnis von Mensch und Gesellschaft," Karl Engisch et al., eds., *Max Weber Gedächtnisschrift* (Berlin: Duncker and Humbolt, 1966), p. 195-243.; *Erläuterungsband* (Tübingen: Mohr, 1976), Winckelmann's volume of annotations to *Wirtschaft und Gesellschaft*.

11. Winckelmann, "Vorbemerkung," *Erläuterungsband, op. cit.*

12. Friedrich H. Tenbruck, "Das Werk Max Webers," *Kölner Zeitschrift für Soziologie*, 27 (1975): 663-702. For the slightly abridged English version see "The Problem of Thematic Unity in the Works of Max Weber," *British J. of Sociology*, 31 (1980): 313-51. Tenbruck includes his own earlier writings in this challenge (cf. p. 695). For a critique of Tenbruck, see Martin Riesebrodt, "Ideen, Interessen, Rationalisierung," *Kölner Zeitschrift für Soziologie*, 32 (1980): 109-129: Johannes Winckelmann, "Die Herkunft von Max Webers Entzauberungskonzeption," *Kölner Zeitschrift für Soziologie*, 32 (1980): 12-53.

Before Tenbruck, Parsons attempted to place Weber in the evolutionary camp in his introduction to Weber, *The Sociology of Religion*, tr. Ephraim Fischoff (Boston: Beacon Press, 1963), p. xxvii. (This manuscript is part of *Economy and Society*.) On the difference between Weber and the new evolutionary approach, including Parsons, see Roth, "Sociological Typology and Historical Explanation," in Bendix and Roth, *op. cit.*, pp. 109ff. and 114ff.

13. Tenbruck, *op. cit.*, p. 670.

strategy of forming ideal types apparently parallels the inner drive toward rationalization to which the religious world view was subject; it is a strategy of emphasizing one or more viewpoints one-sidedly and of integrating them into a unifying structure that possesses logical and teleological consistency. Finally, this interpretation asserts that Western rationalization was not only dependent on world views, but was on that level determined endogenously; it was not a series of historical concatenations, accidents or interest constellations but the very result of an "inner necessity" on the level of ideas.[14] This necessity arose in ancient Judaism and reached its logical conclusion in ascetic Protestantism. After Weber discovered this inner necessity for the sequence of ideas, he allegedly lost interest in analyzing the cumulative processes.

Quite clearly, this interpretation makes Weber's position important for sociological theories based on an evolutionary perspective. It also creates doubts about classifying Weber as a representative of a typological comparative approach. This doubt provides a warrant for reconsidering the philosophical status and the substantive content of Weber's theory of rationalization. However, I believe that Tenbruck's classification of Weber as an evolutionist is as one-sided as some of the interpretations of Weber as a mere typologist. I agree with Tenbruck that Weber formulated an evolutionary perspective. But it is combined with a comparative approach. I agree with him that Weber formulated an autonomous "logic" of ideas, especially religious ideas. But it is combined with an institutional approach. I also agree with him that Weber put forth an explanation of Western rationalization based on the assumption of the inner necessity of the sequence from ancient Judaism to ascetic Protestantism. But it is combined with the analysis of partial processes in between. Weber provides a multidimensional macrosociological theory for the historical analysis of basic social configurations and their variants in evolutionary and comparative perspective. Using his own term I call this kind of analysis "developmental history." In principle, there is not one developmental history, there are several. Weber is interested in the developmental history of the West. Our task, then, is to extract it from some of his writings. This requires a reinterpretation that follows his way of posing the problem without fully accepting his solution. A reinterpretation seeks to improve an answer without abandoning the basis of the original resolution. For this purpose it must resort to other theories—in our case elements of neo-evolutionary theory. Only in this way can we articulate developmental history as an alternative to neo-evolutionary theory as well as to the merely typological comparison. I shall take four steps: identify the basic historical issues of Weber's approach (Ch. II); reconstruct its philosophical background (Ch. III); extensively analyze the substantive content of his developmental history (Chs. IV and V); and clarify his explanation of the transition to modernity (Ch. VI).

14. Cf. *Op. cit.*, p. 675. Here Tenbruck opposes especially the interpretations of Reinhard Bendix.

II
WEBER'S HISTORICAL PROBLEM

The Distinctiveness of Western Capitalism

Capitalism is Max Weber's first theme.* From the very beginning he treats it in historical perspective and as an institutional problem.[1] We can see this already in his first major publication, his study of the history of the trading companies in the medieval Italian cities. Weber dealt with the origin and organizational structure of a legal institution that favored the development of a particular form of capitalism, modern production-oriented capitalism. He analyzed the institution of joint liability of trade partners and the separation of business property from non-business assets, which emerged in complicated ways from the maritime and overland long-distance trade associations and their family basis.[2] This early perspective was retained more than thirty years later in the "Author's Introduction" to the comparative studies of the economic ethics of the world religions, which he assembled and partly extended shortly before his death: the capitalism of the modern business firm (Betriebskapitalismus) is based on a separation of business and personal assets and on an arrangement of risk and liability that has an "elective affinity" to the institution of

*All numbers in parentheses are page references to Economy and Society.

1. When Weber became editor of the Archiv für Sozialwissenschaft und Sozialpolitik in 1904, he described the subject matter of the journal and, at the same time, of social science as "the scientific inquiry into the general cultural significance of the socio-economic structure of human groups and of their historical forms of organization." Cf. "Objectivity," p. 67. If we add to this formulation the notion of the socio-cultural structure—the world views and their social basis—we have in my judgment not only a valid definition of what Weber considered to be the task of social science but also a definition that remains valid today. It is important that Weber always keeps the organizational forms of social life in sight.

2. Cf. Weber, Die Geschichte der Handelsgesellschaften im Mittelalter. Nach südeuropäischen Quellen. (Stuttgart: Enke, 1889), reprinted in Gesammelte Aufsätze zur Sozial- und Wirtschaftsgeschichte (Tübingen: Mohr, 1924), pp. 312-443.

joint liability of the medieval private trading companies.[3] Only this legal differentiation between types of assets made possible the organizational separation of household and enterprise. This separation, as well as that of consumption and production, always remained precarious in premodern economic variants of production-oriented capitalism. Not only the political and technological but also the organizational preconditions were lacking for a sustained commercial exploitation of capital so that there were only "the intermittent ups and downs of wealth-accumulating periods."[4] Obviously, the separation of business and personal property and the related dissolution of the original identity of workshop, counting room and household as well as that of household members and business partners, as they were typical of the "undifferentiated household" (379), had to be accompanied by the creation of other institutions: capital assets in the form of material means of production and formally free labor in the form of wage labor.[5] But even this is not enough. Capital and labor must be brought together in a formally rational organization, the enterprise, "a mode of produc-

3. The continuity of Weber's work can be recognized in the remarkable degree to which he integrated his early writings into his later ones and to which the later questions and concepts developed out of the earlier ones. For the sociology of domination this has been shown by G. Roth, "Introduction" to *ES*. Something similar can be said about the early and late analyses of Imperial Germany. See Wolfgang Mommsen, *Max Weber und die deutsche Politik 1890-1920* (Tübingen: Mohr, 1974), 2nd enl. edition, and David Beetham, *Max Weber and the Theory of Modern Politics* (London: Allen and Unwin, 1974). A more detailed investigation of this connection seems desirable. I have attempted a comparison of Weber's analysis of Imperial Rome and Imperial Germany in "Der autoritär verfasste Kapitalismus. Max Webers, Kritik am Kaiserreich," *Rationalismus der Weltbeherrschung* (Frankfurt: Suhrkamp, 1980), pp. 134-69. Reinhard Bendix, too, has pointed to the significance of the early writings for the crystallization of Weber's sociological perspective. See his *Max Weber, op. cit.*, especially Part I. I do not claim that the development of Weber's work was without any discontinuities. However, I doubt the view (cf. Tenbruck, *op. cit.*, p. 670f.) that dates Weber's "own sociology" only from 1903, from the writing of *PE* and " 'Objectivity' in Social Science and Social Policy." Cf. also Dirk Käsler, "Max Weber," *Klassiker soziologischen Denkens* (Munich: Beck, 1976), p. 174.

4. Cf. Weber, *The Agrarian Sociology of Ancient Civilizations*, tr. R. I. Frank (London: New Left Books, 1976), p. 48. On the most important handicaps for the development of capitalism in antiquity, see p. 65f.

5. Cf. "Author's Introduction," p. 21f. It is important—also for a comparison with Marx—that for Weber this historical form of capitalism, which has technological preconditions, and this historical form of labor, which has political presuppositions, are fused into a kind of capital utilization that contrasts with others. One contrasting type is ancient slave capitalism, characterized by the fact "that the products *become* (at least in part) objects of exchange, at the same time that the means of production *were* objects of exchange" (cf. *The Agrarian Sociology, op. cit.*, p. 48f). Slavery-based capital utilization, however, is specifically irrational in comparison to modern capital utilization: slaves are both constant and variable capital. This creates serious risks for the capital owner. Capital formation is made more difficult, capital turnover is slowed down, and there is danger of the capital dying. Moreover, the value of capital is dependent on noneconomic factors because of the way the market for slaves is supplied. Finally, slaves are part of the

tion which divides and coordinates labor."[6] Only then can a final developmental factor achieve its full effect—rational commercial bookkeeping as the basis of capital accounting. Thus, in Weber's view the historical distinctiveness of the modern capitalist enterprise cannot be comprehended either by the paired concepts of barter versus monetary economy or by the contrast of direct want satisfaction and market orientation, although money economy and market orientation are part of every capitalist economy that is economically and not politically oriented. Rather, only after the combination of these elements—separation of household and enterprise, capitalist organization of labor, and rational bookkeeping—had historically prevailed, could the commercial exploitation of capital take on its rational character and be permanently stabilized by the "methodical use of science for practical purposes."[7] Only then did the Social Question and rational socialism arise. The latter is as removed from its predecessors— religious, military, state and consumption-oriented socialism—as rational capitalism is from all forms of trading, finance and slavery capitalism, on the one hand, and booty and war capitalism on the other.[8]

However, between the perspective of the dissertation and the "Author's Introduction" lie literally worlds of difference. Before Weber arrives at his definition of "the bourgeois capitalism of the business firm with its rational organization of free labor,"[9] he moves through the social and economic history of East and West: from Mesopotamia via the Old, Middle and New Kingdom in Egypt to exilic, post-exilic and Talmudic Judaism,[10] from Hellenism to Rome with its Imperial period, from the decline of the Empire to the Imperial reconstitution of the Middle Ages and the Germanic social structure, from China to India and

---

master's household; there is no separation of household and enterprise. Because of his comparative interests Weber calls even this situation an instance of capital utilization. Only in this perspective can the peculiarity of Western capitalism be recognized. But Weber takes this view also because of the range of his historical knowledge. Throughout the history of mankind there has always been capitalism, including commercial capitalism on the basis of unfree as well as free labor, at least "as far back as the economic records go" (cf. "Author's Introduction," p. 19). The economic counter-concept to the capitalist economy is the *oikos* economy, which is frequently linked to manorialism. Its purpose is rent, not profit.

6. "The Agrarian Sociology," *op. cit.*, p. 66. Therefore, according to Weber, in antiquity there were no permanent large-scale enterprises on the basis of slave labor. The accumulation of slaves satisfied personal, not technical needs.

7. Weber, "Anticritical Last Word on 'The Spirit of Capitalism,' " tr. Wallace Davis, *Am. J. of Sociology*, 83 (1978): 1129.

8. These formulations are grounded in Weber's distinction between economically oriented and politically oriented capitalism and, in the former case, between trading, banking and modern business *(Betrieb)* capitalism. See especially *ES*, p. 164f.

9. Cf. "Author's Introduction," p. 24.

10. See "The Agrarian Sociology of Ancient Civilizations" and the *Collected Essays in the Sociology of Religions*.

back again to ancient Judaism. Along the way Weber continuously enlarged not only the factual basis but also the theoretical horizon of his analysis. At first he was primarily concerned with the distinctiveness of the modern European economy, but increasingly he also dealt with the particularity of modern European science, art, politics, law—in short, with the whole structure of modern European culture. We can go further: this analysis of the whole configuration of a specific cultural manifestation with its possibly world-historical significance impels the comparison and even the confrontation with alternatives. In the course of this analysis the theme of capitalism is transformed into that of rationalism.[11]

The Distinctiveness of Western Rationalism

Like capitalism, rationalism is for Weber not limited to the modern West. Time and again he emphasizes that rationalism and rationalization have existed in all civilizations and that the most diverse areas of social life have been rationalized "from very divergent viewpoints and in very different directions." This implies that what is rational from one perspective appears irrational from

11. Note the different questions posed in "The Agrarian Sociology of Ancient Civilizations" and "The Economic Ethics of the World Religions." In the former, the question is: "Did a capitalist economy exist in antiquity to a degree significant for cultural history?" (*op. cit.*, p. 48). This question facilitates the analysis of the modern Western economy. In the *Collected Essays in the Sociology of Religions*, the question is: "To what combination of circumstances should the fact be attributed that in Western civilization, and in Western civilization only, cultural phenomena have appeared which (as we like to think) lie in a line of development having universal significance and value?" ("Author's Introduction," p. 13). This question raises the issue of alternative historical *(kulturge-schichtlich)* interpretations of culture itself. Thus, I am advancing here the thesis that Weber enlarged his range of interests. On this problem, see also G. Roth, "Introduction" to *ES*, Sec. 6, who points to the parallelism between the analysis of capitalism and rationalism. Tenbruck, too, speaks of an enlargement, but he has in mind primarily the thesis of rationalization. In addition, he remarks that Weber "was continuously preoccupied with the question of rationality" (*op. cit.*, p. 693). Whatever the emphasis, one point is certain: Weber's work requires a genetic and developmental interpretation, as Tenbruck has correctly demanded. See also his "Abschied von *Wirtschaft und Gesellschaft*," *Zeitschrift für die gesamte Staatswissenschaft*, 133 (1977): 703ff.

It is true, however, that Weber himself tied his interests relatively early to the issue of rationalization. Already in the first version of *PE* he states that "Rationalism is an historical concept which covers a whole world of different things. It will be our task to find out whose intellectual child the particular concrete form of rational thought was, from which the idea of a calling and the devotion to labor in the calling has grown, which is, as we have seen, so irrational from the standpoint of purely eudaemonistic self-interest, but which has been and still is one of the most characteristic elements of our capitalistic culture" (*PE*, p. 78). In his anti-critique against Rachfahl he emphasized that

another, both within a given culture and across cultures.[12] Rationalism and rationalization also depend upon the kind of actor—the "theoretician," who pursues the intellectual ordering of reality, or the "practitioner," who wants to actualize a social order.[13] This viewpoint can be further differentiated and specified sociologically. This leads us to a typology of the social carriers of rationalism and rationalization, but one that cannot be a typology of intellectuals in the narrower sense of the term.

However, Weber does not restrict himself to a typology of the social carriers of rationalism and rationalization. He is also interested in the processes that embody the rationality of social action and of social order within and between cultures. He relates the theme of rationalism not only to individuals and social groups but also to inclusive and partial social orders—to the level of social order that has a logic of its own in comparison with the level of social action. Thus, the theme of rationalism and rationalization appears in a dual perspective: the first is the relation of the rationality of social action and social order, the second the variation of rationality within and among cultures.

It would seem, therefore, that Weber's approach leads to a systematic typology and sociology of rationalism and rationalization. But if we follow his own formulation, this is not the case. It is true that he wants to contribute to such a sociology but only insofar as it is related to the solution of his historical problem—"to identify the distinctiveness of Western and especially of modern Western rationalism and to explain its historical origins."[14] For this purpose cultures must be compared with regard to who rationalizes which spheres of life in what directions and which historical kinds of social order result therefrom.

Thus, for pragmatic reasons Weber does not attempt a systematic typology and sociology of rationalism. However, this is only half of the truth. He also has a theoretical reason. Whoever wants to make such a systematic effort must satisfy two criteria: the typology must be complete and must fit into a model of universal stages.[15] But time and again Weber stressed two points. First, histori-

---

his research on the relation of the Protestant ethic and the spirit of capitalism dated back to the 1890s. First results were presented in class as early as 1897 (cf. *PE*, p. 150).

Thus, it is justified to see the question of rationality as Weber's central issue. The early Weber literature was aware of that, but the issue has been given much attention recently. Apart from the literature cited above, see also Manfred Hennen, *Krise der Rationalität—Dilemma der Soziologie* (Stuttgart: Enke, 1976); Stephen Kalberg, "Max Weber's Types of Rationality: Cornerstones for the Analysis of Rationalization Processes in History," *Am.J. of Sociology*, 85 (1980): 1145-79; Donald N. Levine, "Rationality and Freedom: Weber and Beyond," *Sociological Inquiry*, 51 (1981); Ulrike Vogel, "Einige Überlegungen zum Begriff der Rationalität bei Max Weber," *Kölner Zeitschrift für Soziologie*, 25 (1973): 532ff.; Jürgen Habermas, *Handlungsrationalität und gesellschaftliche Rationalisierung*, Ms.

12. "Author's Introduction," p. 26.   13. "Introduction," p. 293.
14. "Author's Introduction," p. 26. Cf. also "Theory," p. 324.
15. "Introduction," p. 292f.

cal concepts cannot be created independently from cultural values; there is no definitive historical conceptualization and no definitive system of the cultural sciences. Second, theories of universal stages have not only failed for this systematic reason but have also been discredited through historical research.[16] It is true that Weber deals with world-historical *(universalgeschichtlich)* issues, but neither with world history nor with universal sociology nor even with the philosophy of world history.[17]

Does this mean that the analysis of the distinctiveness and origin of Western rationalism is a purely historiographic task? This too Weber has denied. He speaks of his unhistorical procedure in the treatment of the ethics of the world religions. For example, these ethics will be "treated systematically as being much more unified than has been true of the flux of actual historical development."[18] Here Weber criticizes naive historism, which believes that the sources speak for themselves and misunderstands the relation of concept and fact. However, this statement has a strategic as well as a theoretical aspect. These ethics are analyzed not on their own terms and not for their own sake but from the perspective of modern economic rationalism. Those elements are emphasized which "characterize them in contrast to others and which are at the same time important for our own purposes."[19] These ethics have their own historical distinctiveness and are to that extent autonomous, but so to speak only with

16. Weber's so-called *Wissenschaftslehre* is a determined effort to demonstrate the *hiatus irrationalis* between concept and reality and to oppose not only a copy or correspondence theory of concept formation but also an emanationist one, whether it be naturalist or idealist. Cf. Weber, *Roscher and Knies. The Logical Problems of Historical Economics,* tr. Guy Oakes (New York: The Free Press, 1975), p. 67. Weber pointed out the historical deficiencies of a theory of universal stages in his analysis of Germanic social structure; he argued against nomadic life as a universal stage of development with the example of the Germanic tribes in Caesar's time. Cf. "Der Streit um den Charakter der altgermanischen Sozialverfassung in der deutschen Literatur des letzten Jahrzehnts" (1904), in *Gesammelte Aufsätze zur Sozial- und Wirtschaftsgeschichte, op. cit.,* pp. 508-556; see also Roth, "Introduction" to *ES*, sec. 4.

17. A problem in universal history would be one that occurs in all known cultural history and the most consistent "solutions" of which could therefore claim universal significance. Such a problem is the discrepancy between fate and merit; consistent "solutions" are the theodicy of Karma, dualism and predestination. But these "solutions" do not exhaust historical reality, just as this problem is not the only one that can be significant for cultural history. Wolfgang J. Mommsen seems to think differently. He perceives in Weber's development a change from cultural historian to systematic universal sociologist, for whom the type is no longer a means but the end of research. Mommsen dates this change from 1913 and illustrates it with the different variants of the sociology of domination. Cf. Mommsen, *The Age of Bureaucracy* (Oxford: Blackwell, 1974), pp. 13-21. This interpretation parallels the thesis of the dialectic of charisma and bureaucratization. In my view this is a misinterpretation of Weber's "late sociology," for it tends to ignore the issues to which the concepts refer and to absolutize one of several possible theories of development.

18. "Introduction," p. 294.   19. *Op. cit.,* p. 292.

reference to Western rationalism. The latter is for us the hermeneutic starting point from which the ethics of the world religions are viewed. However, they must not be seen simply in relation to our own culture. They must also be contrasted with one another. Historical truth can be served only by a series of contrasts, even if modern Western rationalism remains the starting and end point of such a comparison.

For Weber, therefore, there are not only different types of rationalism and rationalization, not only different spheres of life which can be rationalized, not only different carriers of rationalization and, as a consequence, not only different kinds of rational order and types of rationalization; there is above all one special phenomenon of rationalism and rationalization that poses an historical problem of identification and explanation and thus demands an adequate "historical theory." This theory cannot be a theory of universal stages; nor can it be restricted to a typological comparison. The theory must provide a developmental *(entwicklungsgeschichtlich)* perspective. It must be capable of providing a valid explanation for the particularity of Western rationalism and Western rationalization. This leads us to the question of the status and content of this theory.

III

THE PHILOSOPHICAL
BACKGROUND OF WEBER'S
DEVELOPMENTAL HISTORY

The Relation to Neo-Kantian Value Theory

I consider it desirable to place Weber's position more clearly than is usually done in the context of a value theory as it was elaborated in neo-Kantianism, especially by Heinrich Rickert and Emil Lask.[1] This should make it easier to answer the question of the status of Weber's developmental history. In his analyses of the logic and methodology of *Kulturwissenschaft* as an historical social science—a science dealing with the individual and not only with the general— Weber emphasized time and again that his remarks did not imply any decision in matters of epistemology, philosophy of history and value philosophy. But in my opinion he located himself along the philosophical spectrum by sketching a value theory that can be identified at least typologically. Weber follows Kant's critique of dogmatic rationalism, for which concepts are in the last analysis copies of "objective" reality. But he also opposes sharply any kind of emanationist reinterpretation of Kantian Criticism that concepts represent the "true" reality and that the various realities are realizations or emanations of concepts. Although Weber could have criticized Kant's "one-sided formalism of valuation *(Werten)*" the way Emil Lask did, and like him was concerned with a theory of concrete historical values *(Wertindividualitäten)*, he continued to adhere to a

1. The connection between Rickert's epistemology and methodology of the natural and cultural sciences and Weber's studies on the logic and methodology of *Kulturwissenschaft* has often been traced, most recently in the brilliant study by Thomas Burger, *Max Weber's Theory of Concept Formation: History, Laws, and Ideal Types* (Durham: Duke University Press, 1976). Burger points out correctly that without knowledge of Rickert's theory of concept formation Weber's methodology cannot be made intelligible; in fact, he argues that on this score the two positions are identical (cf. p. 7). What Burger says about

Kantian theory of concepts over against an emanationism of concrete values—the view that history is the "unfolding" of values.[2] For Weber the *hiatus irrationalis* between concept and subject matter cannot be resolved. He recognizes only the cognitive ordering of reality as the result of its conceptual transformation. However, he also shares the neo-Kantian critique of Kant—that an abstract value scheme does not suffice to comprehend reality. Rather, reality must be

---

the theory of concept formation will not apply to value theory to the same extent. However, I basically agree with Burger when he speaks in general of an "a priori underestimation of Rickert's influence" in the Weber literature *(loc. cit.)*. To my knowledge the relationship between Weber and Lask has not been studied seriously. A beginning was made by Fritz Loos, *Zur Wert-und Rechtslehre Max Webers* (Tübingen: Mohr, 1970), pp. 106ff. Loos limits himself to legal theory.

Rickert himself was aware of Weber's significance for neo-Kantian value philosophy. Thus, he wrote about Weber in *System der Philosophie*, which contains essays on value theory published in *Logos* and *Kantstudien* between 1910 and 1914: "This outstanding scholar belonged to the few who fully understood the relation between value problems and empirical problems and thus between philosophy and the individual sciences. Therefore, his works are of great importance for value philosophy, even though he deliberately avoided philosophical problems, with the exception of methodological ones"*(System der Philosophy*. Tübingen: Mohr, 1921, Part I, p. 164, n. 1).

My proposal to place Weber's position more clearly than is usually done in the context of neo-Kantian value theory does not mean that I assert his complete dependence on it. In a comparison of Weber's methodological essays with Part I of *ES*, Johannes Winckelmann has correctly pointed out that Weber gradually "abandoned the terminology of contemporary value philosophy even for his methodological purposes" *(Erläuterungsband, op. cit.,* p. 11). But this does not mean that he also abandoned its central premises. By contrast, I consider it a basic misinterpretation to drag Weber into the camp of phenomenology—a fashionable tendency. It is hardly possible to interpret the "Theory of Religious Rejections of the World" consistently without keeping in mind Rickert's distinction between objective value, subjective meaning and historical value *(Wert, Sinn* and *Gut)*. Moreover, an adequate interpretation of Weber's theory of legitimation, as Winckelmann has accomplished it (cf. *op. cit.,* pp. 44ff), presupposes at least a value-philosophical reflection. Winckelmann's thesis that Weber championed an empirical value theory in which, however, justification from "highest" principles played a central role can be justified within a theory of value spheres, a theory which modifies basic elements of the neo-Kantian value theory in a manner peculiar to Weber.

For studies that deal with Weber's value theory, partially by way of the problem of legitimation, see Johannes Winckelmann's writings, especially *Legitimität und Legalität in Max Webers Herrschaftssoziologie* (Tübingen: Mohr, 1952); Fritz Loos, *op. cit.*; Hans Henrik Bruun, *Science, Values and Politics in Max Weber's Methodology* (Copenhagen: Munksgaard, 1971); and Jürgen Habermas, *Legitimation Crisis,* tr. Thomas McCarthy (Boston: Beacon Press, 1975). For a brief review of Rickert and the Southwestern School of neo-Kantianism, see Thomas E. Willey, *Back to Kant: The Revival of Kantianism in German Social and Historical Thought, 1860-1914* (Detroit: Wayne State University Press, 1978), Ch. 6.

2. For this classification, see Weber's *Roscher and Knies, op. cit.,* pp. 64ff., which in this regard largely follows Emil Lask's dissertation, *Fichtes Idealismus und die Geschichte* (1902). Weber called Lask's contribution to the history of philosophy "splendid" (p. 219). In his study (reprinted in *Gesammelte Schriften.* Tübingen: Mohr, 1923, I, pp. 1ff.) Lask

understood in terms of concrete historical value schemes. It can and should be approached not only as nature but also as history or culture. Further, a Kantian theory of concepts must not claim a scientific *(naturwissenschaftlich)* monopoly. Weber considers it a naturalistic prejudice to believe that only the general, only the identification of general laws and the subsumption of individual phenomena as specimen, must guide the ordering of reality.[3] Because we are cultural beings we are interested in not only the general but also the individual features of reality, and we take a special interest in them if we can believe that they are significant and relevant not only for us but for others as well.

In my view, Weber recognizes clearly that at this point certain assumptions could misdirect his analysis. A theory of concrete historical values can be overextended in two directions: a value philosophy that pretends to develop a

---

distinguished between a dogmatic rationalism of the kind advanced by Christian Wolff and Leibniz and a critical rationalism of the Kantian kind. With particular attention to Hegel and Fichte, he reconstructed the historical development that took off from the abstract formulation of the dualism of form and content in Kant's theory of concepts and led to its resolution in an emanationist theory of concepts. Lask's dominant concern was the problem of irrationality in epistemology. He was convinced that the case could not be deduced from the law nor the specimen from the species nor the part from the whole. Thus, he sought to defend the Kantian theory of concepts against both the dogmatic and the emanationist theories. However, at the same time he recognized the limits of the Kantian approach for the solution of the logical problem posed by the study of history. Therefore, Lask accepts the idealist critique of Kant's abstract value scheme for the realm of history and aims at supplementing this abstract scheme with a theory of concrete historical values without sacrificing the Kantian theory of concepts. Lask formulates his program in these words: "We will be able to agree with the logical presuppositions of Kant's transcendental philosophy without approving of the one-sided formalism of valuation which is its psychological consequence. Conversely, we will be able to reject Hegel's theory of the concept without having to disregard his fruitful creation of new value concepts. Our critical approach is justified solely by our conviction that a combination of Kant's and Hegel's theory of concept formation is possible" *(op. cit.,* p. 28). I believe that Weber's thinking goes in the same direction.

3. Friedrich H. Tenbruck, in particular, has correctly emphasized Weber's stand against naturalism. See his study, "Die Genesis der Methodologie Max Webers," *Kölner Zeitschrift für Soziologie,* 11 (1959): 573. Weber's opposition to naturalism had a double thrust: on the one hand, he affirmed that our interest in the particular has equal rank with our interest in the general; on the other, he insisted that the cognition of facts depends upon constructs. For this reason Weber never linked the distinction between the natural and cultural sciences with the thesis of the theoretical particularity of the cultural sciences or even explained the difference between the two in terms of the contrasting principles of explanation and *Verstehen.* This is illustrated very clearly by a quotation that should be the starting point for every analysis of Weber's methodology. After reviewing the various approaches to "a theory of interpretation *(Deutung),* which is today only in its very beginnings" *(Roscher and Knies, op. cit.,* p. 151) but which must be formulated, Weber writes (p. 184f.): "Let us conclude this analysis—unavoidably somewhat monotonous— of the diverse theories of the alleged peculiarity of the subjectifying disciplines and the significance of this peculiarity for history, theories which fairly glitter in the

closed system of general values, and a theory of value realization which closes the *hiatus irrationalis* between values and "value-laden" reality in theory and the gap between moral demand and action in practice. It is true that Weber thinks the task of a "genuine philosophy of value" is to construe a "well-ordered conceptual scheme of values" by means of an interpretive approach that transcends mere value analysis, "identifies the ultimate meaning and consequences of values, . . . locates their place within the totality of all possible ultimate values" and delimits the "spheres of their validity."[4] But he considers a closed

---

variety of their colors and forms. The only result of this analysis is really quite trivial. Nevertheless, its soundness has repeatedly been questioned. Consider any given piece of knowledge. Neither the substantive qualities of its object nor the ontological peculiarities of the existence of this object nor, finally, the kind of *psychological* conditions required for its acquisition are of any consequence as regards its *logical* content and the presuppositions on which its validity is based. *Empirical* knowledge in the domain of the mental and in the domain of external nature, knowledge of processes within us and of those without us, is invariably tied to the instrument of concept formation. From a logical point of view, the nature of a concept in these two substantive domains is the same. The *logical* peculiarity of historical knowledge in contrast to natural-scientific knowledge—in the *logical* sense of this expression—has nothing at all to do with the distinction between the psychical and physical: the personality and action, on the one hand, and the dead natural object and the mechanical process of nature on the other. To identify the self-evidence of empathy in the actual or potential conscious inner experience—an exclusively phenomenological quality of interpretation—with a unique empirical certainty of processes susceptible to interpretation is an even more serious mistake. Physical and psychical reality or an aspect of reality comprehending both physical and psychical components constitutes an historical entity because and insofar as it can mean something to us. Meaningfully interpretable human conduct ("action") is identifiable by reference to valuations and meanings. For this reason, our criteria for *causal* explanation have a unique kind of satisfaction in the historical explanation of such an entity. Finally, insofar as human conduct is oriented to values or can be confronted with them, there is a peculiar sense in which its understanding is self-evident. The question of the special role of the interpretively understandable in history therefore concerns differences in (1) our causal interest and (2) the quality of the self-evidence pursued in the investigation of concrete causal relations. However, it does not concern differences in the concept of causality, the significance of concept formation or the kind of conceptual apparatus employed."

I do not see that Weber abandoned this basic position, which is indebted to Rickert's and Lask's philosophy, in anything but terminology.

4. Weber, "The Meaning of 'Ethical Neutrality' in Sociology and Economics," *The Methodology of the Social Sciences*, tr. and ed. Edward Shils and Henry Finch, (Glencoe: Free Press, 1949), p. 17f. These statements do not date from the early phase of Weber's treatment of methodological issues, but from a study published in 1917 and drafted for a discussion within the *Verein für Sozialpolitik* in 1913. Thus, the statements belong to a time when both Rickert's essay on "*Vom System der Werte*" and Weber's "On Some Categories of Interpretive Sociology" were published in *Logos*, 4 (1913) and Weber planned to write a systematic epistemology of the social sciences as a supplement to the *Outline of Social Economics*. See *1. Abteilung* (Tübingen: Mohr, 1914), p. vii. On the difference between value philosophy and value analysis, see Weber, "Critical Studies in the Logic of the Cultural Sciences," *The Methodology of the Social Sciences, op. cit.*, pp. 143ff.; also

system of general values impossible, as did Rickert before him,[5] and denies the applicability of the concept of system in the theory of values altogether insofar as it tends to a hierarchy of values. Even though value philosophy has the task of establishing an orderly conceptual scheme of values, it has no means for justifying a rank order. Weber points to a basic experience rooted in the history of mankind and especially of modernity: "the possibility of, in principle, unbridgeably divergent ultimate evaluations," an experience not merely of value differences but of value collision and value conflict.[6] No rational or empirical scientific procedure can reconcile these differences. The tremendous existential problem posed by this situation cannot be resolved by either empirical science or philosophy. It is true that according to Weber we are interested in historical reality only because and insofar as it constitutes values. However, Weber resolutely opposes the supposition that this implies "the empirical fact of a world process that objectively works toward the realization of an absolute."[7] Historical cognition and historical action require the evaluating "historical individual" who alone can actualize values and take a conscious position. [8] It is true that the "historical individuals," whether individuals or collectivities, make their history not under chosen but under given conditions and that they remain exposed to the unintended consequences of their actions. For Weber this is fate: "The paradox of unintended consequences—human beings and their fate (fate as the consequence of their actions vis-à-vis their intentions)."[9] But human beings do *make* their history, and in actualizing historical values they obey neither a naturalist nor spiritualist, neither a conscious nor an unconscious, teleology of history.

"Ethical Neutrality," *op. cit.*, p. 22. Value analysis or value interpretation which aims at "establishing the array of *possible* meaningful positions vis-à-vis a given phenomenon" *(loc. cit.)* remains an empirical means, whereas value philosophy or axiology ultimately envisages a complete tableau of values.

5. Cf. Rickert, "Vom System der Werte," *op. cit.*, pp. 195ff.

6. "Ethical Neutrality," *op. cit.*, p. 14. Herein lies the decisive difference between Weber and Rickert. Another difference could be Weber's denial of the primacy of practical reason in logic and epistemology, that is, of moral criteria. This position was shared by Emil Lask. Cf. Lask, *op. cit.*, p. 349.

7. Weber, *Roscher and Knies, op. cit.*, p. 267, n. 77.

8. I deliberately use the term "historical individual" in a nontechnical sense. In Rickert's work an historical individual is any object historically significant to us, i.e., any object constituted by an historical value relation *(Wertbeziehung)*. Cf. Rickert, *Die Grenzen der naturwissenschaftlichen Begriffsbildung* (Tübingen: Mohr, 1913), 2nd ed., pp. 300ff. Weber, too, accepts this definition, as is shown by the quotation in n. 3 above. Here I choose this term in order to link the methodology of history with the theory of action, which includes collective action. This is in line with the definition of action proposed by Talcott Parsons and Neil Smelser in *Economy and Society* (New York: Free Press, 1965), p. 8.

9. *China*, p. 238. The view that sociology and history deal with the unintended consequences of actions plays a central role for Weber, as it does later for Karl Popper.

In order to protect himself against the misunderstandings of a closed theory of general values as an objectivist philosophy of history, Weber championed
a double dualism: the dualism of reality and values and, within values, the
dualism between the sphere of the theoretical and of the practical, between cognitive and value judgment. It would be wrong to identify these distinctions with
the difference between natural and cultural science. Rather, their concept formation is subsumed under the cognitive aspect. Both accomplish a cognitive
ordering of reality, even though cultural science requires historical value relations and is thus linked with the practical sphere, in contrast to natural science.
However, both sciences make cognitive judgments with which they assert
claims of the same kind—claims of logical and empirical, not of normative
truth. Although it would be in line with neo-Kantian value theory to speak of
valuations even within the cognitive sphere, Weber reserves the term for normative truth.[10] This is shown by the range within which he considers value judgments applicable. The value concept implies a clear positive or negative judgment, "something that makes a claim *(Geltung)* on us. That claim is recognized
as a value for us and therefore by us, or else rejected or evaluated in the most
diverse degrees. Whenever an ethical or aesthetic value confronts us, we are invariably expected to render a value judgment."[11]

In this manner Weber emphasizes not only that values make objective demands upon us but also that our responses are *judgments*, and therefore, he
stresses the cognitive aspects of values, their communicability. After all, value
judgments can be discussed scientifically, in contrast to mere feelings, which
are indeterminate and therefore cannot be communicated and discussed. This
aspect of Weber's position has frequently been neglected. Value analysis and
value discussion permit him to deal with the ways in which practical and aesthetic questions can be cognitively rationalized. But another aspect is more important: although Weber permits an ordered relationship between value judgment and cognitive judgment, they belong to different spheres of validity. He
dramatizes the dualism and even antagonism between the two spheres, not the
transfer of validity. It is one of his basic convictions that a value judgment cannot be derived from a cognitive one and follows a logic of its own, both on the
level of philosophy and of empirical science. Whoever does not accept this has in
Weber's eyes neither a philosophically nor scientifically adequate notion of decision-making, freedom and personality. If Panlogism of an Hegelian type can at

10. This is so for neo-Kantianism because of the theory of judgment *(Urteil)*. Every
judgment, including a logical one, is affirmative or negative and thus implies a position
toward a value. Cf. Rickert, *Der Gegenstand des Erkennens* (Tübingen: Mohr, 1904), 2nd
ed. (first published in 1892). Rickert speaks of the "logical priority of ought over is" and
views the ought as "a logical condition of reality" (pp. 148ff). See also Emil Lask, "Die
Lehre vom Urteil," *Gesammelte Schriften, op. cit.,* pp. 283ff.

11. *Roscher and Knies, op. cit.,* p. 182. These considerations are also pertinent to
Weber's substantive sociology; see e.g. Weber's discussion of charisma in *ES,* p. 1116.

least erect a dam against "naturalist monism,"[12] an empirico-historical value theory that replaces a genuine value philosophy and disregards the difference between cognitive judgment and value judgment produces crude naturalism. Such a value theory cannot be anything but a theory of the normative power of the factual, a theory of adaptation.

Value Theory as a Theory of Value Conflict

We must keep this context in mind if we want to understand correctly Weber's demand for freedom from value judgment in science, but also his historical theory of the value-related institutional spheres and his theory of value conflict. It is true that Weber tends to approach the value spheres and corresponding institutional realms descriptively, and as a historian he views validity primarily in terms of historical effectiveness. But in the background of his analysis lies a value theory in which the historical studies must find their anchorage. This is especially true of the historical theory of rationalization. This theory is based on an open value scheme that distinguishes between logical, religious or moral and aesthetic kinds of values—in Talcott Parsons' and Jürgen Habermas' terms this is a difference of cognitive, evaluative and expressive symbolism.[13] Moreover, the scheme subdivides the evaluative sphere. There Weber deals with the possible conflict between otherworldly and this-worldly values and within the latter, with the conflict between the values of various spheres of life.

If we want to systematize, for example, the "Theory of the Stages and Directions of Religious World Rejection," we must attribute to Weber a conceptual scheme of values that distinguishes between cognitive values, religious values, ethical values in politics, economy and family, aesthetic values and, enlarging the expressive sphere, eroticism. This conceptual scheme is similar to Rickert's.[14] However, it is not as systematically organized as Rickert's but only differ-

12. "Objectivity," p. 86.

13. Cf. Talcott Parsons and Gerald M. Platt, *The American University* (Cambridge: Harvard University Press, 1973), esp. Chapter 2; and Jürgen Habermas, *Handlungsrationalität und gesellschaftliche Rationalisierung*, Ms., Starnberg, 1978.

14. Cf. the value spheres or institutional realms distinguished by Weber with the schematic table of values and goods in Rickert's *System der Philosophie*, appendix. Rickert distinguishes between logic, ethics, aesthetics, eroticism and religion, which is divided into mysticism and philosophy of religion. Incidentally, Rickert believes that value philosophy is dependent on an empirical science of values that approaches values inductively. It is the task of philosophy, then, to systematize these values by the manner in which they are actualized. This leads Rickert to the distinction of future, present, and eternal goods, terms that may also be useful for the clarification of Weber's value theory. Here we cannot compare in detail the two value theories, a comparison that would have to establish similarities and especially differences. This must be the task of another essay.

entiated into the basic distinction between cognitive, evaluative and expressive spheres or, even more simplified, between cognition and valuation. Moreover, the historical theory of rationalization also requires assumptions about the actualization of values: only "historical individuals" realize values, and such processes are regulated not only by the inherent claims of the various kinds of values but also by their "value interests." Socially significant value realizations congeal into institutional arrangements, which can have a history of their own. They elaborate symbols and regulate the possession of otherworldly and this-worldly goods.[15] Therefore, institutional realms always consist of relations of legitimation *and* appropriation. They can develop tensions with one another *because* they are based on values with different claims and interests. Only this assumption makes it possible for Weber to speak of the "internal dynamics of the individual spheres" *(innere Eigengesetzlichkeiten)*, without having to fear mechanistic connotations.[16] For he is dealing not with an autonomous logic of the ideas as such but with the dynamics *(Eigenlogik)* of *actualized* ideas, which always require interests and institutions. Under the conditions of value conflict there are two strategies for creating and composing tensions—one-sided articulation and compromise. As a rule, the historical advantage is on the side of compromise, if for no other reason than that individuals and groups have a limited capacity to suffer for their convictions. Weber pointed to this connection when he addressed the example of the possible tensions between religious and political action: "The widely varying empirical stands which historical religions have taken in the face of political action have been determined by the entanglement of religious organizations in power interests and in struggles for power, by the always unavoidable collapse of even the highest states of tension with the world in favor of compromises and relativities, by the usefulness and the use of religious organizations for the political taming of the masses and, especially, by the need of the powers-that-be for the religious consecration of their legitimacy. Almost all religions have been instances of relativizing spiritual values and their ethically rational logic *(Eigengesetzlichkeit.)*"[17]

Weber's theory of value is tailored to the requirements of *Kulturwissenschaft* as an historical social science. Where these are satisfied, the theory ends. It does not offer a system of values nor a systematization of their realization, as it was presented in Rickert's philosophy of value and used for the construction of an open-ended system of values, a tableau of values. Still, Weber's theory has implications for the philosophy of value which are more far-reaching than has generally been perceived by both Weber's critics and apologists. It is these implications that shape historical analysis, especially the theory of rationalization. Only because humans are cultural beings who cannot create culture in the

---

15. Cf. "Theory," p. 328.
16. *Loc. cit.* Cf. Johannes Winckelmann, *Erläuterungsband, op. cit.*, p. 94.
17. "Theory," p. 337f.

broadest sense without bringing about inner and external tensions can the study of these tensions become an essential part of historical and sociological research. Rationalism and rationalization become essential subjects of investigations only because "the development of inner-worldly and otherworldly values toward rationality, conscious endeavor and sublimation through *knowledge*" destroys the "primeval naivete" of human beings about themselves and the world and produces tension as well as the awareness of tension.[18] Insofar as value-guided action is confronted by different and, in principle, antagonistic claims, the rationalization of value spheres and institutional realms must not only develop tensions but also lead to different processes and types of rationalism. This depends upon who makes what value sphere, from which perspective, the object of conscious endeavor and of sublimation through knowledge, and on the resulting relationship of the value spheres to one another.

There is another implication of Weber's rudimentary theory of value. The cognitive unity of history cannot consist of the unfolding of a concept, and its practical unity cannot amount to the progressive reconciliation of the institutional realms and to an ultimate resolution of the conflict of values. It is true that Weber too must postulate the idea of history's unity. Otherwise he could not say that historical social science teaches us to understand "cultural phenomena out of their historical origins," and that we become historical social scientists because we have an interest "in sharing, through this method, in the community of human beings."[19] However, this unity, this community, is a regulative idea that makes it possible to compare alternative interpretations of human existence in terms of how they cope with the practical problems posed by the conflict of values. The mode of articulating conflict, the resulting practical problems and the principles of synthesis in a scientific comparison change for historical social science "with the content of culture itself."[20] This holds true also for the practical cultural problems of modern Western rationalism and the theory of modern Western rationalization as a form of world mastery. They must, in the first instance, be viewed as a set of particular existential problems and as a one-sided and transient conceptual construction. As in all such efforts, such a theory is valuable, among other reasons, because it reveals "the limits of the significance of the very viewpoint" that underlies its construction.[21] It defines a concrete hermeneutic situation, from which we must start. We must never overlook this hermeneutic dependency and the constructivist character of our retrospective designs. Because of his own views in the realm of the philosophy of value, Weber not only rejected naturalism but also a Hegelian version of idealism *(historische Subjektphilosophie)*. In a letter to Franz Eulenburg of May 11, 1909, we find this revealing formulation: "There are only two ways: Hegel's or our own approach."[22] Nothing catches as concisely as this phrase a position

18. *Op. cit.*, p. 328.   19. "Science," p. 145.   20. "Objectivity," p. 105.
21. *Loc. cit.*   22. Cited by H. H. Bruun, *op. cit.*, p. 39.

which is based on a philosophical decision. This is easily overlooked because Weber did not directly criticize Hegel, Marx and Dilthey but instead turned on their epigoni and followers. In Hegel's case he dealt with Roscher and Knies, in Marx's with contemporary vulgar Marxism, and in Dilthey's case with contemporary methodologies of the social and cultural sciences (Münsterberg, Wundt, Croce and others).[23]

Nevertheless, for Weber the historical configuration of modern Western rationalism is more than merely one among many interpretations of the fundamental situation of human beings, and the theory of modern Western rationalization is for him more than just one among any number of criteria of historical reconstruction. Modern Western culture is a *special* interpretation of civilization. The reconstruction of history from the perspective of the origin, development and consequences of a rationalism of world mastery is a special one, which cannot simply be sacrificed to other criteria so long as cultural science intends to understand what is worth knowing (in the sense of getting at the essentials). Weber goes even further: he presents modern Western culture as a "developmental product," which Westerners at least, if they are fully aware of their situation, cannot abandon without becoming unfaithful to themselves. The viewpoint from which alone the special configuration of its rationalism becomes visible is not exhausted as long as the great existential problem posed by it has not become obsolete. This is unlikely as long as we do not flee into new illusions, for the special historical achievement of modern Western rationalism has been the disenchantment of the world, which has led to the most acute actualization of the conflict of values in cultural history. This rationalism firmly established and radicalized a consciousness that had been anticipated before, for instance in the Hellenist world view, and that had accompanied human beings latently ever since they began to symbolize. Today the "many old gods, disenchanted and transformed into impersonal forces," have risen again after recognition of the value conflict had been blurred "for a millennium by the presumably or allegedly exclusive orientation toward the grand pathos of the Christian ethic." For Weber the rise of modern Western rationalism seems to indicate a basic change of consciousness, hence a *development* of consciousness, which is paralleled by the development of a world view. Personal gods have become impersonal forces; the antagonism of values has replaced the polytheistic and even the monotheistic rank order, and the result has been their irreconcilable "perennial conflict." The demands upon human beings have not only been depersonalized, they also make conflicting claims. This is for Weber "the fate of the times," which cannot be mitigated by any theology or science.[24] Only persons who have affirmed their own fate, the meaning of their existence and actions, in a series of clear-eyed decisions can stand this kind of everyday life.[25] This implies not

23. Similarly Bruun, *loc. cit.*, n. 5.　　　24. "Science," p. 149.
25. "Ethical Neutrality," *op. cit.*, p. 18.

relativism, opportunism or arbitrariness but the formulation of a viewpoint that is marked by clarity, consistency and knowledge of the paradox of unintended consequences in the face of the inescapable pressures toward compromise and relativities.[26] This is less the result of an insight into the dialectic of the Enlightment than an insight into the unity of self-awareness and self-preservation, at the same time that it does not claim omnipotence.[27]

We must call this perspective a philosophical implication of Weber's historical theory of rationalization. Weber diagnoses not merely a relatively higher rank of modern Western rationalism on the empirical level but also its superiority over other kinds of rationalism on the level of a philosophy of value. His evaluative viewpoint, which guides his ideal-typical developmental construct, has more than merely heuristic character. It is valid also insofar as the unfolding of the conflict of values and the corresponding consciousness are in his eyes something valuable. Of course, we must carefully specify the status of this implication for the philosophy of history. Weber speaks explicitly of the fate of *our* culture and observes that it "lies in a developmental direction of *universal* significance and validity, at least as *we* like to think."[28] Some Western innovations have a good chance of diffusing into other cultural traditions by virtue of power politics, inter-civilizational contacts[29] or merely because every social order that wants to survive must utilize the adaptive capacities of modern Western rationalism. But this does not mean that the totality of modern Western culture can negate all other cultural configurations. We do not know whether "at the end of this tremendous development entirely new prophets will arise or whether there will be a powerful rebirth of old ideas and ideals."[30] Nor has the rationalism of world mastery incorporated all other forms of rationalism in such a manner that they are mere antecedent stages in the course of disenchantment. This rationalism is *our* viewpoint, with which we direct, so to speak, a searchlight at a slice of world history, and it is valid for *us* as long as we are interested in our historical continuity. This rationalism is part of our hermeneutic base line, which retains special importance. However, modern Western rationalism is also of such a kind that all human beings can take an interest in it, for it has brought forth a novel interpretation of civilization. For this reason it is not only a particular phenomenon, it constitutes a historical problem of significance and validity beyond the West. Even those who do not choose this alternative are

26. On this point, see Dieter Henrich, *Die Einheit der Wissenschaftslehre Max Webers* (Tübingen: Mohr, 1952). Henrich's interpretation still remains pertinent today.

27. Cf. Dieter Henrich, "Über Selbstbewusstsein und Selbsterhaltung," ed. Hans Ebeling, *Subjektivität und Selbsterhaltung* (Frankfurt: Suhrkamp 1976), pp. 122ff.

28. "Author's Introduction," p. 13.

29. Cf. Benjamin Nelson, "Structures of Consciousness from the Perspective of the Comparative Historical Sociology of Sociocultural Process," paper presented at the 1971 annual meeting of the American Sociological Association (Denver).

30. *PE*, p. 182.

forced to recognize it as a possible form of civilization. They need not relativize their values because of it, but they must put their values in relation to it if they want to live with full awareness.[31]

Thus, the viewpoint selected by Weber, the directional criterion emphasized by him, does indeed constitute a sequence. But insofar as it claims not only heuristic utility but validity as well, this holds only *for us*.[32] This sequence also provides the precondition for identifying analogous developments in other cultures. The search for them is not a mere investigation of parallels and contrasts for their own sake[33] nor does it lead to an inclusive stage theory of world history. It remains primarily a diagnostic effort to understand our own culture. Therefore, Weber's perspective lacks completeness in principle and cannot satisfy either prospective or retrospective expectations on this score. Rather, it extends only far enough to help identify the comparisons relevant for Western culture and to reveal its selectivity in turn. In this sense Weber's sociology offers neither a comprehensive typology of world history nor a universal theory of evolution but a developmental history of the West.

31. On this distinction see also Karl Mannheim, *Ideology and Utopia* (New York: Harcourt, Brace, n.d.) p. 78f.

32. Cf. Henrich, *op. cit.*, p. 142.

33. This point has correctly been made by Friedrich H. Tenbruck. He calls it "an annoying blindness of Weber interpreters" that they usually try to understand the studies on the economic ethics of the world religions as a contrast to the study on the Protestant ethic. Cf. Tenbruck, "Das Werk Max Webers," *op. cit.*, p. 676.

IV

THE SUBSTANTIVE CONTENT OF WEBER'S DEVELOPMENTAL HISTORY

A. Presuppositions and Basic Concepts

Value-Spheres and Institutional Realms

In 1919/20 Weber revised his introduction to the "Economic Ethics of the World Religions," which he now called comparative essays, for his *Collected Essays in the Sociology of Religion*. He added a passage that in the eyes of many interpreters has become a key to his work: "Interests (material and ideal) not ideas directly determine man's action. But the world views, which were created by ideas, have very often acted as the switches that channeled the dynamics of the interests."[1] This quotation can also explain the basic concepts and presuppositions of a theory of Western developmental history that is based on his position but goes some steps further. The distinction between material and ideal interests is important for our undertaking. The material interests concern the "happiness" of human beings, their well-being, health and longevity. Ideal interests concern their search for meaning, primarily for "salvation." The distinction between external and internal wants is related to this juxtaposition. Since human beings are not only capable of creating meaning but are also in need of

---

1. "Introduction," p. 280; compare "Die Wirtschaftsethik der Weltreligionen," *Archiv für Sozialwissenschaft*, 41 (1916): 15. The original passage read: "Yet redemption attained a specific significance only where it expressed a systematic and rationalized 'image of the world' and a behavioral response to it. Its potential and actual meaning and psychological quality has depended on such a world image and the response to it. This determined from what and for what one wished to be redeemed." The new passage was inserted before the last sentence.

it, they are caught in two kinds of wants: it is not enough for them to survive physically, they must also be able to give meaning to life. As a rule, therefore, human beings not only battle for the distribution of material goods but also for spiritual goods, and the struggle for the one can but need not be merely a function of the other. Thus, Weber writes about modernity: "It is widely believed today that conflicts among 'class interests' predominate, but there is also a conflict among world views. This is not to deny in any way that the degree of elective affinity with a 'class interest' (if we accept this seemingly unambiguous term here for the moment) tends to be very important, apart from other factors, for the world view embraced by the individual."[2]

Material and ideal interests, interests in happiness and salvation, directly govern the actions of human beings, but the term "directly" must not be misunderstood. Interests are direct insofar as they constitute motivations. However, motives are always mediated historically; they are interpreted and institutionalized. As soon as human beings leave behind the state of "preanimist naturalism,"[3] they create symbols with the help of abstraction, differentiation and systematization. As soon as they reach this state, more and more things and processes acquire meaning apart from the effects that are believed to inhere in them in fact or surmise.[4] Thus, a world of ideas comes into being, which influences how people act. It is such symbolic systems, which may be more or less abstract, differentiated and systematized, that direct our actions, for they inform us for what and from what we want to and can be saved. However, this is not enough to channel the dynamics of interests. We must know the means through which the material and ideal goods selected in a world view can be

2. "Objectivity," p. 56.

3. *ES*, p. 406. Weber contrasts pre-animistic naturalism with symbolism. Its first developed form is represented by mythological thought and magic rationalized by analogy.

4. *ES*, p. 405. The world of ideas is at first a realm of "souls, demons and deities that cannot be encountered in everyday life but exist in a transcendental realm accessible only through symbolism and meaning." In order to be able to influence this transcendental realm symbolic action becomes increasingly more important than real action: man must manipulate symbols if he wants to influence reality. Thereby action is drawn into a "symbolist magic circle," from which it is hard to escape. This consideration provides the background for Weber's theory of disenchantment with which he formulated a central historical interest at the latest by 1913, but probably earlier. The question is under what conditions religious action can emancipate itself from the view that the realities of life can be manipulated symbolically, that is, under what conditions magic can be left completely behind. This was accomplished consistently only by ascetic Protestantism, under which the symbol that connects the world with transcendence, the sacrament, lost any ability to manipulate the religious reality. For the dating of the notion of disenchantment Weber's essay "On Some Categories of Interpretive Sociology" is important. It was published in 1913, but partly conceived at an earlier time. We encounter the thesis of the "increasing disenchantment of the world" in those passages which were apparently written "some time ago" (cf. *Wissenschaftslehre, op. cit.*, pp. 427, 433).

attained. Only the institutionalization of a world view determines which of the symbolically formulated possibilities are selectively used and how action is motivated. It is well known that in his sociology of religion Weber was interested not in theological doctrines but in the "psychological and pragmatic connections" established by a religious order.[5] Thus, an institutional realm mediates between ideas and interests. Although it never fully represents them, it is embedded in constellations of interests and ideas, but it can also claim relative autonomy *(Eigenrecht)* and a dynamic of its own *(Eigengesetzlichkeit)*. Only through institutionalization do material and spiritual wants receive a socially relevant solution. We can say, therefore, that at the center of Weber's sociology lies the analysis of a society from the viewpoint of the functional relations of its partial orders as well as its structural effects on conduct.

We have already mentioned that Weber did not present a systematic account of the institutional realms and value spheres as the locus for the fusion of ideas and interests. In the older parts of *Economy and Society* that have survived he deals primarily with lineage groups, including the neighborhood and ethnic and cultural extensions, and with religious, legal and political orders, and of course with the economy in relation to these institutional realms, insofar as these manuscript fragments are concerned with the relation between the economy and normative and de facto powers.[6] In the "Theory of the Stages and Directions of Religious Rejections of the World" of 1915 and 1920 Weber addressed primarily seven partial orders related to value spheres: the family, religion, the economy, politics, art, sexuality and eroticism, and the realm of cognition, "science."[7] To these partial orders correspond partial world views—in contradistinction to the inclusive "social formation" of Marxism and the "social system" of system theory. Thus, we must view the economic ethics, religious ethics, political ethics, etc., as partial world views. However, Weber also thinks in terms of the total social order and of total world views. How else could he consider the conflict between the institutional and value spheres as a crucial dynamic factor and analyze social change *and* social development in its terms? It is true that he does not proceed from fully integrated systems but from loosely structured societies, which sometimes must live with a lack of integration.[8] However, given his theory of conflict he must not only assume that there are some partial orders that are indispensable for the production and reproduction of life, but he must

5. "Introduction," p. 267.

6. Remember that *Economy and Society* first appeared under the title "The Economy and the Normative and De Facto Powers" in the *Grundriss der Sozialökonomik*. Part III: Economy and Society.

7. "Theory," p. 327ff.

8. On this problem see also Erwin K. Scheuch, "Methodische Probleme gesamtgesellschaftlicher Analysen" and M. Rainer Lepsius, "Demokratie in Deutschland als historisch-soziologisches Problem," ed. T. W. Adorno, *Spätkapitalismus oder Industriegesellschaft?* (Stuttgart: Enke, 1969), pp. 153ff. and 197ff.

also face the problem of mediation that is posed for each society by virtue of the integration of partial orders.

Weber dealt with such issues primarily in the various versions of the sociology of domination, where he discusses not only the internal relations of political associations but also their external relationships—especially with religion and the economy, and also with the "natural" orders of family, sib and neighborhood association.[9] I believe that I do not distort Weber's reasoning, which is partly open-ended and fragmentary on this score, if I assume that he focused on four partial orders in his analysis of society: the "natural" order, which is tied to natural reproduction, especially family and kinship, and which is at the core of a much larger order, the educational order; the economic order, which meets the recurrent, normal wants of everyday life; the cultural order, of which religion is the most important element; the political order, which protects social life on a territorial basis internally and externally. So in his analysis of a society Weber is primarily concerned with the relations of family, economy, religion and politics.

If we look for a justification for this selection, we find it first in a functionalist line of reasoning. For Weber too there are basic functions which must be fulfilled through differentiation, so that a "definite social structure" can emerge from "the lack of any structure" (1119). These functions can be called meaning, protection, want satisfaction and socialization. Each society must define exemplary individual and collective identities and solidarities as well as obligatory standards of obedience; each must protect, internally and externally, territorial life through the successful monopolization of powers of command; each must regulate the production, distribution and consumption of goods; it must also bring about a certain degree of external and internal compliance. For these distinctions we can construct an elementary analytical model of functions and exchange.[10] I assume that we can combine Weber's distinction between

9. Cf. *ES*, Part II, Chapter II and "Theory," p. 329f.

10. Cf. Talcott Parsons and Edward Shils, eds., *Toward a General Theory of Action* (New York: Harper, 1962), pp. 57f. and 65. This elementary model of functions and exchange has certain superficial similarities with Parsons' AGIL scheme (adaptation, goal attainment, integration and latent pattern maintenance). However, my scheme is not based on Parsons' "derived" space and time axes (internal-external, instrumental-consummatory) nor on the distinction between general system and social action system. For the last version of Parsons' position see Talcott Parsons and Gerald M. Platt, *The American University* (Cambridge: Harvard University Press, 1973), esp. Chapter 1. Nor is my scheme intended to dichotomize system (or structure) and action. Constans Seyfarth has correctly pointed out that Weber's sociology can be understood only if this "exclusive distinction" is abandoned. See Constans Seyfarth, "Struktur und Reichweite 'handlungstheoretischer' Ansätze: Das Beispiel Max Webers," in Karl Martin Bolte, ed., *Materialien aus der soziologischen Forschung* (Darmstadt: Luchterhand, 1978) pp. 1100ff, esp. 1103. Weber's thesis of meaningful action and action-oriented meaning cannot be grasped by dichotomizing structure and action, objectively or subjectively oriented theory. A striking example of the barriers to understanding created by such a dichotomy is provided by Veit

material and ideal interests with Parson's distinction between social objects ("actors") and nonsocial (i.e., physical and cultural) objects—see Scheme I.

A functional explanation, however, is not sufficient in itself. Functionalism provides for Weber merely an answer to a preliminary question. Empirical sociology must know "what kinds of action are functional from the viewpoint of 'self-preservation' (but also and especially of cultural distinctiveness) and important from the viewpoint of a specific evolution *(Fortbildung)* of a type of social action." Not least because of its focus on the "whole," functionalist analysis is a useful, even indispensable preliminary. However, historical research is not oriented toward the analysis of the abstract functioning of a "whole" or even merely toward the identification of what is functional for a concrete type of action. Rather, historical research asks: "How does this action come into being? What are its motives?" (18) This kind of question is related not only to the claims of an historical "science of concrete reality" *(Wirklichkeitswissenschaft)* but also to a theory of action. The analysis of a society and of its partial orders must ultimately be based on a theory of action. The reference point for the identification of an order is not the "whole," but "historical individuals," whether individual or collective. A society and its partial orders are not purposive actors. At most they serve a purpose. They merely guarantee "the likelihood that meaningfully related actions took place, take place and will take place" (27). Such a likelihood must be defined and guaranteed. This may lead to strains toward autonomy on the level of the relationship of partial orders and on the level of their relationship to the historical individuals. Weber is not so naive as to believe that actions can be transformed into an order without creating "emergent properties" and "structural effects."[11] The analysis of these phenomena is one focus of his macrosociological research program. But even though Weber recognizes their importance when he analyzes a society and its partial orders, these orders remain for him externally and internally guaranteed orientations for the actions of "historical individuals." He selects the educational, economic, political and cultural—especially religious—realms, because they constitute a framework within which interests of happiness and salvation are so interpreted and institutionalized, and life-chances are so distributed, that the society can provide a collective answer to the problems of material and spiritual needs.

Michael Bader et al., *Einführung in die Gesellschaftstheorie* (Frankfurt: Suhrkamp, 1976), 16ff. See also the well-balanced critique by Johannes Weiss in *Soziologische Revue*, 1 (1978): 119ff. An interesting attempt to use the AGIL scheme for a systematization of Weber's type of charismatic domination has been undertaken by Dirk Käsler, *Revolution und Veralltäglichung* (Munich: Nymphenburger Verlagshandlung, 1977), pp. 165ff. Richard Münch, too, has attempted a "system-theoretical reading" of Weber's work: "Max Weber's 'Anatomie des okzidentalen Rationalismus': Eine systemtheoretische Lektüre," *Soziale Welt*, 29 (1978): 217ff.

11. On "emergent properties," see Amitai Etzioni, *The Active Society* (New York: The Free Press, 1968), pp. 45ff.; on "structural effects" see Peter Blau, "Structural Effects," *ASR*, 25 (1960): 178ff.

Levels and Dimensions of Social Relations

Weber's substantive analysis, however, is not limited to value spheres and institutional realms corresponding to them. Although the four value spheres and institutional realms play an important role, at least as an analytical foil, in *Economy and Society* and "The Economic Ethics of the World Religions," he usually locates his substantive analyses on a lower level of social aggregation. Thus, in investigating Western development, he deals less with the relation of the economic, political and religious order than with the relation of the cities and the political and hierocratic powers. In the case of the political powers, this involves, for instance, the relation of Holy Roman Emperor, the feudal nobility and the patrimonial bureaucracy; in the case of hierocracy, the relation of Pope and Church, the monastic orders and heterodoxy. In addition, the interactions between rulers and their administrative staffs, for instance, between the patrimonial rulers and their benefice-holders or the charismatic leaders and their following, are of great importance to Weber. Hence, he moves along a scale of levels of social relationships.

Weber also analyzes the relation between status groups, classes and parties. In the older part of *Economy and Society* he dealt with the three concepts from the perspective of the power distribution within a community and proposed to specify the concept of the party through his discussion of forms of domination, but in the newer manuscript he incorporated the party into the sociology of domination and treated status groups and classes together in the following chapter. This shift has substantive reasons, for the concept of the party lies on a level different from that of class and status group. In the older manuscript of *Economy and Society* classes appear as part of the economic order, status groups as part of what he then calls the social order, and parties as part of the power sphere. But it is difficult for Weber to maintain their equal rank. Classes are defined in terms of the production of goods and their mode of acquisition, status groups in terms of life-style and mode of consumption, but parties cannot be defined simply by the way power is acquired. Rather, parties are primarily goal-oriented organizations which appear in orders of a higher level of aggregation. Parties are conceptually possible only "within an organization, the leadership of which they try to influence or take over" (285).[12] We can understand this reinterpretation as a more refined specification. Whereas status groups and classes belong to the societal level of social life, parties are found on the level of organizations. This does not preclude us from studying all three from the same viewpoint, for instance, the manner in which they shape a person's life-chances and the typical chances of the external placement and inner fate which depend upon them. Weber's statements on classes and status groups

12. This does not mean that in the older manuscript Weber did not treat parties as goal-oriented organizations, but now he no longer puts them on the same level with status groups and classes.

in the newer manuscript of *Economy and Society* are pertinent here. A class position "derives from the relative control over goods and skills" (302), whereas status "shall mean an effective claim to social esteem in terms of positive or negative privileges"; this esteem rests on conduct shaped by education or on familial or occupational prestige. These definitions permit us to distinguish class and status positions not so much in terms of production and consumption as in terms of the kind and degree of control over the means of production for material and spiritual goods and to apply this viewpoint to parties and organizations in which—on a different level of aggregation—persons can be identified according to the kinds and degree of control of means of organization. If we follow this line of reasoning, the power distribution within a society can be investigated not only from the viewpoint of the relation of partial orders to one another but also from different life-chances within them, and on different levels of aggregation.

Thus, in analyzing society Weber seems to have in mind not only different levels but also different criteria. From the first viewpoint we deal with the power distribution among realms, from the second with the power distribution within them. In the first case the decisive criterion is the place of an institutional realm within a kind of control hierarchy, in the second the place of an actor within an institutional realm in relation to its "means of production" for material and spiritual goods. The first kind of analysis may be called a system analysis of a society, the second a stratification analysis. Both, however, refer to components of its structure.[13] According to the premises of action theory and the plea for an individualist method, actions must correspond to these two perspectives of social order.[14] It is true that a social order circumscribes actions, but actions must realize one of its structural possibilities, or else the order will not exist.

Weber failed to draw a clear analytical distinction between the problems of order and problems of action on different levels of aggregation. Most important for him is the thesis that macrosociological analysis too must be based on individual or collective action, not on the "whole" or the "system." On the basis of this conviction he permits himself a high degree of discretion in the selection of levels of aggregation and units of analysis. This explains in part why the recon-

13. Thus, we combine an aspect of social theory taken from Talcott Parsons with one taken from Marx. In the terminology proposed here both deal with aspects of social order, not of social action. Together they define the action frame that circumscribes the individual act.

14. Cf. *ES*, p. 18. Weber stated emphatically that "it is a tremendous misunderstanding to think that an 'individualistic' method should involve what is in any conceivable sense a set of individualist values," just as the rationalist character of concept formation has nothing to do with a positive valuation of rationalism. But this disclaimer has been of little help. Time and again the literature has resurrected this misunderstanding. Cf. the apposite remarks by Johannes Weiss, *op. cit.*, and his *Max Webers Grundlegung der Soziologie, op. cit.*, pp. 90ff.

struction of his substantive investigations is so difficult. Levels and units of analysis are changed frequently and often without explanation. This gives his work a fragmentary character—beyond the autobiographical aspects, which are of course important too. Therefore, it must be the task of an explication to classify systematically the problems of order and of action and their connections on various levels. We can facilitate such an explication by recourse to recent developments in the literature.

In his review of familiar critiques of normative functionalism, David Lockwood elaborated the distinction between social integration and system integration, social conflict and systemic conflict: "Whereas the problem of social integration focuses attention upon the orderly or conflictful relationships between the actors, the problem of system integration focuses on the orderly or conflictful relationships between the parts of a social system."[15] Lockwood wants also to identify the status of a conflict theory that is merely the opposite of the integration theory it attacks. Its critical arguments, he argues, are valid at best against normative, not against general functionalism. The very case of Marx, who is usually cited against functionalism, shows that it is not sufficient to focus on social conflict as class conflict, that is, on social disintegration. Capitalist societies are conceivable, and have indeed appeared, in which the contradiction between the forces and the relations of production, between the technological potential and the institutions of property and labor, reflect a "growing surplus of productive capacity," and thus systemic disintegration, but without an exacerbation of class conflict or social disintegration. Hence, we must distinguish for both theoretical and practical reasons between problems of systemic and of social integration and specify the elements of both. Because of the importance which Marx attributed to the economic order, he viewed systemic disintegration in terms of the contradiction between the material means of production and the institution of property and labor, and social integration in terms of the relations between bourgeoisie and proletariat. Lockwood, however, points out that this is only one case of systemic and social integration. If we want to take a Weberian position, we must relativize the thesis that the economic order is the ultimate determinant in two respects even for capitalism: 1. We cannot say a priori which value sphere or institutional realm ultimately determines the integration of a society. This is an historical question which is decided by the position of an individual sphere in the control hierarchy of a society. 2. The possible discrepancy between the material means of production and the institution of property and labor is only one source of tension. In other spheres discrepancies may arise, as between the dominant political order and the means of domination or between the dominant religious order and the means of salvation. Life-chances are provided not only by the economic but also by the political and

15. David Lockwood, "Social Integration and System Integration," eds. George Zollschan and W. Hirsch, *Explorations in Social Change* (London: Routledge and Kegan Paul, 1964), p. 295.

social order, and the situation of one order can but need not be a mere function of the situation of another.

From a system perspective Niklas Luhmann has proposed a distinction between interaction, organization and society. The criteria of the distinction are the principles of selection and boundary maintenance which prevail in these three types. Interaction is defined by presence, organization by membership, and society by the extent of possible and meaningful communication.[16] Thus, the types are also distinguished by their levels. The different levels of order are conceived to be "stacked up" in such a way that the order of a higher level guarantees to that of a lower level an environment with a limited number of possibilities. Under these constraints they are free to make their own selections.

If we relate this approach to Weber's theory and combine it with Lockwood's, we gain a clearer picture of the problems of order and action. It is important for our purposes to distinguish between systemic and social integration and between society, organization and interaction. However, both approaches must be modified. By system integration I mean the integration of an action frame with two components: the resolution of the tensions between as well as within orders. The first kind of tension results from the position of a partial order in the control hierarchy, the second from the position of an actor vis-à-vis the means of production of material and spiritual goods. By social integration I mean meaningfully related actions on the basis of this action frame. Society, organization and interaction are combinations of levels of order with levels of action. This means that we must examine for each level not only the system and stratification aspect but also the action aspect.[17] (Cf. Schemes I and II.)

If superimposed on Weber's theory, this scheme has some interesting consequences for research strategy: (1) It makes it possible to draw a clear analytical distinction between the structural and the personal aspect on all levels. The focus is no longer on the relation between individual and society. Rather, we are concerned with elaborating a theory of structure on these levels and with determining the effects which such structures have for one another and for individual actions.[18] (2) It makes it possible to draw a clear analytical distinction between tensions within a level and tensions among levels. (3) It facilitates an

16. See Niklas Luhmann, *Soziologische Aufklärung, op. cit.*, pp. 9ff.

17. My proposal has some similarities with the rationale for analyzing configurations and interdependencies proposed by Norbert Elias. See his *Höfische Gesellschaft* (Darmstadt: Luchterhand, 1975), pp. 215ff.

18. On the theory of social structure, see Anthony Giddens, *The Class Structure of the Advanced Societies* (New York: Harper, 1973) and M. Rainer Lepsius, "Sozialstruktur und soziale Schichtung in der Bundesrepublik Deutschland," in Richard Lowenthal and Hans-Peter Schwarz, eds., *Die zweite Republik* (Stuttgart: Seewald, 1974), 263; Hans Bertram, *Gesellschaft, Familie und moralisches Urteil* (Weinheim: Beltz, 1978), pp. 150ff. On the theory of organizational structure see now also Irene von Wersebe, *Qualifizierte Spezialisierung und Autoritätsstruktur* (Munich: Minerva, 1978) and id., "Demokratisierung durch Professionalisierung?" in *Zeitschrift für Soziologie*, 7 (1978): 157ff.

analytical identification of the restrictive conditions. Not only do structures constitute restrictive conditions for actions, but higher levels of aggregation restrict lower ones. (4) We can regard Weber's research program as a multi-level analysis. Such an analysis relates the functional relations of structures to the conduct of persons on different levels of aggregation.

The distinction between order and action, between the structural and the personal aspect, must not lead to a radical separation. We must always keep in mind that in Lockwood's words the distinction remains "quite artificial." It is artificial above all because order and action, structure and person, must be mediated through subjective meaning. In my view, this is the core of Weber's concept of action: behavior becomes action insofar as the actor attaches subjective meaning to it. This does not deny that people react to a social order—they do so instinctively. Weber was realistic enough to emphasize strongly that "fully conscious and meaningful action is in reality always a marginal case" and that "in the great majority of cases actual action goes on in a state of inarticulate

Scheme I
Basic Functions of a Society

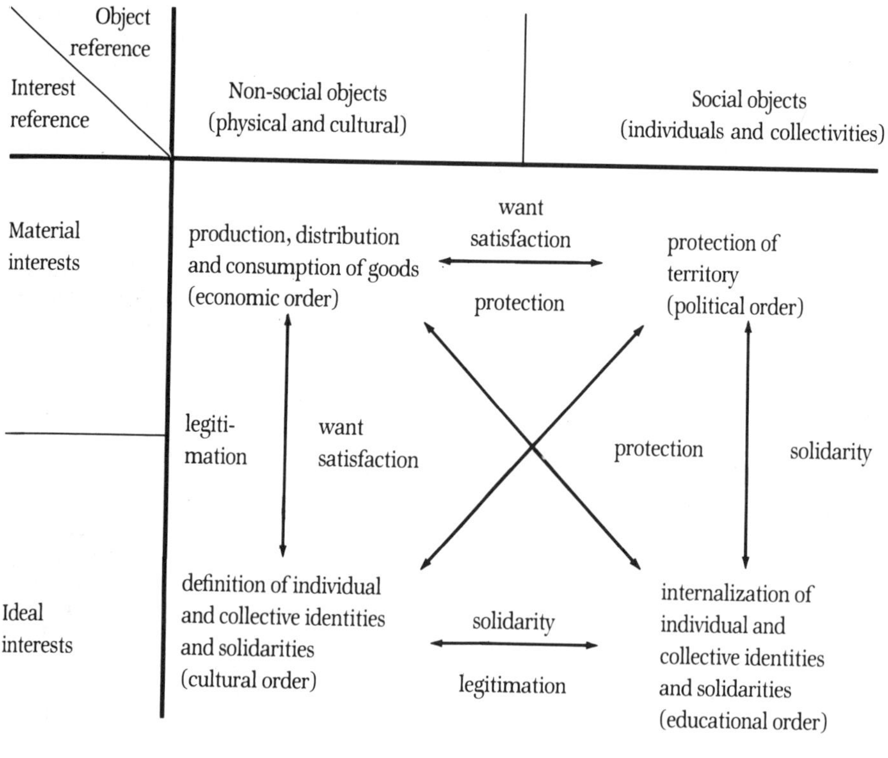

half-consciousness or actual unconsciousness of its subjective meaning" (21f.). But this does not change the fact that actions require symbolic mediation. In Weber's sociology a social order is valid if action is oriented to it in a meaningful way. Social orders are intelligible because they have more or less clearly articulated symbolic components, because they are not merely apparatuses. An order therefore can be understood as a set of institutionalized ideas. Insofar as it belongs to the evaluative sphere, it has an ethical as well as an instrumental component. This explains why actors suit their actions to an order, not only "out of fear or habituation or opportunism" (947) but also because they view the order as "exemplary, binding, and morally desirable" (31).

In elaborating a developmental history that proceeds from Weber, we must not only take into account the connection between system and social integration; we must also avoid viewing the concept of social order in a one-dimensional way. We must distinguish at least between the "apparatus" and the symbols; in this sense every order has an external and an internal component, and the concept of structure applies to both. From this it follows that we must distinguish the structural and the personal aspect in the case of both the external

Scheme II
Dimensions of Integration of Societies

Problem Levels of order and action	system integration		social integration
	power distribution among partial orders	power distribution within partial orders	
societal level	relations among institutional realms	within institutional realms	class and status- oriented action
organizational level	relations among organizations	within organizations	party-oriented action
interaction level	relations among roles	within roles	role-oriented action
	system analysis	stratification analysis	action analysis

The power distribution among partial orders results from their position within the control hierarchy of a society. The power distribution within partial orders results from the position of an actor vis-à-vis the means of production of material and spiritual goods.

and the internal order. Just as persons confront the apparatus, their subjective meanings confront the "objective" meaning of an order. Objective meaning provides a range of possibilities from which the actors must make their choices. Where an order belongs to the evaluative sphere we can clarify this relationship by distinguishing between ethics and morality. An ethic defines an "objective" meaning, which is selectively used by individual moralities. An ethic is compatible with several moralities, just as an apparatus is compatible with different persons. In structural respects a social order must be analyzed from two viewpoints: that of its ethics and their fusion into an overarching ethic of a total world view (Gesamtweltbild) and that of its institutions and their overall integration.

In Jürgen Habermas' terms, we can regard these relationships as aspects of the infrastructure of objective action systems, the subjective correlate of which is the human ability to communicate and to act. However, this does not sufficiently describe the structure of a society. The infrastructure of action systems shows an important differentiation. We "can distinguish the institutions that regulate the normal case from those special institutions that, in case of conflict, re-establish the endangered intersubjectivity of understanding (law and morality)."[19] Whereas the former represent the general action structures of a social order, in which social life follows its routines, the latter constitute the core structures through which a social order asserts its collective identity.

This proposal can be translated into Weber's theory if we assume that the core structure comprises not only the institutional but also the ethical core of a social order. For this purpose we can fall back on a distinction that is fundamental for Weber's sociology: the difference between the ordinary and the extraordinary in social life.[20] As is well known, Weber tends to identify the extraordinary with personal charisma and to contrast it with stable institutionalization. Charisma appears as personal grace "in but not of this world"; it is a power "outside ordinary vocation and daily family duties," it is "the strongest anti-economic force" (1112f.). However, Weber himself as well as his interpreters have pointed out that it does not always make sense to view personal charisma and enduring institutional structures as polar opposites. Weber spoke of institutional charisma in his discussion of the transformation of personal charisma. Among the interpreters Edward Shils and S. N. Eisenstadt

19. Cf. Jürgen Habermas, "Toward a Reconstruction of Historical Materialism," in *Communication and the Evolution of Society, op. cit.,* p. 156.

20. Recently Constans Seyfarth has pointed out the importance of this distinction and attempted to interpret Weber's sociology as a program for the genetic reconstruction of life worlds. Apart from his essay cited in n. 10, see also "Alltag und Charisma bei Max Weber. Eine Studie zur Grundlegung der 'verstehenden' Soziologie," in Richard Grathoff and Walter M. Sprondel, eds., *Alfred Schütz und die Idee des Alltags in den Sozialwissenschaften* (Stuttgart: Enke, 1979), pp. 155ff. Although I share Seyfarth's intentions, I consider the concept of the life world too amorphous for a sufficiently precise characterization of Weber's research program.

have argued convincingly that charisma is a constitutive element of institution-building.[21] Thus, there is no compelling reason to equate personal charisma and the extraordinary. The force of personal charisma, its mission, which Weber links with the distress of human beings, is at least originally, in more or less articulated form, the basis of every social order believed to be legitimate. It is comparable to what Emile Durkheim, from another perspective and for different reasons, calls the sacred character of a collective moral reality. The sacred is characterized by its separation from the profane and by being unconditionally obligatory because it is the locus of collective identity definition.[22] Shils has called this realm of the extraordinary, of the sacred, the center of a social order: "The center, or central zone, is a phenomenon of the realm of values and beliefs. It is the center of the order of symbols, of values and beliefs, which govern the society. It is the center because it is the ultimate and irreducible; and it is felt to be such by many who cannot give explicit articulation to its irreducibility. The central zone partakes of the nature of the sacred. In this sense, every society has an 'official' religion, even when that society or its exponents and interpreters conceive of it, more or less correctly, as a secular, pluralistic, and tolerant society."[23]

This view can be related to another. Especially in his studies on the economic ethics of the world religions Weber points to the bifocal nature of religious ethics—they appear in orthodox and heterodox form. This is a relative distinction, but it reminds us that it would be an inappropriate simplification to think of the core structure of a society as being monolithic. It too shows structural variation.

If we combine these two views, we gain a matrix that in Habermas' sense appears suitable for the interpretation of the structural complexities within a society. Like Habermas I assume that core structures are shaped by notions of justice and equity, whereas general action structures are oriented to notions of reciprocity and "fairness." This distinction says nothing about the frequency, only about the kind of conflicts. Within core structures conflict concerns legitimation; within general action structures it concerns primarily conflicts about procedures and distribution.

21. Cf. Edward Shils, "Charisma, Order and Status," *ASR*, 30 (1965): 199ff. and S. N. Eisenstadt, "Introduction," *Max Weber. On Charisma and Institution Building* (Chicago: University of Chicago Press, 1968). See also the distinction between charismatic leadership and charismatic authority in Reinhard Bendix, *Max Weber, op. cit.*, p. 299f. As early as 1937 Talcott Parsons pointed to the parallel between Durkheim's concept of the sacred and Weber's concept of the extraordinary *(Ausseralltäglichkeit)*; see *The Structure of Social Action* (Glencoe: The Free Press, 1961), pp. 658ff and 669ff. On the difference of the two approaches, see Reinhard Bendix, "Two Sociological Traditions," in Bendix and Roth, *op. cit.*, pp. 282ff, esp. pp. 294ff.

22. Cf. Emile Durkheim, *Sociology and Philosophy* (London: Cohen and West, 1953), pp. 68ff.

23. Edward Shils, *Center and Periphery* (Chicago: The University of Chicago Press, 1975), p. 3.

This scheme is still too simple,[24] but it permits two interesting conclusions for a theory of social change and social development that proceeds from Weber: (1) Extraordinariness is not only a special type of domination but also a constitutive element of every society. Insofar as ideas of justice are linked to it every society has a "mission." Their reinterpretation can become the basis of a change and development of consciousness, of a revolution of consciousness. Only this makes fully understandable why Weber argues that personal charisma revolutionizes not through technical means from the outside but through a "central metanoia of the convictions of the ruled" by destroying notions of sanctity. Personal charisma attacks from inside a dominant core structure. The creator of ideas or works may dramatize traditional notions of justice or try to replace them with new ones.[25] (2) No dominant core structure can be fully immunized against this kind of revolution from within. Such a revolution remains a structural possibility, and its realization does not depend on personal charisma. In Weber's view, therefore, the internal revolutionary transformation cannot be considered a priori a function of external revolution, or vice versa. Both relationships are possible, but the extent to which this happens must remain an historical question.

Core structures are located on the highest level of aggregation of a social order. They have a symbolic, an institutional and an interest dimension. The symbolic dimension comprises not only evaluative, especially ethical, ideas but also cognitive and expressive ones; the institutional dimension not only religious, political, economic and educational institutions but also scientific and artistic ones; the interest dimension not only ideal but also material interests. The major symbolic, institutional and interest components are combined into a basic social configuration, which is comparable to Habermas' "organizational principle." Thus, it consists of highly abstract regulations which describe a social order's range of possibilities. Basic configurations or organizational principles determine the basic modes of social integration. They establish, in particular, "within which structures changes of the institutional system are possible; to what degree existing productive capacities can be used by the society or new productive forces can be mobilized. They also circumscribe the extent to which the complexity of a system and its steering capacity can be increased." As Habermas goes on to say, an organizational principle consists of "such abstract

24. A higher degree of complexity can be achieved by applying the idea of mixing stages, as it has been proposed in developmental psychology, which links low levels of mixtures with developmental stagnation and high levels with dynamic development. Cf. Elliot Turiel, "Developmental Processes in the Child's Moral Thinking," eds. Paul H. Mussen et al., *Trends and Issues in Developmental Psychology* (New York: Holt, 1969).

25. Cf. *ES*, p. 1116. This passage is important also because Weber touches here on the connection between a theory of value spheres and a theory of the actual effects of ideas. A central change of mind is not due to a mere "subjective feeling" or "experience" but "to a being seized by the demands of the work," a psychological effect that is intelligible only if we assume the "objective" character of ideas.

regulations that in the social formation determined by it several functionally equivalent modes of production are feasible."[26] If we follow Weber, this is true of the mode of production and also of the modes of domination and of the ways in which a society satisfies the functions of meaning and socialization.

If we want to extract from Weber's sociology not only a theory of the social changes but also of the social development of the West, we must analytically identify such basic configurations and then locate them in his work. The analytical derivation must again proceed from recent discussions in the literature, but our reference to Weber will be limited primarily to his sociology of religion, law and domination. Other parts could be included, but I have avoided this for the most part, since I am interested not in an interpretation of Weber's work as a whole but in the articulation of his developmental history of the West.

B. Basic Configurations of Social Order

1. The Ethical Component

Typology of Ethics

In order to identify the ethical component of basic configurations I consider it useful to proceed from evolutionary theory based on a logic of development. Such a theory employs the basic concepts of a genetic theory of action and the parallelism of ontogenesis and phylogenesis—the latter, however, only with considerable qualifications.[27] The theory is based on the thesis of a correspondence between the subjective competence to act and objective structures of action. From the actor's development of competence the theory derives criteria for the structural development of symbolic realms within which the development of individual competence occurs. This strategy is justified by the observation

26. Habermas, *op. cit.*,, p. 153.

27. This program of research has been undertaken especially by Jürgen Habermas and his collaborators. They are also interested in a reconstruction of historical materialism along the lines of a theory of action. In addition to previously cited works, see Habermas, *Handlungsrationalität und gesellschaftliche Rationalisierung* (unpubl. ms 1978). In my view this study will advance the discussion considerably. See also Klaus Eder and Ulrich Rödel, "Handlungstheoretische Implikationen des historischen Materialismus," in Karl Martin Bolte, ed., *op. cit.*, pp. 1092 ff.; Klaus Eder, "Zum Problem der logischen Periodisierung von Produktionsweisen. Ein Beitrag zu einer evolutionstheoretischen Rekonstruktion des historischen Materialismus" and Rainer Döbert, "Methodologische und forschungsstrategische Implikationen von evolutionstheoretischen Stadienmodellen," both in Urs Jaeggi and Axel Honneth, eds., *Theorien des historischen Materialismus, op. cit.*, pp. 501ff. and 524ff. On the limits of the parallelism between ontogenesis and phylogenesis, see J. Habermas, "Historical Materialism and the Development of Normative Structures," in *Communication and the Evolution of Society, op. cit.*, p. 102f.

that—if we accept the premises of a cognitive psychology of development—individuals develop their competence through a combination of maturation and learning, which is based on their actively coming to terms with a natural, social and cultural environment. Ontogenetic processes of development are not simplistically determined by the environment, but they are influenced by it. There is no exact correspondence but an elective affinity, a relation of mutual support, between the structure of the environment and the competence of subjects capable of speaking and action. At least it makes heuristic sense to search for structural analogies between the development of the individual and the collective world view. However, there is an important limitation to such analogies: the explanation of development in terms of "maturation" and "age," which is perhaps meaningful for individuals, is not appropriate on the level of collectivities.

The works of Lawrence Kohlberg provide an important foundation for structural analogies between the moral development of an individual and the ethical development of a society.[28] Kohlberg endeavors to show that "there are stages or directed structural age-changes in the area of social-personality development just as there are in the cognitive area."[29] His position is 'cognitivist' insofar as he maintains that "directed sequences of changes in behavior organization or shape always have a strong cognitive component." This is also true of moral development in two respects: 1. Moral development has cognitive preconditions. 2. The analysis of the cognitive dimension of moral development—the analysis of moral judgment and its development—is a precondition for understanding the development of moral action and moral affect. In analyzing moral judgment it is necessary to distinguish between cognitive form and cognitive content. Only the cognitive form of moral judgment permits statements about directed sequences, universal stages and types of moral judgment. Therefore, Kohlberg asserts that "universal and regular age trends of development may be found in moral judgment, and these have a formal-cognitive base. Many aspects of moral judgment do not have such a cognitive base, but these aspects do not define universal and regular trends of moral development."[30]

28. Cf. Lawrence Kohlberg, "Stage and Sequence: The Cognitive-Developmental Approach to Socialization," in David A. Goslin, ed., *Handbook of Socialization Theory and Research* (Chicago: Rand McNally, 1969), Ch. 6, pp. 347-480; "Continuities in Childhood and Adult Moral Development Revisited," in P. B. Baltes et al., eds., *Life-Span Developmental Psychology* (New York: Academic Press, 1973), pp. 179-204. It should be noted that Kohlberg is still revising his theory and that it is quite controversial. On the dangers of an unwary Kohlberg reception see Hans Bertram, "Zur Bedeutung moralischer Entwicklung und Sozialisation für politische Bildungsprozesse" (unpubl. ms, Heidelberg 1978) and his discussion of German literature on the tradition of Piaget and Kohlberg, "Sozialisation oder Entwicklung: Vom angepassten zum handelnden Subjekt?," in *Soziologische Revue* 2 (1979): 9 ff. My remarks are not intended as a contribution to the Kohlberg discussion. I only use his ideas on stage and sequence as heuristic means for reconstructing the developmental aspect of Weber's position.

29. Kohlberg, "Stage and Sequence," *op. cit.*, p. 369.   30. *Op. cit.*, pp. 372, 374f.

Kohlberg has proposed three levels of moral judgment and moral consciousness, each of which has two stages, so that a six-stage scheme results. I am here only interested in the three levels. They denote basic forms of moral judgment, with which the child relates to self and environment. These forms classify actions in terms of which ones can be considered to be good, and for what reasons. Kohlberg calls the levels of judgment pre-conventional, conventional and post-conventional. On the pre-conventional level, an action is considered to be good if it has positive physical or hedonist consequences for the actor. A rule is considered right because it is willed by an overwhelmingly powerful person. On the conventional level an action is considered to be good if it intentionally fulfills the expectations of recognized reference groups, from the family to the nation, and if at the same time the action contributes to the preservation of the social order that is centered around these expectations. It is considered right that this order claims loyalty. A rule is right if it is willed by the group with which the individual identifies. On the post-conventional level an action is considered to be good if in intention or consequence (or both) it follows a principle that is recognized by the individual. A rule is right because it is recognized to be so independently of persons and reference groups. Kohlberg also calls the post-conventional level the autonomous and principled level. The two other levels do not have such other appellations.[31]

If one looks closely at Kohlberg's description of the different levels, it becomes evident that he does not clearly specify their dimensions. Therefore, the levels need to be reconstructed systematically. Since we are dealing with levels and stages of moral judgment, we shall derive our most important criteria from the analysis of the act of judgment. Such an act has at least three dimensions: the subject of judgment, the criterion or basis of judgment, and the object of judgment. Kohlberg's descriptions refer to all three dimensions. First of all, the three levels show that the actor becomes increasingly autonomous. His moral judgment changes with his changing relationship to the environment. As the ego identifies itself more clearly, external control turns into self-control, objective responsibility into subjective, and heteronomy into autonomy. Thus, the three levels describe a process of individuation through which the ego becomes more and more capable of making judgments independently of the authority of persons and groups. Furthermore, this individuation of the subject is paralleled by an increasingly abstract basis of judgment. Concrete "law-giving" persons and social groups turn into abstract principles. Finally, the object of evaluation also changes. Instead of the consequences, the intention of an action moves into the center of judgment.

31. See also Kohlberg and Elliot Turiel, "Moral Development and Moral Education," in G. Lesser, ed., *Psychology and Educational Practice* (Chicago: Scott, Foresman, 1971), p. 415f. In the latter essay the original scheme is modified by a distinction between pre-moral stage and preconventional phase. But the six stages remain, since the premoral stage is designated as stage zero.

Since we want to draw upon criteria of ontogenetic development for the analysis of phylogenetic development, the transformation of the basis of judgment is of special interest among the three dimensions. Moral criteria are not only the objective aspect of the individual moral consciousness, they probably have also a collective component which is a "richer" reality than the individual's.[32] The process of abstraction, which the individual moral judgment experiences with regard to the moral criteria, must have preconditions on the level of ethics. Autonomous individual morality demands an ethic of the highest abstraction, an ethic that satisfies the criteria of ideal-typical abstraction—logical and teleological consistency. At least, we can conclude this from the way Kohlberg describes the sixth and last stage: "Right is defined by the decision of conscience in accord with self-chosen ethical principles appealing to logical comprehensiveness, universality, and consistency. These principles are abstract and ethical (the Golden Rule, the categorical imperative), not concrete moral rules like the Ten Commandments. At heart, these are universal principles of justice, of the reciprocity and equality of human rights, and of respect for the dignity of human beings as individual persons."[33] If we disregard the illustrations and the unclear terminology, we see that here a distinction is drawn between concrete ethical rules and abstract ethical principles. I consider it useful to view for the time being not only the development of moral judgment but also of ethics from this perspective, which involves a central criterion that is also crucial for Weber's sociology. This is not equally true of the shift of moral judgment from the consequence to the intent of an action. It is true that this aspect too appears in Weber's sociology but in reverse, so to speak: the ethic of good intentions (or conviction) is older than the ethic of responsibility.

If we want to assess more precisely the importance of abstraction for a formal characterization of the ethical component of basic social configurations, a suggestion by Jürgen Habermas may be helpful. He has interpreted and systematized Kohlberg's levels in terms of the theory of action. Habermas distinguishes "the stage of symbolically mediated interaction at which speaking and acting are still enmeshed in the framework of a single, imperativist mode of communication" from the "stage of propositionally differentiated speech," at which speaking and acting separate in such a way that an action can be evaluated from the perspective of the observer as well as the participant. Now it is possible to speak about actions, but only on the basis of norms that are taken for granted. On the third level this limitation is removed. Here it is possible to speak not only about actions in the light of given norms but also about these norms in the light of principles. Propositionally differentiated speech becomes argumentative speech. Assertions about the validity of norms can be explained in discourse, and actions can be justified by it. Habermas interprets this communica-

32. See also Durkheim's distinction between collective and individual representations in *Sociology and Philosophy, op. cit.*, Ch. I.
33. Kohlberg and Turiel, *op. cit.*, p. 416.

tive development as "the step-by-step differentiation of a social reality graduated in itself." Through this differentiation the individual shifts the basis of his judgment first from action to norm and then from norm to principle.[34]

This systematic reconstruction immediately points up another limitation of the parallelism between ontogenesis and phylogenesis. There cannot be a preconventional ethic, for an ethic presupposes the differentiation of actions and norms. This does not mean that pre-ethical actions are not guided by symbols and do not contain "demands." But these symbolic representations remain intertwined with the action level. Against the background of this persepctive we must read Weber's "systematic" sociology of religion in *Economy and Society*. Weber distinguishes between preanimist naturalism and symbolism, and on the level of symbolism between magic and religious ethic, between belief in demons and faith in gods, taboos and divine commandment. It is true that he also speaks—in my view misleadingly—of magical ethics, especially because within the mythological world view demands exist in the form of taboos, the violation of which will be punished by retribution.[35] However, in this case cognitive and evaluative symbolism are still fused and the relations of human beings to their symbolic world are "forced." They have not yet developed a relationship of distance, of supplication, of sacrifice and veneration toward their symbolic representations. They cannot yet understand the violation of prescriptions as sin. Demons don't allow themselves to be supplicated and venerated; they need to be compelled. These "compelling" symbolic relationships are sundered by religious ethics. Compared to magic it is *the* new principle, and it is linked to the formation of a "rational metaphysics," that is, to a cognitive development (427). The cognitive preconditions for the development of ethics are rational metaphysics, and the displacement of the mythological world view by a metaphysical one, of monism by dualism, and of the unity of natural and ethical causality by their difference. Ethics is at first religious ethics and as such "law ethics." Thus, it belongs to the class of normative ethics, in contrast to principled ethics.[36] But this means a profound transformation of the relation between human beings and their symbolic world: "Hitherto, there had been two primordial methods of

34. Habermas, "Toward a Reconstruction of Historical Materialism," *op. cit.*, p. 154f.

35. Cf. *ES*, p. 437. However, the distinction between magical and religious ethics is paralleled by the distinction between belief in spirits and faith in gods, and magical and ethical religiosity. In general, Weber tends to conflate the objective and the subjective component of meaning. I will try to avoid the difficulties resulting from this inclination by looking at Weber from Durkheim's perspective.

36. Weber's distinction of types of religious ethics is implicit. See, for instance, *ES*, p. 576: "The more a religion of salvation has been systematized and internalized in the direction of an ethic of conviction *(Gesinnungsethik)*, the greater becomes its tension in relation to the world. This tension appears in less consistent fashion and less as a matter of principle as long as the religion has a ritualistic or legalistic form. In this form the religion exerts the same effects as those of magical ethics."

influencing supernatural powers. One was to subject them to human purposes
by means of magic. The other was to win them over by making oneself agree-
able to them not by the exercise of any ethical virtue, but by gratifying their
egotistic wishes. To these methods was now added obedience to the religious
law as the distinctive way to win the god's favor" (432). This means that a new
moral level has been achieved. Action has been differentiated from norm and
cognitive from evaluative symbolism.

If we follow the remaining criteria of Kohlberg's scheme, it appears that
for Weber there is only the distinction between conventional and post-conventional ethics, between an ethic of norms and and an ethic of principles. There is
much in favor of this view. This distinction suffices to reconstruct systematically
what is perhaps the most crucial aspect of Weber's sociology of religion, the
contrast between the "law ethic" and the ethic of conviction *(Gesinnungsethik)*.
Large parts of his sociology of religion are concerned with this difference, but
also with the developments that brought it about. This is especially true of the
comparative studies on the world religions, insofar as they deal with the character of their religious ethics. At the same time Weber also treats this problem in
the context of the question: under what institutional conditions do religious ethics of conviction shape autonomous, subjectively responsible individuals, and
how do these affect the world?

I believe that the religious ethic of conviction can indeed be classified as an
ethic of principles. To begin with, this is made clear by Weber's description of
its cognitive context. It consists of a "metaphysically rationalized religion"
(426), which in the form of theodicies has worked out systematic and "formally
perfect" solutions to the problem of the perfection of transcendence and the
imperfection of this world by "splitting the world into two principles" (523f.).
This occurred in the cognitive form of an ontological, spiritualist and ethical
dualism, that is, in the historic manifestations of Zoroastrian dualism, of the
Buddhist and Hinduist doctrine of karma and of the Calvinist doctrine of predestination. At least among intellectuals, in all these cases a collective cognitive
level has been achieved, which in Piaget's sense has formal and operative features.[37] This means that moral judgments of an abstract and principled kind
have become possible, especially where religious thought embraces the idea of
salvation and follows the path of universalist monotheism. The emergence of an
ethic of abstract principles is particularly likely when the idea of salvation, universalist monotheism and the ethical interpretation of dualism are combined.
This happened in the Judeo-Christian tradition, which is founded on the idea of
a personal ethical god with "absolute unchangeableness, omnipotence and om-
niscience—in brief, with an absolutely transcendental character" (518). This
idea leads to a tremendous increase in the power of such a god and of the ethi-

37. Cf. Lawrence Kohlberg, "Continuities in Childhood and Adult Moral Development Revisited," *op. cit.*, pp. 179ff.

cal principle championed by him. Such an emphasis on the ethical in the shape of a personal god constituted a profound difference between the Judeo-Christian tradition and the other great religious traditions. For spiritualism the gods are "light" and for the believers in karma personal gods can t rivaln o'the super-divine character of the eternal order of the world" (525). In comparing the Near Eastern and Asian traditions with the special phenomenon of the Judeo-Christian tradition Weber came to the conclusion that from the beginning the latter had been weighted on the side of an "ethically integrated personality" (533).

However, these considerations are not yet sufficient for an adequate characterization of Weber's "theory of ethics." Two more aspects must be taken into account. 1. Weber knows not only a religious but also a secular ethic of conviction, especially an ethic of responsibility, 2. In central passages of his sociology of religion he analyzes the dualism of in-group and out-group morality and its resolution. The second aspect is of fundamental importance particularly for a discussion of Western religious development. It makes intelligible the reasons for distinguishing between a Judaic and a Christian component in this tradition.

At first sight, we might be inclined to consider the first aspect as relatively unimportant. Because we want to distinguish between basic configurations and variants, development and change, we might be tempted to view the religious and secular ethic of conviction and the ethic of responsibility as three forms of one and the same configuration. However, such a view is systematically unsatisfactory. In my opinion, the ethic of responsibility is, from a systematic perspective, part of a basic configuration in its own right. Only in this manner can we understand what Weber meant by the transition from a religious to a secular abstract ethic—not so much the transformation of principles of faith into those of reason as the transition to the use of a reflexive principle. Weber's diagnosis shows us how he views the destruction of the Christian illusion. For Weber not only Christian ethics but ethical principles as such have become problematic. In Western modernity the morally evaluating and acting individual is forced to choose his own moral fate. To modify a formulation by Niklas Luhmann, even in the moral realm modern man is forced from representation into reflexivity— or which ethics can be understood no longer in substantive terms but only in terms of structurally conditioned selectivity. Ethics becomes a transparent contingency formula.[38] It transcends itself and points to other contingency formulas. To put it paradoxically: in principle, ethics has become incapable of constituting meaning nonselectively. The contingency experience of moral consciousness is based no longer, as was true in the case of theodicy, on the felt experience of the world's imperfection, but on the imperfection of the "other," the transcendent world. This is the systematic reason for Weber's perception that modern Western rationalism constitutes a consciousness that has universal

38. Cf. Niklas Luhmann, *Funktion der Religion* (Frankfurt: Suhrkamp, 1977), esp. Ch. 2.

meaning and validity, without its content—its particular interpretation of civilization—being binding on all people for all times. The principle that controls this consciousness points to, and even requires, substantive alternatives.

If we want to state this idea systematically, we must not be content with the distinction between action, norm and principle. We need another level on which ethical principles become reflexive and change from the state of divine or rational givenness to one of contingent generation. Strictly speaking, Kohlberg's sixth and last stage of individual moral judgment and consciousness rests on such a basis. For "right is defined by the decision of conscience in accord with self-chosen ethical principles." It remains true, however, that Kohlberg's scheme does not let us clearly separate a choice between given principles from one which constitutes principles in turn. This is another limitation of the parallelism between ontogenesis and phylogenesis.[39]

If we look at the second aspect, we can gain another criterion for the formal systematization of ethics, apart from the criterion of abstraction. Weber's distinction between in-group and out-group morality refers not to the basis but to the realm of validity of an ethic. This criterion is already contained in Kohlberg's scheme and in its systematization by Habermas: the more abstract the basis of validity, the more comprehensive its realm of validity. However, in Weber's sociology of religion this dimension of the realm of validity, which can be defined in terms of particularism and universalism, must not be linked too rigidly with the dimension of the basis of validity. At least on the level of historical variants Weber recognized ethics of principle that are not completely universalist. In this respect, too, the Judeo-Christian tradition has a special place. Its idea of a universal god, no matter how diluted or combined with other ideas, was not only directed from the very beginning against the particularism of local and functional deities with their concrete norm-oriented ethics, but also made possible the idea of world history.

These considerations can be sketched in the following scheme, which classifies ethics according to the dimensions of the basis and realm of validity (see Scheme III).

39. Cf. J. Habermas, "Moral Development and Ego Identity," *Communication and the Evolution of Society, op. cit.,* p. 90. In his revision of Kohlberg's scheme Habermas points out that Kohlberg's sixth stage contains two qualitatively different ethics of principle, which can be called formalist ethics and universal ethics of speech *(Sprachethik):* "The principle of justification is no longer the monologically applicable *principle* of generalizability but the communally followed *procedure* of redeeming normative validity discursively. An unexpected result of our attempt to derive the stages of moral consciousness from the stages of interactive competence is the demonstration that Kohlberg's schema of stages is incomplete." I agree with Habermas, but my analytical strategy is different. For me the difference between the two ethics of principle rests primarily on their different bases of validity and only secondarily upon whether they have the form of monologue or dialogue.

Scheme III
Ethical Components of Basic Social Configurations

Realm of Validity / Basis of validity	particularist	universalist
action	magical "ethic"	--------
norm	particularist law ethic	universalist law ethic
principle	particularist ethic of conviction	universalist ethic of conviction
reflexive principle	--------	ethic of responsibility

In this scheme I use Weber's concepts, but omit the adjective "religious" before law ethic and ethic of conviction for three reasons: 1. Under the heading of religious ethics Weber collapsed two social ethics that should be kept separate: law ethic as norm-oriented ethic and ethic of conviction as an ethic of principle. For example, Confucianism[40] is for Weber a religious ethic, but it is also the polar opposite of an ethic of conviction based on a salvation religion, such as ascetic Protestantism, which is definitely an ethic of principle.[41] 2. Next to religious ethics, there are secular ethics, especially political and economic ones, which also must be comprehended in structural terms. This is true even if a religious-metaphysical world view, that is, a theocentric or cosmocentric dualism with its variants from polytheism to monotheism, is dominant.[42] 3. In distinguishing a religious from a nonreligious ethic of conviction Weber seems

40. Cf. *ES*, p. 526. Weber notes that Confucianism is a "religious ethic" but with no need for salvation.
41. See the comparison between Confucianism and Puritanism at the end of the study on *China*, pp. 226ff. There are two versions of the study.
42. On the concept of theocentric dualism, see Schluchter, "The Paradox of Rationalization: On the Relation of Ethics and World," in Roth and Schluchter, *op. cit.*, p. 30f. and p. 53f. In this essay I still identified the religious-metaphysical world view with the theocentric world view. This is justified if one conceives of the notion of god broadly, so that the personal god as well as the impersonal divine are subsumed. However, these are two basic alternatives for elaborating the idea of the divine on the level of a religious-metaphysical world view. Since Weber assumes that they have far-reaching consequences, it is preferable to distinguish between theocentric and cosmocentric dualism. I owe this point to Jürgen Habermas. Cf. Habermas, "Handlungsrationalität und gesellschaftliche Rationalisierung," MS, II, p. 4.

to suggest the conclusion that the transition from principles of faith to principles of reason was a crucial step in ethical development. However, this is compatible neither with his intent nor with our systematic argument. In my view the decisive step has been the transition from principle to reflexive principle.[43]

Ethics and the Idea of Compensation

On the basis of these considerations, it should be possible to link concepts of equity to these ethics. The direction in which we should move is indicated by the "Theory of the Stages and Directions of Religious Rejections of the World." There Weber contrasts the religious ethic of brotherhood with the primordial rules of ethical *(sozialethisch)* conduct in the neighborhood association, which shape the "inner-worldly bands of piety." These rules are, first, the previously mentioned "dualism of in-group and out-group morality; second, for in-group morality, simple reciprocity: 'As you do unto me I shall do unto you.' " The dualism of in-group and out-group morality was broken down by universalization, and simple reciprocity by abstractions. The ideas of rebirth and salvation played a crucial role in these processes. The idea of salvation, in particular, had special developmental significance. "The more rational it became and the more it was sublimated in the direction of an ethic of conviction *(Gesinnungsethik)*, the more those commandments that grew out of the ethic of reciprocity in the neighborhood association were intensified externally and internally. Externally, those commandments became a communism of loving brethren; internally, they produced the stance of charity, love for the sufferer, for one's neighbor, for man, and finally for one's enemy." Abstraction and universalization of the simple "principle of helping brothers in distress," which was originally restricted to the neighborhood association, tended to lead in the long run not only to the destruction of group boundaries, "frequently including one's own religious association," but to the transformation of the idea of salvation itself into the idea of liberation and self-fulfillment, to the idea of emancipation.[44]

Following Durkheim, we can distinguish those obligations required by charity from those required by equity.[45] Equity, however, is concerned with compensation. Weber, too, speaks of compensatory causality: the actor expects

43. Here I follow the argument of Friedrich H. Tenbruck (in "Das Werk Max Webers," *op. cit.*, pp. 662ff), who points out that for Weber religion is not simply "the great cognitive Fall of mankind"; hence, it is not the great antagonist of rational cognition; religion is also not merely a first step toward rational knowledge, nor a lesser form of it, but it constitutes a possibility in its own right of understanding the world and oneself. See also Gottfried Kuenzlen, "Unbekannte Quellen der Religionssoziologie Max Webers," *Zeitschrift für Soziologie*, 7 (1978): 215 ff.

44. "Theory," p. 329f.

45. Cf. Emile Durkheim, *Professional Ethics and Civic Morals* (London: Routledge and Kegan Paul, 1957), p. 218f.

that good deeds be rewarded and bad ones be punished. We can use ideas of equity for a further characterization of ethics. An idea of compensation can be simple and concrete or complex and abstract, in which case compensations must be derived from them by enactment, and it can apply to some persons or to all people. If it is limited to certain persons, it is incomplete insofar as it does not demand the same compensation for two comparable actions in comparable situations. In this case it proclaims not equality but inequality. As long as the dualism of internal and external ethic persists, ideas of equity remain tied to ideas of an incomplete compensation. Only on the level of universalist principles does equity imply complete compensation.

We can affirm, therefore, that ideas of equity formulate ideas of compensation. Human beings expect and hope that all people get what they deserve. These expectations may be directed toward external goods, such as wealth, health and long life, or toward internal goods, such as happiness, and they may be oriented toward this world or the world beyond. Robert Bellah has pointed out that "for over 2,000 years great pulses of world rejection spread over the civilized world," but that "world rejection is no more characteristic of the modern world than it is of primitive religion."[46] According to Bellah, this has to do with the relations of these religions to the idea of salvation. When it emerges, the interest in compensation can shift from this world to another which is transcendental, truer and more valuable. From this perspective the inadequacies and injustices of this world are proof of its inferiority. However, salvation is not identical with expectations about the hereafter. Time and again Weber emphasized that not "every world religion knows of a 'beyond' as a locus of definite promises." Even where this is so, it remains true, from a psychological standpoint, that "man in quest of salvation has been primarily preoccupied with attitudes of the here and now."[47] Furthermore, the idea of salvation has magical antecedents. This is especially true of the idea of rebirth, which "appears in classical form already in the magic belief in spirits" (529). However, only the sublimation of the idea of rebirth and redemption into a doctrine of salvation (*Heilslehre*) could provide a countervaling force against the world on the level of world images. Only this could create the motivational potential for overcoming the monism of the mythological world view and the attendant naive affirmation of the world. The rise of the salvation religions led indeed to the tendency to shift the interests in compensation from this world to another. But as the idea of salvation was transformed, a this-worldly orientation gained importance again. At the least we can recognize a major swing of the pendulum. However, the historical process, the direction of which depended to a considerable extent on the "carriers" of the historical social orders, was linked with an increasing rationalization of the ideas of compensation: myth was replaced by theodicy.

46. Robert Bellah, "Religious Evolution," *ASR*, 29 (1964): 359f.
47. "Introduction," p. 277f.

Myth safeguards the unity of the world by means of classifications in such a way that paired concepts, which describe the different spheres of reality, can substitute for one another. Myth also interprets natural event and human action in terms of a single scheme of time and causality.[48] Theodicy, by contrast, safeguards the dualism of the world by differentiating the scheme of causality and temporality. As a rule, theodicies distinguish between nature and human action and between the time horizons of a transitory and an eternal order. They no longer narrate the origin of a social order simply by means of exemplary stories. Rather, they link the origin to a revelation, which tends to be amenable to "rational proof." Once the dualism of natural event and human action has been conceptualized and also the dualism of the contingent and the eternal realm, the idea of compensation for fate in this world by life in the other can arise. Whoever suffers very much in this world will attain bliss in the next. When such ideas were transformed into the idea of liberation and self-fulfillment, theodicy was replaced by anthropodicy.[49] Anthropodicies too endeavor to provide answers for "the need to compensate for the inadequacy of life in this world."[50] However, they cannot locate the place of compensation in a world beyond, but only in the future of this world.

Thus, we can describe notions of compensation in terms of their implicit expectations and of the cognitive structures within which they have been rationalized. We can distinguish ideas of incomplete from ideas of complete compensation, and ideas that are this-worldly from those that are otherwordly. Myth, theodicy and anthropodicy are the most important cognitive structures within which they are rationalized. Wealth, rebirth, salvation and liberation are the most important goods to which the promises of compensation refer. However, these ideas of compensation are also related to conceptions of what actions justify claims for compensation.

In Weber's sociology of religion we can find four kinds of action: 1. observing sacred taboos in the rite; 2. observing sacred laws in the cult; 3. following sacred principles and acquiring holiness through methodically producing a state of mind or good works, hence by living life "objectively"; and 4. choosing one's own fate through a series of ultimate decisions, through satisfying the demands for clarity and consistency and translating them into subjective conduct. This scheme shows that the zones of the sacred shift with the pattern of action. At first ideas of compensation refer equally to the social and the natural world. Then natural and social environment are differentiated with the transition from

---

48. See the studies in the tradition of Claude Levi-Strauss by Rainer Döbert, *Systemtheorie und die Entwicklung religiöser Deutungssysteme, op. cit.*, pp. 87ff. and 99ff. and Maurice Godelier, "Mythe et histoire," *Annales*, 26 (1971): 541-558.

49. Cf. Karl Loewith, *Meaning in History* (University of Chicago Press, 1949); Hans Blumenberg, *Säkularisierung und Selbstbehauptung* (Frankfurt: Suhrkamp), 1974. For the choice of terminology see Schluchter, "The Paradox of Rationalization," *op. cit.*, 50.

50. "Introduction," p. 276.

rite to cult, and this shifts the center of the sacred from the *one* concrete world to *one* concrete social order. Something similar happens with the transition from cult to conduct. At first legality is distinguished from morality and then individual from collective morality. All these changes are related to the great developmental transformations on the level of world views. The mythological world view, which has a monistic and sociocentric structure, is replaced by the religious-metaphysical world view with its dualist and theocentric or cosmocentric structure. Its variants extend from polytheism to universal monotheism and from law ethics to ethics of conviction, without magical ethics dying out completely. The secular-metaphysical world views develop out of the religious-metaphysical ones. They remain dualist but take on anthropocentric features and are threatened with disintegration particularly under the pressure of modern science.

Thus, the structure of the four ethics can be identified more closely through their elective affinities with certain ideas of equity and through their embeddedness in general world views that also include cognitive and expressive symbols. We can now summarize our presentation in a scheme that helps us specify part of the conceptual basis for a developmental history of the West derived from Weber. (See Scheme IV.)

The process of abstraction and universalization of ethical ideas is paralleled by that of ideas of collective equity, the subjective correlate of which is individualization or, in Weber's terminology, sublimation. This process also implies a shift of the ideational centers through which a society defines its collective identity. In Durkheim's terms, we can describe the most general feature of this shift as the replacement of the sacredness of the collective by the sacredness of the person and of the cult of the group by that of the individual. More and more spheres of the natural and social world become subject to instrumental rationality and are ethically neutralized. First, ethics applies no longer to nature, then no longer to large parts of the social order. This does not mean that they need no longer be regulated. Quite the contrary. In Durkheim's sense, the need for regulation increases with the division of labor and the differentiation of the social order. Therefore, ethical neutralization is accompanied by increasing "legalization," which removes more and more spheres of social action from regulation by usage, custom and convention. The increased need for regulation is satisfied primarily through law, not through ethics. Within the legal realm cooperative law with its restitutive sanctions gains ascendancy over penal law with its repressive sanctions.[51] In our terminology, more and more social spheres in need of regulation can be controlled by conceptions of reciprocity and "fairness," whereas equity considerations recede into the background. It is true that ideas of reciprocity remain ultimately tied to equity considerations. In the case of penal law the connection is direct. But principled ethics, which provide a

51. Cf. Emile Durkheim, *The Division of Labor* (New York: Free Press, 1964), Ch. III.

Scheme IV
Typology of Social Ethics

Ethic	Idea of equity and compensation	Ground of adherence (basis for action)	Emphasis (center/periphery)	World View
Magic 'ethic'	incomplete compensation realized in this world by means primarily of material goods. *Myth* ('rebirth')	adherence to 'sacred' taboos. Magic rites	from the identity of nature and society to their differentiation	mythological (monistic, socio-centric)
Law ethic	incomplete compensation in this world and beyond; compensation with material and spiritual goods. *Doctrines* (rebirth and salvation)	adherence to 'sacred' laws. Cult		religious metaphysics (dualist, theocentric, from polytheism to monotheism)
Ethic of conviction	complete compensation in the beyond; compensation primarily with spiritual goods. *Theodicies* (salvation)	adherence to 'sacred' principles and 'holiness.' "Objective conduct"	from legality (external compliance) to morality (internal compliance to social norms)	
Ethic of responsibility	complete compensation in this world with material and non-material goods. *Anthropodicies* (liberation)	choice of one's own fate on basis of ultimate decisions. "Subjective conduct"	from collectivist to individualist morality	secular metaphysics (dualist, anthropocentric, from monocentrism to polycentrism), disintegration of integrated world views

basis for a differentiated social order, not only tend to be individualist, they must also define their "laws" through enactment, in contrast to norm-oriented ethics, which are given. These laws become socially effective only to the extent that they are validated by an agency that enacts them and a special staff that enforces them. This idea of the growing instrumentalization of spheres of action in a social order, in connection with the idea of their growing autonomy, lies at the root of what Weber called depersonalization *(Versachlichung)*. On the basis of market association, for instance, the economy "follows its own rules, disobedience to which entails economic failure and, in the long run, economic ruin. Rational economic association always brings about depersonalization, and it is impossible to control a universe of instrumentally rational activities *(Gesellschaftshandeln)* by charitable appeals to particular individuals. The functionalized world of capitalism certainly offers no support for any such charitable orientation. In it the claims of religious charity are vitiated not merely by the refractoriness and weakness of particular individuals, as happens everywhere, but because they lose their meaning altogether" (585). This statement about the capitalist economy also applies to other spheres in Western modernity. There, too, interpersonal relations have also been largely depersonalized. "Neither ethical nor anti-ethical, but simply non-ethical considerations . . .determine action in crucial respects and interpose impersonal agencies among the persons involved" (1187). It is true that Weber tends to some extent to identify not only ethics and morality but also obligations of charity and obligations of equity. However, this identification can be dissolved and thus the direction of the argument made clearer. The more human relationships are depersonalized, the less they are amenable to direct ethical regulation and the less does equity find fulfillment in charity. In a process of abstraction ideas of compensation become impersonal and formal, and they require complex translations if they are to be relevant at all in the control of a depersonalized world.

Weber's assertion of a special development of modern Western rationalism refers not least to this version of the thesis of depersonalization. Therefore, its reach and depth are only partially contained in the thesis of the bureaucratization of all spheres of life in Western modernity.[52] But not for this reason alone would it be a theoretical foreshortening to locate modernity's problem of order in the dialectic of charisma and bureaucratization and even to regard this as a developmental law in world history.[53] The development of ethics and of the compensatory ideas connected with them modifies the role that charisma can play as an historical force in modernity. For Weber charisma is first of all "the

52. On this perspective see Wolfgang Schluchter, *Aspekte bürokratischer Herrschaft* (Munich: List, 1972); Theodor Leuenberger, *Bürokratisierung und Modernisierung der Gesellschaft* Bern: Haupt, 1975); Rolf-Richard Grauhahn, *Grenzen des Fortschritts?* (Munich: Beck, 1975).

53. This is Wolfgang J. Mommsen's tendency. See *The Age of Bureaucracy, op. cit.*, pp. 80ff.

specifically 'creative' revolutionary force in history" (1117) because of its opposition to tradition and regulation. But this statement must be properly understood. It is decisive that charisma is a *creatively* revolutionary force, not just a revolutionary one. As such it appeared for the last time as the charisma of Reason: the "charisma of 'Reason,' which found a characteristic expression in its apotheosis by Robespierre, is the last form that charisma has adopted in its fateful historical course" (1209).[54] Its most visible expression was revolutionary natural law and the Enlightenment's belief in reason. This belief represented a nonreligious principle. It is "the sum total of all those norms which are valid independently of, and superior to, any positive law and which owe their dignity not to arbitrary enactment but, on the contrary, provide the very legitimation for the binding force of positive law. Natural law has thus been the collective term for those norms which owe their legitimacy not to their origin from a legitimate lawgiver, but to their immanent qualities. It is the specific and only consistent type of legitimacy of a legal order which can remain once religious revelation and the authoritarian sacredness of a tradition and their bearers have lost their force" (867). Thus, the legitimacy claimed in this way is based on an ethic of conviction, and this type of natural law is indeed abstract and formal. A particularly prominent form is the individualist contract theory, which came into being in the seventeenth and eighteenth centuries. Its claim rests on reason insofar as it derives from the idea that "the knowledge gained by human 'reason' is regarded as identical with the 'nature of things,' with the 'logic of things' " (869). This kind of justification, which is not restricted to individualist contract theory, not only puts logical formalism "in the right," it also removes the element of arbitrariness from compensation. For "these norms, which are arrived at by the logical analysis of the concepts of the law and ethics, belong, like the 'laws of nature,' to those generally binding rules which 'not even God Himself' could change,' and with which a legal order must not come into conflict" (869). This does not mean in any way that the difference between natural and compensatory causality is abandoned. On the contrary, the fully developed natural law of reason retains the dualism of the law of nature and of liberty, of the technical and the moral rule. However, just like the laws of nature, those of freedom must be general and necessary, because reason is capable of "becoming practical for itself," to put it in Kantian terms.[55] Reason can be understood as a law-giving capacity that is a force in its own right vis-à-vis not only nature but also man's arbitrariness. Not least because of convictions of this kind, the formal natural law of reason did its part in transforming once and for all the "feudal" world of the status contract based on piety into the "bourgeois" world

54. Guenther Roth has pointed to the significance of this formulation for Weber's historical theory of charisma. See Roth and Schluchter, *op. cit.*, Chs. III and IV. This passage provides a stimulus to look for a developmental history of charisma.

55. Immanuel Kant, *Werke in zehn Bänden*, ed. W. Weischedel (Darmstadt: Wissenschaftliche Buchgesellschaft, 1975), Vol. 7, p. 318.

of the instrumental contract based on enactment. This "bourgeois" world believed in the formula: *veritas, non auctoritas facit legem*.[56] At least it believed it as long as the formalism of reason could be considered an arbitrator in practical matters. Weber seems to have viewed the "a priori rigorism" of Kant's theory of ethics and law as the limiting case of such a construction,[57] for in Kant the formalism of reason reaches its apex. This leads to the "cool matter-of-factness" of an ethic,[58] which not only coordinates morality and legality "reasonably," but also settles the conflict between duties in a reasonable way. According to Kant, legislation must not contradict the inner moral law nor is it possible that two contradictory rules can be general and necessary without reason becoming self-contradictory. Through such ideas the formal natural law of reason became an "independent component of legal development" (873). But as these ideas are pushed to their logical conclusions, they clash with the realities of life, and the "formal rationalist natural law of freedom of contract" develops "strong class implications"; it becomes a natural law of groups interested in market transaction, especially for those interested in the "definitive appropriation of the means of production" (871). The result is that such natural law constructs come under pressure from two directions: from above through a substantive interpretation of natural law, through the explicit introduction of "substantive axioms of natural law" that lead an "irremediable conflict" (874) with formal axioms of natural law; from below, through the restriction of law to an *instrument* of the pragmatic reconciliation of interests. When both tendencies, which can have different origins, combine into a critique of the formal natural law of reason, the close connection between ethical and juristic formalism must disintegrate, the dialectic of ethics, law and power must unfold, and even the concept of reason must change in the direction of a utilitarian position. These are undercurrents that accompany the formal natural law of reason from the beginning. In part, its very emphasis on a formal approach is a reaction to them. But in Weber's view this undercurrent became a main current at the latest with the rise of socialism. Then the ideal and material interests of a class combined with the critique of formal natural law in such a manner that the struggle against economic disadvantage became a struggle in the name of reason itself. From then on the formal principle of equity based on exchange value was not only confronted by the material principle of equity based on use value, but a conflict among the postulates of substantive equity arose. For instance, it can be debated "whether one . . .owes much to those who achieve much or whether one should demand much from those who can accomplish much."[59] This confrontation between formal and substantive natural law and between axioms of sub-

56. Cf. Jürgen Habermas, *Strukturwandel der Öffentlichkeit* (Neuwied: Luchterhand, 1962), pp. 118ff.

57. "Theory," 341. There Weber distinguishes between the religious ethic of brotherhood and a priori rigorism. The passage was inserted in 1920.

58. "Ethical Neutrality," p. 16.   59. "Ethic Neutrality," p. 16.

stantive natural law finally discredited all axioms of natural law. Gradually, law separated from ethics and lost its "metaphysical dignity." It was "unmasked all too visibly as the product or the technical means of a compromise between conflicting interests" (875). The belief in the "sacredness of the purely objective legal formalism" (893) became the only survival of the formal natural law of reason. This is a belief in the value of formal legality as such, a belief that has received its theoretically strongest support for instance in Kelsen's theory of legal positivism with its idea of juristic monism, the unity and consistency of the legal system, and the subsumption of the concrete fact under the general rule.[60]

It is possible to read a confession of a decline of reason into Weber's view of the separation of ethics, law and power and into his emphasis on the "incompatibility that exists between the intrinsic necessities of logically consistent formal legal thinking" (885) and the material and ideal expectations of private parties, and to argue that Weber not only diagnoses this process but also considers it irreversible and even right.[61] Without doubt, this interpretation would touch upon a basic feature of Weber's thought. For instance, he declared it to be our "inescapable fate" that law becomes more and more the "specialists' domain" at the same time that it is increasingly regarded as "a rational technical apparatus, which is continually transformable in the light of expediential considerations and devoid of all sacredness of content" (895). However, Weber's diagnosis is not so simple as this interpretation suggests. He points to the irresolvable tension among equity, due process, morality and legality after the disintegration of the natural law of reason, but he also makes it clear that countervailing tendencies must arise because of the autonomy of legal formalism. There are two processes that merge in this situation to favor the deformalization of modern positive law: 1. an internal critique of formal legal reasoning, which points to the gaps in positive law, denies its systematic unity, doubts the manner in which positivist theory views the rationale of law—in brief, confronts legal positivism with the demand that jurisprudence accept a "sociological foundation" (887); and 2. an external critique, which exposes technical law and the belief in formal legality to the pressure of "emotionally charged moral postulates" (886) and material class interests. Precisely because positive law tends to cut itself

---

60. See also Hans Kelsen, *Hauptprobleme der Staatsrechtslehre* (Tübingen: Mohr, 1911). Weber probably knew this work when he wrote his sociology of law. On the relation betwen Weber and Kelsen, see Fritz Loos, *Zur Wert- und Rechtslehre Max Webers*, *op. cit.*, pp. 106 ff.

61. This is again Wolfgang Mommsen's tendency in his *Max Weber und die deutsche Politik 1890-1920, op. cit.*, insofar as he deals with systematic questions. See esp. Ch. X and the excursus, which deals critically with Johannes Winckelmann. Time and again Mommsen interprets diagnostic remarks by Weber as expressions of his political beliefs and thus neutralizes them from the viewpoint of the critique of ideology. Habermas, too, usually classifies Weber under the rubric of the decline of reason. See Jürgen Habermas, *Legitimation Crisis, op. cit.*, pp. 95-102. However, it seems to me that Habermas has now turned away from this interpretation. Cf. his study, *Handlungsrationalität und gesellschaftliche Rationalisierung*, MS, II.

loose from ethics and power, it creates the nostalgia for a "higher" law at the same time that it calls attention to its economic effects. In this manner it favors not only utilitarianism and social eudaemonism, but also the revitalization of the charisma of reason. However, if we take Weber seriously, it is only the conflict between "demands for substantive justice by certain classes and ideologies" (894) and formal legality, only the retention of legal formalism in the face of ethical, utilitarian and technical demands, that can prevent regression into a kind of neo-patriarchalism that would merge administration and pastoral care. After natural law has, so to speak, transformed itself from a formula of substance into one of contingency, logical formalism cannot be dispensed with as a means of correction. However, because in a modern society the relation of ethics, law and power has become more and more complex, the chances have increased for interest groups to orient themselves not only toward postulates but even toward prophecies. Yet the revitalization of the charisma of reason cannot transcend the situation creatively. Since it is based on an ethic of conviction, it is bound to fail when faced with the dialectic of ethics, law and power, as well as the formal requirements of Western modernity. These requirements are incompatible with the drive toward substantiveness on the part of this attempted revitalization. It is part of the contemporary state of affairs that we must attempt to maintain a tense equilibrium between legality and collective and individual morality. An ethic of conviction cannot accomplish that. The ethic adequate to this situation is the ethic of responsibility, which takes over the individualism of formal natural law—and develops it further under changed conditions. The central idea of freedom of contract is replaced by an extensive formulation of the idea of freedom of conscience, which provides a new basis for the former.

Historically, the freedom of conscience was championed first by the consistent sects as "an inalienable personal right of the governed as against any power, whether political, hierocratic or patriarchal." Then it was transformed into "the most basic Right of Man because it is the most far-reaching, comprising all ethically conditioned action and guaranteeing freedom from compulsion, especially from the power of the state." It is true that this logically first right of man has been interpreted in the most diverse ways, especially through the manner in which it was linked with the other civil and basic rights. For instance, its connection with the "inviolability of individual property," the freedom of contact and the freedom of occupational choice "made it possible for the capitalist to use things and men freely" (1209). But this is a specific historical connection. Individualism need not be identical with economic individualism, with "possessive individualism."[62] It is true that the ethic of responsibility and the ethic of conviction usually presuppose the freedom of conscience, but

62. On the concept of possessive individualism and its tradition in political philosophy, see C. B. MacPherson, *The Political Theory of Possessive Individualism: Hobbes to Locke* (Oxford: Clarendon, 1962): also Hartmut Neuendorf, *Der Begriff des Interesses. Eine Studie zu den Gesellschaftstheorien von Hobbes, Smith und Marx* (Frankfurt: Suhrkamp, 1973).

only with qualifications. The ethic of conviction claims freedom of conscience for itself, but not for dissenters, especially if they are a minority or powerless. Its mission is to protect its principle against dangers, and the greatest dangers come from dissenters. By contrast, the ethic of responsibility must accept the idea of freedom of conscience unconditionally. It includes "freedom of conscience for others" (1209). It must do this because it operates with reflexive principles. Therefore, it must preserve and even elaborate the complex relation of ethics, law and power, formalism and substantiveness, legality and collective and individual morality. The ethic of responsibility requires an extraordinarily complex institutional structure. Charismatic movements carried by an ethic of conviction can easily damage this structure, but they cannot creatively extend it.

However, Weber failed to link the ethic of responsiblity with the characteristics of reflexive principle, individual morality and freedom of conscience for others in such a way that it would be free of the connotations of "possessive individualism." Had he done this, he could have provided an alternative to the ethic of conviction and thus contributed a possible ethical component to the basic configuration of modern Western rationalism. On the one hand, he tended to equate the erosion of natural law—for which "general propositions about regularities of factual occurrences and general norms of conduct" (869) coincide—with the erosion of reason as such and to assume that the non-ethical character of a depersonalized world makes belief a private matter in modernity. A modern ethic would then be possible only as a kind of existentialist ethic of personality,[63] and it would be irrelevant on the level of the social order. On the other hand, his reflections on the difference between ethic of conviction and ethic of responsibility remain ambivalent. Sometimes he distinguishes between intention and consequences, at other times he claims that the ethic of conviction is primarily a religious ethic of brotherhood, whereas the ethic of responsibility is a secular 'political' ethic. In the first case two formal ways of realizing ethical claims are identified independently of the content of any given ethic; in the second two ethics are distinguished from one another, so that they either refer to different spheres or follow one another. We must attempt to resolve this ambivalence through an explication which we can achieve only if we argue with Weber against him.[64] The ethic of conviction and the ethic of responsibility are two different ethics, the latter more complex than the former. This is clear already from the observation that Weber expects the believer in an ethic of responsibility

63. See esp. Karl Loewith, "Max Weber und Karl Marx," *Gesammelte Abhandlungen* (Stuttgart: Kohlhammer, 1960), translated in two parts, "Max Weber's Interpretation of the Bourgeois-Capitalistic World in Terms of the Guiding Principle of 'Rationalization,' " ed. Dennis Wrong, *Max Weber* (Englewood Cliffs, N.J.: Prentice-Hall, 1970), pp. 101-122; "Man's Self-Alienation in the Early Writings of Marx," *Social Research*, 21 (1954): 204-230.

64. Here I elaborate some ideas first presented in "Value-Neutrality and the Ethic of Responsibility" and "The Paradox of Rationalization," Roth and Schluchter, *op. cit.*, Chs. I and II.

to assess not only the consequences but also the intent of an action. This kind of believer, too, must be able to say: "Here I stand. I cannot do otherwise." Thus, instrumental knowledge and enlightenment are equally important for the ethic of responsibility. It requires the knowledge of means-end relations and of consequences as well as the results of value analysis. It requires exchanges between the evaluative and cognitive sphere which are still possible under the conditions of modernity. In this sense, the ethic of responsibility is dependent on science. At the same time it is based on the freedom of conscience for others, which it must accept because it is aware of the significance of value conflict for Western modernity.[65] By contrast, the ethic of conviction devalues the ethical significance of enlightenment and of instrumental knowledge. It tends to negate the exchange between the cognitive and the evaluative sphere and the inescapability of value conflict. It is committed to its own freedom of conscience, not that of others. Therefore, in acting upon revealed or right principles, it is not concerned with the consequences for others. In this sense we can call the ethic of single-minded conviction a monologic ethic, and the ethic of responsibility a dialogic ethic that develops its guiding principles by taking into consideration other principles as well as the consequences of one's own actions for others.

Ethics and Types of Conscience

Our explication of Weber's sociology of religion has discovered four evaluative components of basic social configurations: pre-ethical evaluations (magical ethics), law ethics, ethics of conviction and ethics of responsibility. Only the last three can be considered social ethics in the strict sense. Only they constitute objective ethical structures, to which "subjective" moral attitudes should correspond on the level of the individual. In fact, Martin L. Hoffman has distinguished three types of conscience that closely resemble the three ethics.[66] Hoffman contrasts the external and the internal type of conscience and divides the latter into a conventional-rigid and a humanistic-flexible type. Whereas for the first distinction the degree of internalization of rules or, in Weber's terms, the degree of

65. Weber once gave a concrete description of the ethic of responsibility—in the address in memory of Georg Jellinek, when he sketched a portrait of this scholar who was so important for the development of his own ideas. Cf. Marianne Weber, *Max Weber*, tr. Harry Zohn (New York: Wiley, 1975), pp. 474ff.

66. Cf. Martin L. Hoffman, "Moral Development," in P. E. Mussen, ed., *Carmichael's Manual of Child Psychology* (New York: Wiley, 1970), pp. 336ff. and "Conscience, Personality, and Socialization Techniques," *Human Development*, 13 (1970). The following remarks are indebted to Birgit and Hans Bertram. See Birgit Bertram, *Typen moralischen Urteilens* (dissertation, U. of Düsseldorf, 1976) and Hans Bertram, *Gesellschaftliche und familiäre Bedingungen moralischen Urteilens* (dissertation, U. of Düsseldorf, 1976). See also Hans Bertram, *Gesellschaft, Familie und moralisches Urteil* (Weinheim: Beltz, 1978).

sublimation is decisive, the second distinction depends on whether the application of an internalized system of rules takes into account the consequences of one's actions for others. The formation of these three types of conscience is connected with the prevalence of certain techniques of socialization. In the case of the external type compliance with rules builds on external sanctions, especially reward and punishment with external goods; in the case of the internal type it rests on inner sanctions, reward and punishment with internal goods, either primarily though manipulation of affective components, that is, through withholding or demonstration of love, or primarily through the manipulation of cognitive components, that is, through the justification of rules and through pointing out the consequences of compliance. In the first case the control types "power" and "money" prevail, in the second value commitment and influence. Especially in the case of the autonomous-flexible type influence is obviously the preferred form of social control.[67]

If we follow Hoffman's suggestion, we can characterize types of conscience or types of moral orientation in two respects: their orientation toward a rule or toward a situation. Moral subjects can orient themselves either toward external or internal rules or toward the significance which a situation has for them or others. I propose to use Hoffman's terms "external" and "internal" for the first dimension of orientation, and the terms "restricted" and "elaborated" for the second. It is possible that both dimensions vary independently, that not three but four types of conscience can be construed.[68] We will not decide this issue at the moment. It should be clear that the elective affinity between objective ethics and subjective morality is not treated here as an empirical relationship; it logically reflects the definition of the moral subject from the perspective of ethics. Yet Hoffman's findings encourage us to specify one aspect on the level of ethics which up to now has been treated only superficially: the object of evaluation to which an ethic refers. Kohlberg has pointed to the significance of the distinction between intent and consequence of an action. For Weber, too, this distinction is important and tied to that between the ethic of responsibility and the ethic of conviction. But the theory of ethics proposed here, as well as Hoffman's description of types of conscience, motivates us to take a further step. The distinction between intent and consequence does not permit a sufficient differentiation between the ethics and their moral objects. In the transition from the norm-oriented ethic to the principled ethic, from the heteronomous to the autonomous type, the grounds of evaluation become more abstract and universalist, and the object of evaluation becomes more complex. It is true that the ethic of responsi-

---

67. On these control types cf. Talcott Parsons, *Sociological Theory and Modern Society* (New York: Free Press, 1967), Chs. 10 and 11.

68. This is the result of the theoretical and empirical work of Birgit Bertram. See *op. cit.*, p. 146. However, she chooses as the second dimension ego-oriented and alter-oriented instead of restricted and elaborated.

bility accentuates the evaluation of the consequence, but not without taking into account the intent, from which paradoxical consequences may result.

Weber's contrast of the Confucian and the Puritan ethic, as he presented it at the conclusion of his study on Confucianism and Taoism, can give us a clue for the direction in which an analysis of objects of ethical evaluation can be carried further. If we look at the two ethics from the outside, so to speak, they appear to prescribe rational conduct on the basis of sobriety. But if we look more closely, the two historical phenomena represent two diametrically opposed ethics with diametrically opposite consequences for action—rational adjustment to the world versus rational world mastery.[69] The Confucian ethic recognizes only individual duties.[70] In contrast to the Puritan ethic, it lacks a criterion according to which the world "is viewed as material to be fashioned ethically according to the norm."[71] The objects of evaluation are individual actions and individual qualities of character related to them, not the systematic unity of conduct and the total ethical personality: "Conduct regulated by a unified attitude constitutes the basic contrast to the limitations imposed on Chinese conduct by innumerable conventions."[72] In contrast to the Confucian, for the Puritan life is not a series of discrete events but "a whole placed methodically under a transcendental goal."[73] It is not enough for the Puritan ethic to evaluate as good virtues that are inculcated according to the adaptive needs of the external world. Rather, it demands conduct that provides a countervailing force against the world as it is. Its object of evaluation is not so much the individual act as the unity of conduct. It is concerned not with convention, as is the Confucian ethic, but with conduct founded on "principles controlled from a unified center" and subject to the "peculiar confinement and repression of natural impulse which was brought about by strictly volitional ethical rationalization."[74] In brief, whereas the Confucian ethic evaluates the individual act, the Puritan ethic evaluates total conduct and the total personality that sustains it.

If we combine this criterion—individual action as against total conduct—with the distinction between consequence and intent of action, we can classify the three ethical components of basic social configurations according to the basis and realm of their validity and also according to their objects of evaluation. Norm-oriented ethics focus on the intent or consequence of individual actions. Principled ethics focus on the conviction behind total conduct or on its consequences.

We can now summarize our explication of Weber's theory of ethics. We began with the components of moral judgment: its subject, base and object. Ethics can be distinguished according to their basis of evaluation: norm, princi-

---

69. *China*, p. 248.   70. *China*, p. 230.   71. *China*, p. 235.

72. *China*, p. 232. The meaning of this sentence is reversed in the old English translation.

73. *China*, p. 235.   74. Cf. *China*, p. 240, pp. 244.

ple or reflexive principle. They can further be distinguished according to which object is evaluated under what criterion: the intent or consequence of an act, and intent as a conviction deriving from unified conduct, or conviction in the light of the consequences resulting from it. Ethics can also be distinguished according to the type of conscience, the type of moral orientation: a heteronomous, an autonomous-rigid or an autonomous-flexible type of conscience. It is in this sense that I propose to distinguish among law ethic, ethic of conviction and ethic of responsibility and to set them off from pre-ethical evaluation (magic ethics), to which no type of conscience can correspond. (Cf. Scheme V.)

The development of the basis of evaluation follows processes of abstraction, universalization and unification. The development of the object of evaluation follows processes of increasing complexity. The development of the subject doing the evaluation follows the process of individuation, which is at the same time a process of sublimation and of increased autonomy. A good deal of Weber's research is focused on this process. He is also interested in the conditions under which an integrated moral personality comes into being and under what conditions this leads to world mastery.

Revised Typology of Ethics

Weber interpreted the transition from magical ethic to law ethic and especially of both to the ethic of conviction as a development, but he clearly did not analyze the transition from the ethic of conviction to the ethic of responsibility as a breakthrough. This has to do with his historical focus, but there are also systematic reasons, which can be understood from our explication. The ethic of responsibility remains tied to principles; its subjective correlate is an autonomous type of conscience. However, I am inclined to assume a sequence from the ethic of conviction to the ethic of responsibility. From the perspective of developmental history, the ethic of responsibility cannot be simply understood as a consequence of the ethic of conviction. The ethical development of the West has apparently not come to a close with the Reformation and its unintended consequences. The Reformation still had not overcome the cognitive and evaluative symbolism of the hierarchical and dualist world views typical of the great world religions. This was not achieved until Kant, as Robert Bellah has suggested: "By revealing the problematic nature of the traditional metaphysical basis of all the religions and by indicating that it is not so much a question of two worlds as it is of as many worlds as there are modes of apprehending them, he placed the whole religious problem in a new light."[75] Only after this change of cognitive perspective was the road free for the formation of an ethic of responsibility.

Bellah's reference to the significance of the Kantian Revolution for the development of the evaluative component of basic social configurations suggests

75. Robert Bellah, "Religious Evolution," *op. cit.*, p. 371.

Scheme V
Evaluative Components of Basic Social Configurations

Characteristics Type	Basis of evaluation	Object of evaluation	Type of conscience
Pre-ethical evaluation (magic)	Consequences of actions as retribution		
Law ethic	norms	consequences or intentions of actions	heteronomous
Ethic of conviction	principles	intent of conduct ('conviction')	autonomous-rigid
Ethic of responsibility	reflexive principles	consequences of conduct	autonomous-flexible

to me that the systematization proposed here can be taken one step further. Although Kant rendered the traditional metaphysical basis of all revealed principles problematic, although he was decisive in giving ethics a reflexive foundation and thus in facilitating the rise of an ethic of responsibility, he was critical of two views which in our scheme are crucial for the ethic of responsibility: 1. value conflict is irremediable, and 2. good intention is constituted through reflection on the anticipated consequences of an action. This would make it appear from our perspective that we must classify the Kantian ethic as an ethic of conviction that does not differ from that of ascetic Protestantism. In turn, this raises the question whether our scheme can be improved to cope with this difficulty.

Again, Weber himself gives a hint about the direction in which we might proceed. In discussing the relationship of the ethic of conviction and the ethic of responsibility he points out that "all ethically oriented conduct may be guided by one of two fundamentally differing and irreconcilably opposed maxims"—by the ethic of conviction which in religious terms means that "the Christian does right and leaves the result with the Lord," or by an ethic of responsibility, "in which case one has to give an account of the foreseeable results of one's action." In the same context he emphasizes that "an ethic of conviction is [not] identical with irresponsibility," and an ethic of responsibility is not identical "with unprincipled opportunism."[76] In my view, this is because an ethic of conviction

76. "Politics," p. 120.

can open itself dialogically, whereas an ethic of responsibility can close itself monologically without abolishing the fundamental difference between the two— the one rests on principle, the other on reflexive principle. In both cases the component of conviction or of responsibility can be emphasized. This ambiguity can be resolved easily if we assume that in the case of principled ethics the basis and the object of evaluation can vary independently. This may even be true of norm-oriented ethics. Thus, we should be able to distinguish between a monological and a dialogical variant of law ethic, ethic of conviction and ethic of responsibility, although within the principled ethics the monologic ethic of conviction and dialogic ethic of responsibility remain the consistent types. Then the difference between the ethic of ascetic Protestantism and the Kantian ethic would consist in the fact that with Kant the basis of evaluation becomes reflexive, even though he retains the monologic quality of the ethic of ascetic Protestantism. This is the reason for the revolutionary role of the Kantian ethic, making it a precursor of a dialogical ethic of responsibility.

If we follow this line of reasoning, we can moderate the attributions we have made for the ethics and types of conscience. Then we can envisage two principled ethics which reward a restricted (self-oriented) situational orientation and two which reward an elaborated (other-oriented) one. Something similar can be said for norm-oriented ethics. They too demand that the moral subject react to a situation in restricted or elaborated terms. This suggests that we can distinguish four types of conscience (and not just three): a heteronomous-rigid and a heteronomous-flexible type, which in Kohlberg's scheme is located on the conventional level; and an autonomous-rigid and an autonomous-flexible type, which for Kohlberg is located on the post-conventional level. Thus, not only are alternatives built into the ethical stages, but it becomes clear that the

Scheme VI

Ethical Components of Basic Social Configurations

Basis of evaluations Object of Evaluation	Norm	Principle	Reflexive principle
Intent	monologic law ethic	monologic ethic of conviction	monologic ethic of responsibility
Consequence	dialogic law ethic	dialogic ethic of conviction	dialogic ethic of responsibility

formation of an autonomous-flexible type of conscience does not require the transition to an ethic of responsibility. In other words, ethical development and moral development are not synchronous. (Cf. Scheme VI, VII, VIII.)

We can draw three conclusions from this scheme: 1) As soon as ethics of conviction arise, the objective ethical "supply" to the individual allows autonomous types of conscience to develop, at least on the level of competence. The "inner-directed" personality is by no means an invention of the Reformation or even of Western modernity. It must be possible to locate it also in non-European salvation religions that have produced an ethic of conviction. 2) The individual's development from pre-conventional to conventional moral judgment, the development of the heteronomous type of conscience, again appears to occur relatively independently of the ethical "supply." It may depend primarily on the development of cognitive abilities that can emerge in every natural and social environment endowed with symbolic representation, at least up to the level of concrete-operational reasoning in Piaget's sense. Even the representative of the "savage mind" and of "magic judgment" is capable of developing a heteronomous conscience, difficult as this may be in a "preconventional" environment. 3) The development from the ethic of conviction to the ethic of responsibility does not promote ontogenetic moral development. However, it offers an objective ethical structure that requires an autonomous-flexible type of conscience. This type is not dependent on the rise of the ethic of responsibility. Rather, the dialogic version of the ethic of conviction is sufficient. Moreover, it is true in general that ethics can relate to types of conscience that have no elective affinity with them. This is the analytical meaning of the distinction—taken from linguistics—between competence and performance, which recently has received considerable attention in the social sciences. The type of conscience depends not only on the type of ethics but also on the other components of basic social configurations, especially on the institutionalization of the ways of salvation and on

Scheme VII
Moral Orientations ('Types of Conscience')

Orientation to rules / Orientation to situation	External	Internal
Restricted: actors take only themselves into account	heteronomous-rigid (conventional I)	autonomous-rigid (post-conventional I)
Elaborated: actors also take others into account	heteronomous-flexible (conventional II)	autonomous-flexible (post-conventional II)

whether a distinction is drawn between heroic and average ethics, between the ethic of the virtuosi and of the masses.[77]

Weber's developmental history is concerned mainly with the monological ethic of conviction and its consequences. Moreover, he operates mainly on the level of historical variants, not of basic configurations. This is quite sufficient for an empirical analysis. Basic configurations only provide an abstract range of possibilities within which historical variants arise under contingent conditions. That is, the historical variants cannot simply be deduced from the basic configurations. Nevertheless, we need to identify basic configurations in order to avoid the inappropriate attribution of historical variants and mistaken assessments of their developmental potential. Weber did not always avoid this danger. This is true even if we take into account that he did not analyze ethics as such but in their institutional articulation and that his interest was focused on the relation between religious ethics and economic ethics.

Scheme VIII
Relation of Ethical and Moral Development

Ethical stages	Moral stages
	preconventional I preconventional II
law ethic I law ethic II	conventional I conventional II
ethic of conviction I ethic of conviction II	post-conventional I post-conventional II
ethic of responsibility I ethic of responsibility II	

77. Distinctions of this kind are found as early as in Weber's letter on Otto Gross of September 13, 1907. See Eduard Baumgarten, ed., *Max Weber. Werk und Person* (Tübingen: Mohr, 1964), pp. 644ff. On the ideas of Otto Gross and the relation of Weber and Gross, see Martin Green, *The von Richthofen Sisters* (New York: Basic Books, 1974), pp. 32ff., pp. 62ff. The distinction between the religiosity of the virtuosi and of the masses is central for Weber's sociology of religion. Of course, by religious "mass" Weber does not understand "by any means those who occupy the lower ranks of the secular status order," but those who "are unmusical in matters religious." Cf. "Introduction," p. 287.

Questionable Classifications: Confucianism and Judaism

In my view Weber made a misleading attribution in his study of Confucianism. Until the very end he classified Confucianism as a magic ethic.[78] It is true that he seems to distinguish between ethic and morality, between an ethical doctrine as a normative structure that is set off from the action level, and the "purely magical religiosity" of actual behavior.[79] At the same time, however, he tends to perceive the objective structure of Confucianism in magical terms: individual duties are under the protection of the spirits, and there is no idea of salvation, no ethic that has a "transcendental mooring."[80] The notion of sin, too, is barely developed; it has an aesthetic coloration and is equated with indecency and lack of taste. The world appears as a magic garden, the preservation of which is one of "the most characteristic tendencies of the Confucian ethic."[81] In 1920 Weber summarized his view in this way: "Completely absent in the Confucian ethic was any tension between nature and deity, between ethical demand and human shortcoming, consciousness of sin and need for salvation, conduct on earth and compensation in the beyond, religious duty and socio-political reality. Hence, there was no leverage for influencing conduct through inner forces freed of tradition and convention. Family piety, resting in the belief in spirits, was by far the strongest influence on man's conduct."[82]

However, Weber's own description indicates that this attribution must be insufficient. The coercive symbolism of the pre-ethical evaluative system was destroyed by Confucianism. Its world view is dualist in spite of the dominant harmonizing tendencies, and an idea of salvation develops at least to the point at which the beginnings of a theodicy can emerge as well as a "constant and alert self-control in order to maintain the dignity of the universally accomplished man of the world" as a central virtue.[83] It is true that this Confucian ethic remains affirmative of the world, in contrast to the ethics of the salvation religions, but its "radical optimism"[84] differs from the world affirmation of pre-

---

78. *China*, pp. 229, 240. See also Benjamin Nelson, "Sciences and Civilizations, 'East' and 'West': Joseph Needham and Max Weber," in R. S. Cohen and M. Wartofsky, eds., *Boston Studies in the Philosophy of Science*, XI (Boston: Reidel, 1974), pp. 225-73.

For a critical examination of Weber's study on Confucianism and Taoism see Schluchter, ed., *Max Webers Studie über Konfuzianismus und Taoismus* (Frankfurt: Suhrkamp, forthcoming in 1982). This volume is based on the proceedings of the conference on Weber's intrepretation of China at the Reimersstiftung, Bad Homburg, Nov. 5-7, 1981.

79. *China*, p. 229. Here we encounter again the difficulties which result from the mixing of the objective and the subjective components of structures of meaning.

80. *Op. cit.*, p. 228f.

81. *Op. cit.*, p. 227. Thus, according to Weber, Confucianism enchants the world, whereas ascetic Protestantism disenchants it.

82. *Op. cit.*, p. 235f.   83. *Op. cit.*, p. 240.   84. *Op. cit.*, p. 235.

ethical evaluation. This optimism is tied to refined education, to the "cultivation of the self as a harmoniously balanced personality."[85] Doubtless, this ethic does not yet destroy the ties of kinship, and therefore a "personalist barrier to depersonalization" remains.[86] But this barrier must be understood not in terms of pre-ethical evaluation but only in terms of norm-oriented ethics, which accentuates the dialogic as against the monologic variant.[87]

I also believe that Weber did not move beyond an ambivalent attribution in his analysis of Judaism.[88] The question is whether Judaism is primarily a norm-oriented ethic or principled ethic. Quite clearly, Judaism has traits of principled ethics because of the idea of the transcendental, personal god and his expressed will as well as the development of these elements in prophecy. However, late Judaism, especially in its Talmudic form, seems to remain in Weber's eyes on the level of a norm-oriented ethic. Moreover, this seems to be true not only of the Talmud but also of parts of the Old Testament (623). In the latter there are even pre-ethical survivals; as in Chinese, Indian and Islamic sacred books, "legal prescriptions are treated in exactly the same manner as are ceremonial and ritual norms" (527). Ultimately Judaism seems to have appeared to Weber as an ethic of norms for the following reasons: its core is the sacred law, the casuistical knowledge of law, obedience to the letter of the law and—not to be forgot-

---

85. *Op. cit.*, p. 227.   86. *Op. cit.*, p. 236.

87. *Op. cit.*, p. 237: "The greatest achievement of ethical religions, above all of the ethical and ascetic sects of Protestantism, was to shatter the fetters of the sib. These religions established the superiority of the community of faith and of ethical conduct in opposition to the community of blood, even to a large extent in opposition to the family." This passage captures precisely the goal of Weber's sociology of religion, that is, the investigation of the "inner" factors that must exist before the principle of filial piety and personal loyalty can be overthrown. However, the formulation also points to serious conceptual ambivalences. The concept of ethical religion has two reference points: it is the counter concept to magical religion and also to intellectual religion *(Gedankenreligion)*. In the first case we deal with a sequence, in the second with an alternative. I believe that only the second interpretation is correct. Confucianism cannot be viewed in monistic terms, it must be considered dualist. Its affirmation of the world is not naive but reflexive. The relation to the world advocated by Confucianism represents an alternative in the context of religious-metaphysical dualism. However, it points more in the direction of the enchantment than of the disenchantment of the world.

88. This probably has to do with two facts. Weber moved back and forth between the different phases of Jewish religious development, and his study of ancient Judaism is a fragment. Moveover, his perspective is a reaction to Sombart. Cf. Werner Sombart, *The Jews and Modern Capitalism*, tr. M. Epstein (Glencoe: Free Press, 1951) and *The Quintessence of Capitalism*, tr. M. Epstein (London: Unwin, 1915). See also *ES*, pp. 612ff. and a number of footnotes which were added to the revised version of "The Protestant Ethic." This passage has now been superseded by my essay "Altisraelitische religiöse Ethik und okzidentaler Rationalismus," in Schluchter, ed., *Max Webers Studie über das antike Judentum: Interpretation und Kritik* (Frankfurt: Suhrkamp, 1981). This volume is based on the proceedings of the conference on "Max Weber's Study of Ancient Judaism" at the Reimersstiftung, Bad Homburg, Nov. 8-9, 1979. The volume contains contributions by S. N. Eisenstadt, Eugène Fleischmann, Freddy Raphael, Abraham Malamat and others.

ten—fear of the law. Judaic law fostered "a tendency to compare individual actions with each other and to compute the net result;" it did not equally promote "a methodical and ascetic orientation to the conduct of life on the scale that such an orientation developed in Puritanism" (621). For this reason, but also because of the religious pariah character furthered by Yahweh's promises, Judaism did not produce a "systematization of religious obligations in the form of an ethic of conviction" (578). Other historical forces were necessary to bring about this systematization, powers that were capable of promoting further abstraction, especially universalization and unification. For Weber such forces were, among others, Jesus' sermon, the Pauline mission, Western monasticism in the form of the Benedictines, Cluniacs and Cistercians, Scotism, the theology of the Quattrocento represented by such authors as Bernardino of Siena and Anthony of Florence, and medieval heterodoxy in the form of pre-Reformation sects such as the Waldensians, the early Franciscans and the movements of Wyclif and Huss.[89] These forces had to appear before ascetic Protestantism, by reviving "God's will" as expressed in the Old Testament and by linking it with the norms of the New Testament, could radicalize those elements of a principled ethic which for Weber were, so to speak, the "non-Jewish" element of Judaism (623).

If a clear classification of Judaism in terms of basic configurations is feasible—as a norm-oriented ethic rather than a principled ethic—we gain a systematic reason for why Weber could not drop his planned study of early and medieval Christianity.[90] Ethical variants, however, are not only "subordinated" to basic configurations but are also tied to a concrete social order, in which they are differentiated into the ethics of various institutional spheres. Thus, Puritanism was not only an ethic in the religious realm, wherever it became the orthodoxy of a concrete order; it also penetrated the economic ethic, the political ethic and the realm of socialization. Of course, such specific ethics can nowhere be easily integrated. They are always values in their own right. According to Weber, this explains the attractiveness that the "organic social ethic" has had for all traditional societies.[91] More easily than others, the organic social ethic concedes to the ethics of the individual spheres their "individual rights," without abandoning their integration into a given historical variant. However, every variant always implies its own negation. Heterodoxy emerged beside orthodoxy. As a rule, the former too is oriented toward the basic configuration which it shares with the latter.

89. This is a conjecture. It is supported by Weber's statements in *ES* as well as in the footnotes to the revised version of "The Protestant Ethic," especially in the remarks on Troeltsch, Sombart and Brentano, whose studies were relevant for Weber's thesis.

90. Moreover, a comparison between the two versions of "The Protestant Ethic" and his outline for the *Collected Essays in the Sociology of Religion*, which he sketched at the end of his life, show that he did not intend to abandon his projected study, contrary to Tenbruck's suggestion. See the letter of Fall 1919 in the Mohr-Siebeck archive in Tübingen.

91. "Theory," p. 338 and *ES*, p. 600.

2. The Institutional Component

Typology of Differentiation

In order to identify the institutional component of basic configurations, I consider it useful to proceed from the functionalist theory of evolution advanced by Talcott Parsons and Niklas Luhmann. In the early 1960s Parsons began to transform his structural functionalism into a kind of diachronic functionalism. He did this partly through a reconsideration of Weber's work. According to Parsons, Weber's thesis was that the development of Western modernity, of the system of modern societies, is not only of universal significance for the history of humankind but has also a specific direction and is in this sense not accidental.[92] However, Parsons wanted more than merely to bring Weber up-to-date. He chose a wider frame of reference, his own general system of action. One aspect of this frame is the paradigm of evolutionary change or, in our terminology, of social development. The central directional criterion is the adaptive capacity of a society.[93] This paradigm has four components that constitute a logical sequence: differentiation, adaptive upgrading, inclusion, and value generalization. Differentiation means that a unit is divided into two or more units that differ from the original unit in structure and function. Differentiation is progressive when the new units fulfill functions better than the old unit, when in Parsons' terms the process of differentiation is at the same time a process of adaptive upgrading of all units concerned. Thus, not every differentiation is progressive. However, progressive differentiation does more than simply resurrect the old unit in a reduced form, it elevates it to a new level. It would be a misunderstanding to speak of the loss of function in the course of social development. For the original unit cedes functions in order to fulfill its primary function. But the new units must be integrated. Only if they gain full membership in a society do they increase their own adaptive capacity as well as that of the society-at-large. Such inclusion in turn has consequences for the institutionalized values through which collective identities and ideas of the good social order are defined and made obligatory. Progressive differentiation enlarges a society's possibilities in the realm of goals and functions. Therefore, the society needs a more abstract and universalist base of legitimation. According to Parsons, this is achieved through value generalization.

Parsons does not assign primacy to one of the four processes in the course of social development. Only when all four processes occur simultaneously can adaptive capacities be augmented "either within the society originating a new type of structure or, through cultural diffusion and the involvement of other

---

92. Cf. Talcott Parsons, *The System of Modern Societies, op. cit.*, p. 139.

93. Cf. Talcott Parsons, *Societies, Evolutionary and Comparative Perspectives, op. cit.*, pp. 21ff.

factors in combination with the new type of structure, within other societies and perhaps at later periods."[94] In the perspective of developmental history, all new types of structure, whether they arise endogenously or by diffusion, are breakthroughs; they are innovations that fundamentally change the relations among units. Although Parsons emphasizes that a combination of all four processes is necessary for a breakthrough, I consider it appropriate to give particular attention to two: differentiation and value generalization. The processes of adaptive upgrading and of inclusion can be clearly identified only in reference to the value dimension. Adaptive upgrading is a category of productivity and inclusion one of legitimacy. Thus, they presuppose standards of reciprocity and equity. If we accept this point, it should be possible to find breakthroughs, new structural types or, in our terminology, new basic configurations especially along the dimensions of value and differentiation. The value dimension includes as one of its aspects evaluative symbolism, the ethics of which we have analyzed. Thus, Parsons' paradigm of evolutionary change gives us an indication of where we can locate the institutional component of principles of social structure—in a theory of differentiation, which supplements the theory of ethics.

However, in matters of differentiation we are inclined to think not of Max Weber but of Herbert Spencer and Emile Durkheim. Even on the level of explication the criterion of differentiation does not appear to be an important part of Weber's work. Yet our analysis of the relationship of value spheres and institutional realms has shown that Weber assumes differentiation at least implicitly. At times he even does so explicitly. In discussing the dissolution of the household and of patriarchal authority, he distinguished between their inner dissolution through exchange with the outside and their inner differentiation in the form of the *oikos*, the extended household. In the last analysis, these two developments are interpreted in terms of a theory of differentiation. This example is also of special interest because the dissolution of the household with its kinship and agrarian basis is the exemplary case for the illustration of processes of differentiation in functionalist sociology. By analyzing Weber's passages against the background of the functionalist theory of differentiation one can show in what way they are deficient in terms of this theory.

Weber perceives the household as one of the "undifferentiated forms of life" (375) that solve the material and ideal problems with regard to social and nonsocial objects on the basis of a certain degree of "organized cultivation of the soil," (358) but primarily through ancestor worship. The household is an economic group *and* a group based on authority and solidarity. As an economic group it is engaged in consumption and production. As a solidary group it obeys the rules of the dualism of in-group and out-group morality. Internally, it follows the rule of simple reciprocity. In its purest form the household involves "solidarity in dealing with the outside and the communist use and consumption of everyday goods within the group. This is household communism. In both

94. *Loc. cit.*.

respects the household remains an undisputed unit on the basis of strictly personal relations of filial piety" (359). The undifferentiated unity begins to dissolve under external and internal pressures. Two dimensions are conceivable and of historical interest. Weber even gives them the status of an "evolution of the household" (381). There is external differentiation into household and enterprise and patriarchal and political authority; and there is internal differentiation in the form of the *oikos*,[95] which also makes these distinctions but interprets them in the context of the more encompassing notion of the patrimonial household.[96] If we pursue the first line of development, we move in the direction of the capitalist economy and the modern state *(Anstaltsstaat)* on the societal level, and in the direction of the commercial enterprise and the private household on the organizational level. Thus, there is a functional separation of economy and politics, production and consumption. If we follow the second line of development, on the societal level we encounter organized want satisfaction and traditional patrimonialism, on the organizational level "the authoritarian household of a prince, manorial lord or patrician" (381) to which other households and enterprises are attached through various kinds of duties and taxes. In this case the economy remains subordinated to the polity, and production to consumption. Instead of functional differentiation, stratified differentiation of the units prevails.

Of course, Weber did not use the terms functional and stratified differentiation. He spoke instead of external and internal differentiation and viewed them as alternatives, not as two sides of a single process. This terminology could be justified by the argument that the dissolution of a unit can mean two things, either that similar or that dissimilar units arise. However, according to Weber, the development of the household into the *oikos* as well as its development into the capitalist enterprise and private household involved the emergence of dissimilar units. We need a more complex framework than the one proposed by Weber if we want to reconstruct clearly in terms of the theory of differentiation what he only implied along these lines. We can avail ourselves of such a framework on the basis of the arguments presented thus far and with the help of Niklas Luhmann's writings. In this manner we can also identify more clearly the institutional components of basic configurations that are central to a Weberian developmental history of the West.

System theories usually contrast segmentation and differentiation. However, Niklas Luhmann has proposed a distinction among three forms of systemic differentiation: segmental, stratified and functional.[97] He argues that sys-

95. Weber borrowed the term *oikos* from Karl Rodbertus. It refers to a large princely or manorial household in contrast to a commercial enterprise. See also "Author's Introduction," p. 22.

96. Cf. the study by Otto Brunner, *Land und Herrschaft* (Vienna: Rohrer, 1965), pp. 240ff.

97. Cf. Niklas Luhmann, "Differentiation of Society," *Canadian Journal of Sociology*, 2 (1977): 29-53.

tem differentiation can be understood as the repetition of the process constitutive of every system formation—establishing a boundary by distinguishing environment and system. Differentiation appears then as a reflexive kind of system formation, through which a system's complexity and its adaptive capacity can be increased. In systems that apply the distinction between the external and the internal to themselves, internal environments emerge. Environments specific to each subsystem arise, in addition to the environment shared by all subsystems. To conceptualize the relation between system formation and the constitution of external and internal environments, Luhmann introduces the dichotomy "equality-inequality" next to the dichotomy of the external and the internal. It refers to the way systems treat their environments and communicate with them, whether as equals or unequals, symmetrically or asymmetrically. If both dimensions are combined, three forms of differentiation can be described. Segmental differentiation means that a society splits into subsystems that treat one another as equals. This internal differentiation does not give rise to the dualism of in-group and out-group morality. Rather, the decisive boundary for this dualism is the external environment, which for this reason is treated unequally by all subsystems. This does not mean that subsystems cannot in fact be unequal. Indeed, their relations to the external world lead sooner or later to inequality. But this is not a systemic function of reflexive system formation; it does not follow from the internal, but from the external structure of communication. Stratified differentiation means that a society splits into subsystems that treat one another unequally. Thus, next to the external boundaries, internal ones emerge which bring about the dualism of in-group and out-group morality. Equality tends to apply only within the subsystems because their functions have become unequal. In order to insure that unequal communication among the subsystems does not impair their necessary interaction, the subsystems must be related in a hierarchical manner. This requires that a rank order is more or less accepted. At the same time, the subsystems must define their identities in relation to one another by accepting their super- or subordination. Thus inequality becomes a systematic function of reflexive system formation. It no longer results from the external, but from the internal communications structure. Finally, functional differentiation means that a society splits up into subsystems that treat one another equally in spite of unequal functions. Subsystems need not define themselves in terms of their specific relations to other subsystems. Rather, each subsystem can now tolerate an open and fluid inner environment "as long as the other subsystems in its environment fulfill their function."[98] At the same time the need for a firm and durable hierarchy disappears and is replaced by a high degree of indifference. It is true that the inequality of the functions increases the internal dependencies between the units and thus the need for integration, but since the specific attributions and structural complementarities have been loosened, there is more leeway for integration. There-

98. *Op. cit.*, p. 36.

fore, a system based on functional differentiation can absorb a much higher degree of structural heterogeneity than a segmental or stratified system. In addition, such a system tends to overcome the dualism between in-group and out-group morality within itself and in relation to the outside.[99]

Luhmann has given these classifications an evolutionary twist. Social development proceeds from segmental to stratified to functional differentiation. This is in line with the views that have dominated the functionalist tradition since Spencer. However, Luhmann advances a novel interpretation. Spencer still embraced the evolutionary principle that "evolution is a change from a state of relatively indefinite, incoherent homogeneity to a state of relatively definite, coherent heterogeneity."[100] Luhmann obviously tends to reverse this principle: evolution is a change from a state of relatively definite, coherent homogeneity to a state of relatively indefinite, incoherent heterogeneity. It is true that the growing complexity of a system also increases the internal tensions and the need for integration, but it also enlarges the possibilities for institutionalizing values in an equal manner, that is, without having to resort to a firm and durable hierarchy.[101] I believe that this is also Weber's perspective, as we find it in the "Theory of the Stages and Directions of Religious Rejections of the World." Western modernity has carried value conflict further than any other civilization. Therefore, functional differentiation as we understand it here is an institutional component of its basic configuration.

Luhmann's distinctions are informative in other respects as well. His concept of segmental differentiation is useful for conceptually reconstructing Weber's treatment of the household. Weber did not deal with the household in isolation. Rather, he viewed it in the context of the neighborhood, as village or commune, and of the kin group. For Weber, too, the kin group is of special interest. It is not simply an "extended or decentralized household or a superordinate structure uniting several households" (365); it is a relatively loose grouping of households related by belief in common descent from a natural object, by the incest taboo, by the prohibition to engage in combat with one another, and by the liability to blood revenge. The kin group is therefore "a complex of obligations and loyalties, which derives from actual or fictitious common descent or a bond created through blood brotherhood" (366). The kin group presupposes not only other kin groups but also an external boundary, with the help of which they can be organized into kin associations. However, within kin associations

99. In this sense the world society is the goal of this development. However, the world society still needs an external environment, in relation to which it represents "reduced complexity."

100. Cf. Robert L. Carneiro, ed., preface to Herbert Spencer, *The Evolution of Society* (Chicago University Press, 1967), p. xviii.

101. See also M. Rainer Lepsius, "Modernisierungspolitik als Institutionenbildung: Kriterien institutioneller Differenzierung," in Wolfgang Zapf, ed., *Probleme der Modernisierungspolitik* (Meisenheim: Hain, 1977), pp. 17ff. and Richard Münch, "Max Webers 'Anatomie des okzidentalen Rationalismus,' " *op. cit.*, pp. 235ff.

households and kin groups treat one another as equals. This is most visible in internal conflict regulation. Whereas the blood feud regulates conflict with the outside, the principle of composition applies internally. In the household composition is in the hands of the holder of patriarchal authority, in the kin group in the hands of the elders. Among several households and kin groups conflict is regulated by arbitration, not by the discretion of a master. Thus, the kin group, which often does not engage in more than discontinuous social action, can sometimes take over the function of protection internally and externally. In this case it competes strenuously against the emergent or existing political association. Weber points out that "especially in periods in which social action is otherwise scarcely developed, household, kin group, neighborhood and political community typically overlap in such a manner that the members of a household and a village may belong to different kin groups, and the kin members to different political and even language communities. Hence it is possible that neighbors or members of the same political group and even of the same household are expected to practice blood revenge against one another. These drastically conflicting obligations were removed only when the political community gradually monopolized the use of physical force" (367). This tangle of internal and external boundaries among different groups, which is typical of stages of relatively undeveloped social action, must not make us overlook the fact that we are dealing with social orders whose institutional component is segmental differentiation and incipient stratified differentiation.

The three differentiations, then, can be distinguished by the manner in which they regulate the relations among the various partial orders of a society. If we slightly modify Luhmann's proposal, we can say that in the case of segmental differentiation the various spheres or orders have equal rank, in the case of stratified differentiation there is inequality between either similar or dissimilar spheres, and in the case of functional differentiation there is equality between dissimilar ones.[102] However, the regulation of the relation among the

102. Strictly speaking, four kinds of differentiation should be distinguished, because the concept of stratified differentiation applies to two constellations. This becomes clear if we use in our own way the dimensions proposed by Luhmann. Societal differentiation has a structural aspect and a coordination or control aspect. A unit can be divided into similar or dissimilar units. This alternative can be represented by the paired concepts segmental and functional. The units divided in this manner can be coordinated in an egalitarian or a hierarchical fashion. This alternative is represented by the paired concept "horizontal and vertical." Through cross tabulation we arrive at four principles of societal differentiation: horizontal-segmental and vertical-segmental versus horizontal-functional and vertical-functional differentiation.

In this way we can combine the distinction between segmental and functional differentiation that is well-known in general sociology and the distinction between horizontal and vertical differentiation familiar from organizational sociology. We can also make the concept of stratified differentiation more precise and further "differentiate" it in a vertical-segmental differentiation, on the one hand, and a vertical-functional differentiation on the other. Thus, a group united by common descent or a sib is based on

spheres of a society is only one criterion for identifying the three kinds of differentiation. It is especially interesting from an evolutionary perspective to examine Weber's treatment of the competition between kin groups and political associations and of the gradual monopolization of physical force by the latter. We can understand this process as a differentiation of functions and as a reminder that the similarity or dissimilarity of the various partial orders is linked to the degree of functional specification. The kin group and its units fulfill all basic functions simultaneously—protection, meaning, want satisfaction and socialization. Only as long as this is true can household and patriarchal authority remain stable. When the basic functions are separated, "the functional position of the household is radically changed," a process that occurred only in Western modernity. As this happens, the individual has less and less reason "to submit to a large communist household." Protection is guaranteed no longer by household and kin group, but by the compulsory political association, and education is taken over by "enterprises" of all kinds. Like Durkheim, Weber viewed the changed position of the household in Western modernity as the consequence of a differentiation of the partial orders and the loosening ties of household and kin group as the consequence of a specification of functions. Today the individual "can no longer regard the household as the bearer of those objective cultural values in whose service he places himself, and the decrease in the size of the household is not due to any increase of 'subjectivism,' understood as a 'stage' of social psychological development, but to the *objective* conditions" (375f).

Thus, Weber kept two kinds of differentiation separate, at least relatively so: the differentiation of the "primeval" groups, which rests on equal rank among similar units and on functional fusion, and the differentiation of the "modern" groups, in which equal rank between dissimilar units is combined with the differentiation and specification of functions. The difference can best be illustrated by the development of the protective function. In the primeval groups it is distributed among many kin groups; in modern groups the state successfully monopolizes it: "The claim of the modern state to monopolize the use of force is as essential to it as its character of compulsory jurisdiction and of continuous operation" (56). In between lies that form in which unequal rank between similar and especially between dissimilar units is combined with the more or less far-reaching differentiation and specification of individual functions. This is a kind of stratified differentiation which for analytical reasons must be expected to appear in manifold guises. As Weber's sketch of the transition from the household to the *oikos* shows, he seems to perceive the difference between segmental and stratified differentiation primarily in the changed func-

---

horizontal-segmental differentiation and an *imperium* ranges from vertical-segmental to vertical-functional differentiation (cf. Schemes IX and X). This distinction permits us to pair the concepts "segmental" and "community of descent" as well as "functional" and "modern state" *(Anstaltsstaat)*.

tional position of the protective and the meaning function, that is, those functions which, according to our scheme, can be assigned to the institutions of politics and law and the institutions of religion and culture. It seems to be true at least of the early forms of stratified differentiation that the economic function is not only subordinated to the protective and meaning functions but also remains partially fused with them. Something similar can be said of the socialization function, which is primarily controlled by religious institutions. Thus, the increasing independence of these functions, in connection with their specification, points to developmental possibilities within the framework of stratified differentiation. However, the increasing independence of *all* functions and their specialization must be viewed as the problem of the transition from stratified to functional differentiation. There is a third viewpoint that further clarifies the kinds of differentiation (segmental, stratified and functional). A social order can be differentiated not only into the four basic functions but also into the three levels of aggregation (roles, organizations, and institutional realms). In this regard, too, Weber gives us a pointer. He discussed the dissolution of the household in the sociology of domination, in the chapter on patriarchal and patrimonial domination, which he labeled "pre-bureaucratic structural principles" (1006). The difference between patriarchal and patrimonial domination is explained primarily in terms of two dimensions, legitimation and organization. The social relationships become more complex under patrimonialism. Although Weber retains the "specific personal loyalty, the filial and servants' piety" (1009) as a criterion for legitimation, the patrimonial relations become increasingly dependent on "the subjects' claim to reciprocity" and "custom" and the "stereotyping force of tradition" (1012). A political association emerges with a staff and "organization," that is, "action continuously oriented toward the enforcement of its order" (264). Moreover, in the course of establishing territorial rule over large areas, centralization and decentralization occur simultaneously. The result is the rise of the "patrimonial state" proper, the empire. In the realm of the meaning function as well, there are trends toward monopolization, though not of physical but of psychic coercion. Just as the patriarch and the elder lose the protective function, so the necromancer and magician lose the meaning function. Their place is taken in the one case by the prince and patrician, and in the other by the priest and teacher. The crucial conflicts tend to erupt no longer among kin groups but between political and hierocratic powers. Not roles, but organizations and increasingly institutional realms become the decisive level of social order. In the case of segmental differentiation the important level is primarily defined by roles; in the case of stratified differentiation we encounter organizations and institutional realms, which may still be fused; in the case of functional differentiation, however, organizations and institutional realms are definitely separated. This is a developmental precondition for the capacity of an organization to become formal and thus a modern bureaucracy.

Classes and Status Groups

The three kinds of differentiation can be summarized under the heading of relations among parts, degree of independence and specification of functions, and levels of order (cf. Scheme IX). However, this identifies only one aspect of the institutional component of basic configurations. As Luhmann has shown, the differentiation of a system means the application to established systems of the dichotomy "external/internal" as well as "equal/unequal." Thus, it refers to what has been called here the power distribution among partial orders in a society. It involves system analysis not stratification analysis. If we want to take into account the power distribution among the partial orders, we must supplement the theory of differentiation with a theory of stratification. We can resort to Weber's discussion of status groups and classes, even though it remains fragmentary.

The contrast between status groups and classes seems to imply a developmental thesis: classes appear as a modern phenomenon, status groups as pre-

Scheme IX
Kinds of Differentiation

Characteristics / Types of differentiation	Relations among partial orders	Degree of independence and specification of function	Levels of order
Segmental	equal rank among partial orders	far-going fusion of the political, religious, economic and educational orders	'roles' patriarchs and elders, special military and religious roles
Stratified	unequal rank among similar and esp. dissimilar partial orders	differentiation esp. of political and religious spheres; development of economy slowed down by its subordination to politics and religion	'organizations' political and hierocratic powers; special economic and educational organizations (such as 'commercial cities' and 'universities')
Functional	equal rank among dissimilar partial orders	differentiation of all orders	'institutional realms' (pluralism)

modern. Weber indeed seems to think so. Western modernity is distinctive because of modern science based on rational proof and rational experiments, rational harmonious music with its counterpoint and harmony, the modern civil service with its systematic training and formal organization, the modern state with its rationally enacted or imposed constitution, and modern capitalism with its rational organization of labor. The burgher, too, is a Western phenomenon, and the bourgeois only a phenomenon of Western modernity, just as the proletariat as a class did not arise outside the West. There were class struggles in other epochs "between creditor and debtor classes; landowners and the landless, serfs and tenants; trading interests and consumers or landlords." But these were not class struggles in the strict sense. For Weber the class struggle seems to be limited to "the modern conflict of the large-scale industrial entrepreneur and free-wage laborers."[103]

However, this first impression must be modified. As the newer part of *Economy and Society* in particular shows, Weber recognizes classes outside of Western modernity and, by implication, status groups within it, although classes and status groups have a different character in each case.[104] Commercial (or acquisition) classes, first in the commercial city, then in the market economy, are distinctive of the West. Whereas a market economy is a precondition for commercial classes, property classes are also found in "organizations which satisfy their wants through monopolistic liturgies, or in feudal or *ständisch*-patrimonial fashion." Their positive or negative privileges derive from the disposition of "consumer goods, means of production, assets and resources" (306) but not from skills. The positively privileged members of property classes typically consist of rentiers, not entrepreneurs, the negatively privileged consist of the unfree, the declassed, the debtors and the poor, not unskilled, semi-skilled, or skilled workers. It is true that there is no privileged commercial class without the "monopolization of entrepreneurial management" (304). This requires not only marketable managerial skills but also the appropriation of the means of production in the enterprise. But the persons who have managerial skills and those who own the means of production need not be identical. Therefore, even when an association has appropriated the means of production, commercial classes can emerge as long as the economy remains market-oriented.

What we have said about the concept of class can also be said about the status group. For Weber, status groups are, in the first instance, defined by "rules of conduct" (307). The difference between a property class and a status group can be illustrated with the example of feudalism. The member of a property class and the vassal as well have property rights, rights over rent-producing objects. But only in the case of specifically Western feudalism *(Lehensfeudalismus)* is this property right infused with a "very demanding code of duties and

103. "Author's Introduction," p. 23.
104. Cf. Anthony Giddens, *The Class Structure of the Advanced Societies, op cit.*, pp. 41ff. and pp. 69ff.

honor" (1074). Here too Weber makes at least an implicit distinction between cases in which conduct, which produces social prestige and social honor, is a matter of ascription and those in which it is a matter of achievement. Therefore, he distinguishes between status groups that are hereditary and those that are based on conduct, especially occupation. The additional notion of political and hierocratic status groups is also connected with Weber's decision in the newer part of *Economy and Society* to retain the association of class situation with market position and economy, and of status situation with conduct and society—an association which in my view is not analytically satisfactory. However, if we distinguish between classes and status groups primarily in terms of the kinds and extent of disposition over external and internal goods, then property classes correspond to hereditary status groups and property-based status groups and the commercial classes to occupational status groups. Kind and extent of disposition depend first of all on birth, property and occupation. These three factors provide the outline of a stratification theory that can be combined with the theory of differentiation presented above. As Weber's own remarks show, with growing differentiation the decisive criterion shifts from birth to property and then to occupation. On the level of segmental differentiation descent determines the social position of the individual; on the level of stratified differentiation social position is determined by both birth and property; and on the level of functional differentiation occupation becomes increasingly important. It is well known that for Weber a basic feature of Western modernity was

Scheme X
Institutional Component of Basic Social Configurations

Type of association · Characteristics	Power distribution among partial orders (system analysis)	Power distribution within partial orders (stratification analysis)
Groups based on descent (sibs)	segmental	hereditary position (hereditary status groups)
Imperium (city states, patrimonial empires)	stratified	property position (property classes, property status groups based on life style)
Rational state	functional	occupational position (acquisition or commercial classes, occupational status groups)

the rise of the trained specialist who is incapable of relating the dutiful exercise of his vocation "directly to the highest cultural values."[105]

We can now conclude the analysis of the institutional components of basic configurations. In accordance with the distinction between the power distribution among and within partial orders, between system analysis and stratification analysis, we had to separate and recombine two aspects. We did this by identifying three principles of differentiation and of stratification and by coordinating them. We distinguished segmental, stratified and functional differentiation as well as birth, property and occupation (cf. Scheme X).

Both the ethical and the institutional components of basic configurations provide possibilities that are historically utilized under contingent conditions. Community of descent, empire and state denote institutional components of basic social configuration, to which several historical variants correspond. The community of descent made possible the neighborhood and the kin group, but also the patrician polity. The empire underlay sultanism, feudalism and the *Ständestaat*. The modern state is compatible with plebiscitary *Führerdemokratie* as well as the administrative state, as long as continuous social action is based on an enacted or imposed rational order. We will now turn to Weber's sociology of domination in order to pursue further the difference between basic social configurations and historical variants. Weber's analysis deals with their connection and also their relation to ethics, insofar as it encompasses both the organization and legitimation of domination.

105. *PE*, p. 182.

V

TYPES OF LAW AND
TYPES OF DOMINATION

1. The Relation Between the Sociology of Domination and of Law

Max Weber's sociology of domination, of which there are several versions, has crucial significance for his developmental history.[1] This is true in biographic as well as systematic respects. It is true biographically because Weber seems to have focused his contribution to the "Outline of Social Economics" from the very beginning on this part of his work. On January 23, 1913, he wrote to his publisher, Paul Siebeck, that if Karl Bücher would soon deliver his manuscript, he would "try to send his own sizable contribution (economy and society, inclusive of state and law) very soon or toward the end of April. It depends on Bücher. Incidentally, I hope that my contribution will be among the better, or even best, things I have written. In a way, I am offering a complete sociological theory of the state. It is fair to say that it cost me much sweat." Somewhat less than a year later, on December 30, 1913, he wrote to Siebeck after Bücher's article had arrived: "Since Bücher's treatment—on the 'developmental states'—is totally inadequate, I have worked out a complete theory and exposition that relates the major social groups to the economy: from the family and household to the enterprise, the kin group, ethnic community, religion (comprising all religions of the world: a sociology of salvation doctrines and of the religious ethics—what Troeltsch did, but now for all religions, if much briefer), finally a

1. Wolfgang J. Mommsen, in particular, has called attention to the several versions of the sociology of domination and has interpreted them in terms of a shifting relation between sociology and history in Weber's work. See *The Age of Bureaucracy, op. cit.*, p. 15f. Mommsen identifies three versions, one each in the older and new manuscript of *Economy and Society* and a brief summary first published posthumously in 1922, "The Three Types of Legitimate Rule" (H. Gerth tr., in A. Etzioni, ed., *Complex Organizations*. New York: Holt, 1961, pp. 4-14). Strictly speaking, one must speak of four versions. The

comprehensive sociological theory of state and domination. I can claim that nothing of the kind has ever been written, not even as a 'precursor.' "[2] Weber's sociology of domination also has crucial significance in systematic respects for his developmental history. It treats basic social configurations from the evaluative as well as the institutional view, and gives equal rank to the modes of legitimate domination as well as to "domination through organization" (952). In his judgment, the structure of a given case of domination must be seen from two viewpoints: (1) its "justification through an appeal to principles of legitimation" and (2) "the relation of the master or masters to the apparatus, and of both to the ruled, and the principle of 'organization' specific to the case, that is, its specific way of distributing the powers of command" (953). The combination of principles of legitimation and organization yields the " 'pure' types of the structure of domination," and "the forms of domination occurring in historical reality constitute combinations, mixtures, adaptations, or modifications of these 'pure' types" (954). This approach amounts not only to a distinction between the evaluative and institutional components of basic social configurations but also, at least implicitly, to a distinction between basic configuration and historical variants, even though we must recognize that Weber tends to identify this latter distinction with that of pure types and mixed types. However, this misconstrues their analytical status.

Weber's sociology of domination has been discussed, especially in the German literature, from three viewpoints, which are partially in conflict with one another: (1) the relation of the types of action, bases of legitimacy and types of domination; (2) the number of the types of legitimate domination; and (3) the

---

fourth is found at the end of the introduction to the essays on the economic ethics of the world religions (see "Introduction," pp. 295-301), which Weber published in 1915 and revised in 1920. Finally, we must take into account the "stages" in Weber's work which preceded the sociology of domination: the 1904 essay on "The Debate About the Character of Ancient Germanic Social Structure in the Literature of the Last Decade" (see *Gesammelte Aufsätze zur Wirtschafts-und Sozialgeschichte, op. cit.*); and the 1908 manuscript, *The Agrarian Sociology of Ancient Civilizations, op. cit.* On this "prehistory," see Roth in *ES*, sec. 4-8. Weber's idea that sociology can be focussed on a theory of the state was greatly influenced by Georg Jellinek. Weber acknowledged Jellinek's impact on him with regard to "the separation of naturalistic and dogmatic thinking . . . for problems of methodology; the creation of the concept of the 'social theory of the state' for the clarification of the blurred tasks of sociology; the demonstration of religious influences in the genesis of the Rights of Man for the investigation of the importance of religious elements in areas where one would not expect to find them." In Marianne Weber, *Max Weber, op. cit.*, p. 476. In view of Jellinek's importance for Weber, a study of their relationship would be desirable. A beginning was made by Roth, "The Genesis of the Typological Approach," in Bendix and Roth, *Scholarship and Partisanship, op. cit.*, pp. 260ff.

2. Both letters are from a transcription of the correspondence between Weber and Siebeck made available to me by Johannes Winckelmann and Franz Bonfig. Weber's formulations should be read against the background of his high esteem for Jellinek.

relation between empirical and normative validity, and the question of the "truth value" of Weber's sociology in general.[3] The subject of the first perspective is the way in which Weber combines the three theoretical aspects with one another: the typology of social action with its distinction between traditional, affectual as well as value-rational and instrumentally rational action; the typology of the bases of legitimacy with its distinction between tradition (the valid is what has always been), affect or emotion (the valid is what is newly revealed or exemplary), value rationality (the valid is what has been deduced as an absolute), and positive enactment (the valid is what has been enacted through contract or imposition); and the typology of the structures of domination with its distinction between traditional, charismatic and rational domination, which Weber also calls legal and bureaucratic domination. The question is how types of action can be translated into types of domination and especially how the types of rational action can be related to the type of rational domination. The subject of the second perspective is the way in which Weber elaborated his third type of domination: the typology of law with its distinction between traditional, revealed, deduced or natural and enacted law. The central question is whether he had in mind two basically different modes of legitimation under the heading of rational domination when he contrasted the natural law of reason and a positive law enacted by the legislature, and whether an explicit distinction should therefore be made between types of value-rational and instrumentally rational legitimation, that is, between enactment on the basis of value-rational and of instrumentally rational domination *(Satzungsherrschaft)*.[4] This leads to the further question of whether the other pure types of legitimate domination are also in need of a further differentiation: patriarchal versus *ständisch* domination in

3. See on the last point esp. Jürgen Habermas, *Legitimation Crisis, op. cit.*, also Johannes Winckelmann, *Legitimität und Legalität in Max Webers Herrschaftssoziologie* (Tübingen: Mohr, 1952); Wolfgang J. Mommsen, *Max Weber und die deutsche Politik, op. cit.*; id., *The Age of Bureaucracy, op. cit.*; Fritz Loos, *Zur Wert- und Rechtslehre Max Webers, op. cit.*; Friedrich Wilhelm Stallberg, *Herrschaft und Legitimität* (Meisenheim: Hain, 1975); Dirk Käsler, *Revolution und Veralltäglichung* (Munich: Beck, 1977). For an overview of the sociology of domination, see Reinhard Bendix, *Max Weber, op. cit.* For a detailed annotation and further literature see Johannes Winckelmann's *Erläuterungsband* to *ES*, pp. 44ff.

4. Cf. Mommsen, *Max Weber und die deutsche Politik, op. cit.*, p. 430: "Max Weber puts next to this type of domination by legal enactment, which has a purely instrumentally rational basis, a type that is based on a normative system of a value-rational kind. The major example of this type is the old democracy with its natural law foundation." See also id., *Max Weber. Gesellschaft, Politik und Geschichte, op. cit.*, p. 205, where Mommsen divides legal domination into a type based on instrumentally rational rules and one based on value-rational rules (such as natural law). Johannes Winckelmann has argued against this view *(Erläuterungsband, op. cit.*, p. 45): "The basic errors of the (predominantly juristic) critics is the assumption of a fourth, 'legal' type, which is merely technical and not norm-oriented and is supposed to stand next to the three original types of legitimate domination. This error results from the failure to understand the double meaning of the term 'legality.' In one sense the term refers to the activity of the legisla-

the case of traditional domination, and charismatic leadership versus charismatic authority or personal charisma versus office charisma in the case of charismatic domination.[5] The subject of the third perspective is the manner in which Weber links two theses of his sociological theory of legitimation: the thesis that legitimacy is the idea of the exemplary and obligatory nature of an order and that in the case of a legitimate order action occurs to "a socially relevant degree as if the ruled had made the content of the command the maxim of their conduct for its own sake" (946); and the thesis that the correctness of norms is not subject to sociological validation, since for an empirical science norms are not a "cosmos . . . that can be logically deduced as being 'correct'; rather they are a complex of empirical grounds for actual human conduct" (312). This perspective becomes more troubling if it is combined with the other two, especially the second one (that is, the question of the typology of law). Then the question arises whether "enactments which are formally correct and which have been made in the accustomed manner" (37), whether legality as such, independently of the highest legal principles and of the ideal interests of the ruled, can create at all that idea of the exemplary and obligatory character of an order without which, in Weber's view, the existence of every structure of domination is endangered. The stability of a given case of domination requires that the ruled are motivated not merely by a "sense of duty, or by fear, or by 'dull' custom, or by a desire to obtain some personal benefit" (947), but by a conviction of the rightness of an order. An order which is "upheld only for instrumentally rational reasons" belongs to the most unstable structures conceivable, exactly because it cannot operate "with the prestige of exemplariness and obligatoriness—we want to say, of 'legitimacy' " (31). Even if a legal domination aims merely at stability, it must develop a principle of justification that permits a normative orientation and a corresponding motivation on the part of the ruled. This raises the question of the legitimacy of legality, and the further question of whether it is necessary to transform Weber's theory of legitimation from the "subjective legitimating ideas" of the actors into "objective justifications" of actions.[6]

Before we can adequately answer these questions, we must introduce a fourth perspective that has been given less attention. In his sociology of domination Weber interwove the analysis of the political order with that of the "whole" social order. This has two consequences: (1) Weber tends to approach the social order from the political order. (2) We must not isolate the analysis of the sociol-

---

ture, which creates legality by passing laws (domination by enactment); in another it refers to the rational form of legitimacy, which is based on the principles of formal and substantive rationality." In the following I shall take a similar position, but with a rationale that is quite different from Winckelmann's.

5. Cf. Mommsen, *op. cit.*, p. 205, and Bendix, *op. cit.*, Part III.

6. Jürgen Habermas, *Zur Rekonstruktion des Historischen Materialismus* (Frankfurt: Suhrkamp, 1976), p. 260.

ogy of domination from his other sociologies, especially from the sociology of religion and of the economy. Moreover, we must read it in close connection with the sociology of law. Law is the authoritarian embodiment of those cultural traditions which are anchored both in world views and in the socialized individuals. This is evident from the fact that Weber makes the existence of law dependent upon an enforcement staff. In a sociological sense law exists only when norms are externally guaranteed. This distinguishes the legal norm from the ethical norm, legal compulsion from the compulsion of conscience. An ethical norm is defined by the very absence of external guarantee as a necessary condition. It is true that ethical norms as well may be guaranteed externally. Most of the time, however, this happens not through legal but through conventional enforcement: an identifiable group reacts disapprovingly to the violation of an ethical norm (33f).

Only when we combine the first three perspectives with the fourth can we adequately understand the significance of the sociology of domination for Weber's work as a whole; only then does it become clear that it is a socio-historical constitutional theory of a new type, quite different from the traditional constitutional theories. It is a theory of "empirical constitutional law," insofar as it demonstrates the way legitimacy develops historically as a "justification from the highest legal principles."[7] It is an empirical theory of constitutional organization, insofar as it shows the ways lawmaking, lawfinding and administration and the structure of their *"organs"* are historically related. It is also a theory of political sociology, insofar as it deals with the historical relationship of the political order to the other orders, especially the relationship of politics and religion, on the one hand, and politics and economy on the other. Thus, we can identify in Weber's sociology of domination not only the evaluative and institutional aspect of basic social configurations but also the juxtaposition of stratification and system analysis. His sociology of domination enables us to carry our analysis further.

If we can view Weber's sociology of domination as an historical theory of constitutional law and organization as well as an historical theory of the relations among the institutional realms, this should lead us to look for the link with his theory of legal development, not only because cultural traditions are embodied in authoritarian structures but also because structures of domination have a legal underpinning. This link is constituted by the sociology of law.[8]

It seems that Weber deliberately focused his analysis on private law. He is primarily concerned with the "extent and nature of the rationality of the law

7. Loos, *op. cit.*, p. 105 and Winckelmann, *op. cit.*, p. 46.

8. Although Talcott Parsons considers the sociology of law the core of Weber's sociology and Johannes Winckelmann writes that "all strands of his opus magnum come together in it," the literature is very small. See Parsons, "Value-Freedom and Objectivity," in Otto Stammer, ed., *Max Weber and Sociology Today* (New York: Harper and Row, 1971), p. 40 and Winckelmann, *Erläuterungsband, op. cit.*, p. 197. The sociology of law is

and, quite particularly, of the branch of it which is relevant to economic life, namely private law" (655). However, there are also a considerable number of references to public law, especially to the legal limits of political rule, to the problems of the internal and external limits of legitimacy, and hence to the limitation and division of powers—this alone is sufficient to show the close connection between the sociology of law and of domination. Moreover, the history of private law can only be written in the context of the history of public law. It is of considerable significance for this history that "a systematic theory of public law was developed only in the West" (653). Only Western society demonstrates a consistent differentiation of the various spheres of law. We distinguish penal and civil law, sacred and secular law, and especially private and public law. This has to do with the Western cultural traditions and with "the intrinsic intellectual needs of the legal theorists" (855). In particular, it has to do with the fact that in the West the political association turned at an early time into the rational *(Anstalt)* state. This required the combination of several factors: "In the realm of historical facts . . . the consociation of privileged persons in public corporations of the *Ständestaat*, which increasingly combined both separation and limitation of powers with rational state features, in the realm of legal theory . . .the Roman concept of the corporation, the ideas of natural law and, finally, French legal theory" (653).

2. The Sociology of Law

Types of Law

In his sociology of law Weber analyzed the relation of ethics, law and "authoritarian powers"—primarily theocracy and patrimonialism—as well as the relation of the various fields of law. His overarching question was: Why did a temporary logical elaboration of law occur only in parts of modern Western society? In order to classify the types which are of interest here, he resorted to a distinction that looks simple enough but is actually complex and sometimes ambiguous in its application. Weber classifies the types of lawmaking and lawfinding in terms of whether they are rational or irrational either in procedural *(formell)* or substantive respects. Law is procedurally irrational "when in

---

discussed in Max Rheinstein's introduction to *Max Weber on Law in Economy and Society*, tr. Edward Shils and Max Rheinstein (Cambridge: Harvard University Press, 1954); Karl Engisch, "Max Weber als Rechtsphilosoph und Rechtssoziologe," in id. et al. eds, *Max Weber* (Berlin: Duncker and Humblot, 1966), pp. 67-88; David M. Trubek, "Max Weber on Law and the Rise of Capitalism," *Wisconsin Law Review*, 3 (1972): 720-53; Julien Freund, *The Sociology of Max Weber* (New York: Random House, 1968), pp. 245-66.

lawmaking or lawfinding one applies means which cannot be controlled by the intellect, for instance recourse to oracles or their substitutes. Lawmaking and lawfinding are substantively irrational to the extent that a decision is influenced by concrete factors of the particular case as evaluated upon an ethical, emotional, or political basis rather than by general norms" (656). This relatively clear definition of "irrational" and "rational" is not paralleled by an equally unambiguous definition of "procedural" and "substantive." Weber's terminology suggests that "procedural" refers to the legal form, whereas "substantive" refers to legal content. If the procedural criterion is emphasized, we are interested in how decisions are made; if the substantive criterion is emphasized, we are interested in the content of decisions. In the first case a decision is legitimated by its procedure, in the second by its content. Since the procedural and the substantive aspects of law can be rational or irrational, there should be four kinds of legitimating legal decisions—two by virtue of procedure, two by virtue of purpose. However, the matter is complicated by the fact that Weber distinguishes between procedural and formal (*formell* and *formal*). He writes: "Every formal law is relatively rational at least in procedural (*formell*) respects" (656). This statement makes sense if we assert that the types of lawmaking and lawfinding can be characterized according to whether the procedural or substantive aspect is dominant. I believe that Weber indeed made this distinction. This is indicated not only by the contrast between the formal and substantive rationalization of law, but also by the fact that he distinguishes law in terms of being procedurally irrational, substantively irrational, procedurally rational and substantively rational. With these basic cases of law he apparently anticipates the types of revealed, traditional, positive and deduced law and the related bases of legitimacy (36). Revealed and positive (or enacted) law can be viewed as formal, traditional and deduced law as substantive. This is clarified by Weber's illustrations. Thus, revealed law with its divine judgments and oracles is much more formal, despite its procedural irrationality, than the "concrete equity" of patriarchal law (845); and positive law with its legal logic is more formal than the natural law of reason, the logic of which rests on the identity of reason and reality and on "the directly binding force of certain legal principles" that cannot be relativized by any legal procedure (866).

We can now see that Weber's typology of law makes two assumptions: (1) The procedural and substantive components of law are not equal, at least in the historically interesting types. Either the procedural or the substantive component predominates. We may speak in shorthand fashion of formal and substantive law, but we must not understand this to mean that formal law is without content and substantive law without form. (2) Both formal and substantive law are subject to rationalization. (See Scheme XI.)

These two theses can be linked to two further observations, one systematic and one historical. Weber did not give equal space, contrary to what the scheme would suggest, to the formal and the substantive rationalization of law. In the

Scheme XI
Types of Law

Level of Rationality / Relation between form and content	non-rational	rational
formal	revealed law ("charismatic")	positive law
substantive	traditional law	deduced law ("natural")

Sociology of Law he is primarily interested in formal rationalization, whereas substantive rationalization remains largely residual. Moreover, he asserted that formal and substantive rationalization stood in an antithetical relationship: the more legal development progresses, the less compatible are procedural and substantive rationality. In "primitive" law they were one, but in modern law a dualism, even an antagonism, seems to have developed. The more consistently legal formalism, which is controlled by the intellect, articulates itself, the more procedural rationality rejects substantive rationality, "because the latter means that the decision of legal problems is influenced by norms different from those obtained through logical generalization of abstract interpretations of meaning. The norms to which substantive rationality accords predominance include ethical imperatives, utilitarian and other expediential rules, and political maxims" (657). These norms break through the confines of legal formalism. Procedural and substantive rationality appear to be antagonistic and to have different origins as well. However, modern law has largely emancipated itself from all external authorities and gained a high degree of consistency on the basis of its procedural rationality.

Formal Modes of Law

We shall briefly elaborate on these two observations. First, what exactly does Weber mean by formal and substantive rationalization of law? As is his wont when he discusses questions of rationality, Weber stresses also in the *Sociology of Law* that law can be rational in different senses of the term, "depending on which of several possible courses legal thinking takes toward rationalization" (655). However, he points to two modes of thought that as a rule are involved: the generalization and systematization of the legal subject matter. Generalization means "the reduction of the reasons relevant in the decision of concrete individual cases to one or more 'principles,' i.e., legal propositions" (655) and the isolation and abstraction of the relevant facts. This analytical penetration of an existing legal situation can be complemented by a synthesis that construes a new legal situation. The result of these analytical and synthetic efforts are the legal casuistries that appear in so many varieties. They range from the mere collection of legal materials to attempts at systematization, from empirical lawbooks to sacred books and finally to bodies of deduced law. These legal casuistries can be classified according to the way in which they treat and order legal matters, whether in an associative or constructive way, whether under transcendent or immanent criteria. Law must become the subject of a continuous literary enterprise if legal thought is to move beyond "unsystematic occasional productions" (854). As in the case of every rationalization, that of law too is decisively dependent on how this enterprise is organized and who operates it. Systematization means "an integration of all analytically derived legal propositions in such a way that they constitute a logically clear, internally consistent, and, at least in theory, gapless system of rules" (656). The "ultimate legal principles" and the factual criteria must be formulated in such an abstract way that "deductive arguments" can be derived from them (854). Thus, systematization means more than generalization. It results not just in a legal casuistry but in a legal system. It presupposes that legal thought changes from empirical and concrete to logical and abstract interpretation and that this systematization by and large abandons criteria from outside the legal realm. Thus, the transition from generalization to systematization is linked to a cognitive development. For Weber systematization is "in every form an historically late product" (656). In this regard Roman law was, among the old kinds of law, relatively far advanced. Therein lies its importance for economic development, not in any affinity between its substantive stipulations and the economic interests of the Western bourgeoisie (853).[9] In Weber's eyes this special position of Roman law was not accidental. A major reason for it was the fact that Roman law was "a product of theoretical-literary juristic training" (865).

The rationalization of law, then, amounts to the generalization and systematization of the legal subject matter, whether it results from lawmaking or lawfinding or from both. Rationalization implies that questions of fact and of law are separated and that the latter are treated from two viewpoints: the legally relevant facts and the legally relevant principles. Rationalization means generalization and systematization in both regards. It aims at unambiguous general criteria of facts and at unambiguous general principles. Beyond that, it also aims at an unambiguous application of both. Only then can a concrete legal decision be a *calculable* application of an abstract legal proposition to a concrete "fact" (657). A law that cannot transcend the "irrationality of the indi-

9. Cf. Weber's early article on "Römisches und deutsches Recht," *Christliche Welt*, 9 (1895): 521ff.

vidual case" is not calculable. In classifying the concrete fact it does not take into account general criteria, and in subsuming the fact it disregards general norms. All decisions that resort to "magical means of legal revelation" show this incalculability, but the same is true of a law that has left behind the magical means, yet has not been formally rationalized in a juristic manner (758). This includes much of traditional law, especially patriarchal law, which takes into account only the person and the concrete situation. Such *khadi* justice is overwhelmed by the concrete legal purpose, not by the concrete legal form, as was true of primitive law. The justification does not transcend the concrete case. It cannot be generalized and formulated as a rule. This can be accomplished only when "the decision becomes the subject matter of discussion" and when it appears justifiable in terms of generalized rules.

Legal rationalization, then, is for Weber the isolation and abstraction of characteristics of the facts and of legal propositions. Law is formally rational to the extent that "exclusively unambiguous and general characteristics of a set of facts are taken into account in substantive and procedural terms" (656). Law is substantively rational—at least we can draw this conclusion—to the extent that exclusively general norms are taken into account in substantive and procedural terms. Weber subsumed this kind of substantive rationality—the fact that in the course of legal development general norms arise, that the maxim of a legal decision gains importance beyond the single case and becomes subject to generalization and systematization—under formal rationalization. Legal development isolates, abstracts and hence formalizes both the formal *and* substantive components of law, both legal procedure and legal purpose. Thus, the concepts of formal and substantive rationalization of law refer to an internal relationship, on the one hand, and a external relationship on the other: to the relationship between formal and substantive components of law, on the one hand, and the relationship between legal norms and norms of other qualitative distinctiveness on the other (657). The more legal development progresses, the more isolated and abstract are the formal and substantive components of the law. Their claims to validity are specified at the same time that the possibility increases of conflict with the claims of other norms, especially with ethical imperatives, utilitarian and other instrumental rules and political maxims, which are recognized in addition to the valid legal rules. When Weber speaks of the opposition betwen the formal character of a professionally sublimated legal system and substantive rationality, he has in mind not the conflict between form and content but the conflict among different kinds of norms. This conflict is articulated in the legal systems. Weber illustrates the dualist character of formally rational legal systems with the example of the *code civil*, which is to him the third great system of law next to vulgar Roman law and Anglo-Saxon law (865). The abstract structure of legal systematics with its "somber legal rules" has built-in postulates of an extralegal distinctiveness. They imbue the legal system with an "epigrammatic and dramatic" quality which is also characteristic of the "rights of man and citizen" in the American and French constitutions (866). This dramatic element is indicative of the fact that a legal system of formal rationality can be autonomous, but never autarkic, that the logical formalism of law is based on extralegal presuppositions in spite of its tendency toward logical closure.

This leads us to the second observation which is connected with the two assumptions (or theses) noted above. The dialectic of legal rationalization must be viewed as a process that is internal as well as external to the legal realm. As soon as mythological thought and magical action have been superseded, the conflict between the procedural and the substantive components of law can arise. As soon as the kin group has lost its predominance, the conflict between law and ethical postulate, law and utility, as well as law and political maxim can erupt, and with it the conflict between the legal order as part of the system of domination and the religious, economic and political spheres. The legal order is the medium within which the claims of the partial orders meet and are mutually limited. This is the systematic reason for the fact that the differentiation and integration of the partial orders must be reflected in a differentiation and integration of the various legal fields. It is also the systematic reason for the close connection between the sociology of law and of domination and for the need to add the sociology of religion and of the economy. Weber analyzes the internal legal process primarily on the basis of the types of legal thought and of their carriers, and the external process primarily on the basis of the three great political powers, theocracy, patrimonialism and democracy, and of their relation to the law. In the first case the emphasis is on the rise of new legal institutions, in the second their diffusion. According to Weber, "the specific type of techniques used in a legal system or, in other words, its modes of thought are of far greater significance for the likelihood that a certain legal institution will be invented in its context than is ordinarily believed. Economic situations do not automatically give birth to new legal forms; they merely provide the opportunity for the actual spread of a legal technique if it is invented" (687). What Weber says here about economic situations also applies to political ones, to civil and to public law. The central question is which modes of thought and which political, economic and religious situations further the development of the formal qualities of law, and under which conditions formal rationalization gains ascendancy over the substantive rationalization within and beyond the legal realm.

I shall turn first to the internal legal development. Here we can follow Weber's ideas on the origins of law. In the main, he distinguishes between two sources, which can be called law imposition and consensual legal practice. In the history of law they parallel one another, they must not be put in a sequence. However, in the course of legal development law imposition gains increasing importance. Today it is so great that almost all law is purposely created, either by imposition or on the basis of a constitution, which in turn can be either more imposed or more agreed upon. The reason for this development lies in the fact that originally the concept of the norm did not exist and, after it had been created, the norm was considered a given (760). New law could be created only through the interpretation of given norms. This placed narrow limits on legal imposition. However, from very early times law imposition existed also in the form of charismatic revelation by magicians and prophets, either from case to case or through the establishment of sacred law. Therefore, charismatic revelation has not only been a revolutionary force in the face of interpreted tradition but also "the source of all law imposition" (761). As its "successors" not only the modern state but also the traditional authoritarian powers of theocracy and patrimonialism imposed law purposely. In contrast to imposition which introduces law from the top down, so to speak, consensual legal practice creates law from the bottom up. Here law results from certain understandings becoming standardized, understandings which derive from the interests of the participants and rest on "private" initiative (759). For a long time this civil law can remain without legal enforcement. Only in the course of societal differentiation does legal enforcement become necessary in view of the need for calculability. However, this prepolitical form of lawmaking also favors the rise of acquired personal rights, which decisively circumscribe the discretion of "political" law. Acquired subjective rights, especially when they become political, constitute the most important limitations on political power, apart from tradition and enactment. However, legal practice is pursued not only by private interests, but also by judges (in the broadest sense). In the case of private agreements new law comes into being most frequently in the form of cautelary reservations, in the case of judges in the form of precedents. Consensual legal practice thus results in a clearly empirical law. Against this background Weber can arrange "the general development of law and procedure" in "theoretical stages of development": "first, charismatic legal revelation through 'law prophets'; second, empirical creation and finding of law by legal *honoratiores*, i.e., law-making through cautelary jurisprudence and adherence to precedent; third, imposition of law by secular or theocratic powers; fourth and finally, systematic elaboration of law and professionalized administration of justice by persons who have received their legal training in a learned and formally logical manner" (882).

Legal thought can now proceed from these two sources and elaborate them: it can be oriented more toward practice or more toward imposition. In the former case it will be primarily empirical and inductive, in the latter theoretical and deductive. In the former it will aim at more or less consistent casuistry, in the second at the legal system. In Weber's view, Western legal development not only used both possibilities, it also brought them to fruition—the first especially in the English tradition, the second at first in the Roman tradition, then in parts of northern European tradition. That does not mean that they were limited to these traditions. The Continental legal development, in particular, is much too diverse to be identified unreservedly with the theoretical and deductive type. Next to the reception of the Roman law in the Middle Ages, which furthered the orientation toward this type, stood the justice of the folk community *(Dinggenossenschaft)*, which contributed to the preservation of traditional sodality forms of association. The new stratum of legal *honoratiores* that came into being with the reception of Roman law managed at first to produce only empirical law books, like the *Mirror of Saxon Law*, which were "oriented more towards concrete techniques of distinction than towards the abstract interpretation of meaning or legal logic" (794). Nevertheless, if we look at the internal development of law, it was not the English, but the northern European Continental tradition that favored the logical elaboration of the law. Only where this happened was there a chance that the formal rationalization of the law could permanently prevail over the substantive rationalization.

In the last analysis, the formal qualities of modern law were brought about not by law tied to precedent, but by law based on principle. There is a general affinity between theoretical and deductive thought and the formalism of legal logic, on the one hand, and between empirical and inductive thought and the weakness of this formalism on the other. The fact that England developed rational capitalism in spite of its "nonformal" law demonstrates that "modern capitalism prospers equally and manifests essentially identical economic traits" under different legal modes which "differ profoundly from each other in their ultimate principles" (890). It also shows that external factors are important for the rise of capitalism, among others the relation between law and structure of domination. If legal thought does not provide the potential for the unification and systematization of a legal system, the structure of domination can accomplish this to some extent, especially in the case of bureaucratic patrimonialism which creates a legal unity through political unification of the realm. However, at first this unity was greater in England than on the Continent. Weber points to the position of the corporate groups which in England were organized more through compulsion than on a voluntary basis and whose ability to resist the central power was at first weak on this account. From this viewpoint, English and Continental legal history began at opposite poles: "In consequence of the rigorous partrimonial central administration this integration of all associations in the state was at its maximum at the beginning of English legal history and from then on had to undergo a gradual weakening. In Continental legal history, on the other hand, it was the bureaucratic princely state of modern times that broke the bonds of the traditional corporate autonomy; subjected to its own supervision the municipalities, guilds, village communities, churches, clubs, and other associations of all kinds; issued patents; regulated and controlled them; cancelled all rights that were not officially granted in the patents; and thus for the first time introduced into actual practice the theory of the 'legists,' who had maintained that no organizational structure could have juristic personality or any rights of its own except by virtue of a grant by the *princeps*" (724).

Thus, English and Continental legal development apparently represent formal modes of law that are related to types of legal reasoning. The formal rationalization of law should therefore consist of a sequence of such formal modes, and in fact, Weber has given us criteria for their identification. To begin with, the primitive legal process has a "strictly formal character," even though its bases of judgment are irrational. Strictly speaking, there are no legal maxims. There are verdicts *(Wahrsprüche)* and sometimes a tradition of verdicts. But they do not constitute an objective law, the norms of which can justify a concrete decision. Even at the primitive level the legal process consists of at least two steps, the determination of disputed facts and finding the law. However, in matters of proof the facts as such are not the issue, but "which party should be allowed or required to address to the magical powers the question of whether he was right and in which of the several ways this might or ought to be done" (762); and in the process of finding the law there is no subsumption under a general legal rule but a concrete revelation of the will of the magical powers, a concrete decision which does not even set a precedent. It is true that the determination of who is permitted to ask questions of the magical powers constitutes "the first stage in the development of technical-legal concepts. But there is as yet no distinction between questions of fact and questions of law; or between objective norms and subjective 'claims' of individuals which they guarantee; or between the claim for performance of an obligation and the demand for vengeance for a wrong . . . or between public and private rights; or between the making and the application of the law. Nor is a distinction always made between 'law,' in the sense of norms which allot 'claims' to the individual interested party, and 'administration,' in the sense of purely technical dispositions which 'automatically' benefit the individual by giving him access to certain opportunities" (764). The strictly formal quality of this primitive kind of trial derives from the fact that in leading up to a verdict only concrete criteria and ritual acts are allowed to play a role, so much so that "even the slightest error by one of the parties in his statement of the ceremonial formula will result in the loss of the remedy or even the entire case" (761).

Thus, the formal nature of the primitive trial is based on external criteria and on the impossibility of distinguishing form and content. The external form is the content, and the correctly employed procedure brings about a substantively correct verdict. The legal reasoning that goes with this formalism is irrational insofar as it remains concrete and does not employ any means that can be controlled by the intellect. It supports a "magically conditioned formalism" (882) that contrasts diametrically with the formalism of modern law. The legal reasoning that infuses modern formalism is rational insofar as it proceeds in an abstract and logical way and permits only the employment of means that can be controlled by the intellect. Hence, it supports a logically conditioned formalism "where the legally relevant characteristics of the facts are disclosed through the logical analysis of meaning and where, accordingly, definitely fixed legal concepts in the form of highly abstract rules are formulated and applied" (657). This presupposes that a distinction is made between acquired subjective rights and objective rights, criminal law and civil law, legal principle and administrative regulation, and especially between the factual and the legal issue and, within the latter, between procedural norms and substantive law. Correct procedure alone does not lead to a substantively correct verdict. Therefore, procedural error is cause for revision on formal or substantive grounds. Form and content, procedure and substance are equally important. Although both primitive and modern legal procedure are formal, they stand at opposite poles of historical development. As Weber summarizes it: "The formal qualities of law emerge as follows: arising in primitive legal procedure from a combination of magically conditioned formalism and irrationality conditioned by revelation, they proceed to increasingly specialized juridical and logical rationality and systematization, sometimes passing through the detour of theocratically or patrimonially conditioned substantive and informal expediency. Finally, they assume, at least from an external viewpoint, an increasingly logical sublimation and deductive rigor and develop an increasingly rational technique in procedure" (882).

Thus, Weber distinguishes concrete from logical formalism—the concrete from the logical modes of law. As in the sociology of religion in which Weber treated the 'demagicalization' of the means of salvation as a consequence of the rationalization of the basic conceptions of salvation, he now treats the transition from concrete to logical formalism as a 'demagicalization' of legal procedure. And as in the sociology of religion, legal rationalization involves not only procedure but also content. At the end of his study on Confucianism and Taoism when Weber tries to assess their rationality in comparison with Puritanism, he points out that the stage of religious rationalization depends on "two primary yardsticks which are in many ways interrelated. One is the degree to which the religion has divested itself of magic; the other is the degree to which it has systematically unified the relation between God and the world and therewith the individual's ethical relationship to the world."[10] This observation can be transferred to the analysis of law. Legal rationalization involves not only the 'demagicalization' of procedure but also the systematization of legal content: "the collection and rationalization by logical means of all the several rules recognized as legally valid into an internally consistent complex of abstract legal

10. *China*, p. 226. Weber distinguishes here clearly between the basic conception and the means of salvation, just as he distinguishes in the sociology of law between the conceptual foundation and the means of law. The theory of disenchantment refers primarily to the means, although there is an affinity between foundation and means. However, a systematic foundation does not lead 'automatically' to the disenchantment or demagicalization of the means, as can be seen in the case of the Indian salvation religions.

propositions" (657). This is possible only if concrete formalism is overcome and the legal substance takes on the character of objective norms. However, as is shown by Weber's distinction between generalization and systematization, legal casuistry and legal systematics, not every objective body of law is equally suited for systematization. This raises the question of whether Weber distinguished substantive as well as formal modes of law.

Substantive Modes of Law

In contrast to the formal modes, substantive modes of law relate not to the development of legal procedure but to that of legal norms and thus of objective law under which "principles" become the basis of decision. As our review of the primitive stage has shown, there is no objective law on that level. A judgment is a concrete verdict, which cannot be generalized. The concept of the objective norm as an expectation juxtaposed to the facts has not yet developed. Therefore, there is also no concept of guilt and no gradation of legal consequences in proportion to guilt. Attitude and intention are not taken into account. The notion of expiation predominates; with its help all wrongs are interpreted, whether they concern persons or things, a killing or a piece of real estate. There is no distinction between "crimes requiring revenge" and "wrongs requiring restitution" (647). Moreover, the enforcement of a verdict is not up to a staff but to those involved. The notion of expiation is mitigated only after a distinction is made between acquired subjective rights and objective laws, only after some "rules have been established as a set of factually binding norms" (652). Only then can institutionalized guarantees come into being. This typification and stabilization of norms emerges when legal revelations become traditions. Then generalization becomes feasible, although concrete formalism has not yet been superceded.

This fact has to do with the character of traditional objective law. It is viewed as a given, not as something intentionally created or deliberately introduced. Existing rights are, so to speak, sanctified by tradition, and generalization can go only to the point where it is still compatible with the "pluralism of sacred matters." Moreover, traditional objective law is a conglomeration of special rights: in general, it is the right of certain groups, "the privilege of a person as a member of a particular group" (696). In short, it is a law of privileges, and as such remains particularist. It is based on the dualism of in-group and out-group morality and has a precarious relationship to a *lex terra* that aims at formal equality. This creates another barrier to generalization. As a set of special rights traditional objective law has limited applicability. When primitive law and legal revelation are left behind, it becomes possible to formulate a notion of objective laws and of legal enforcement. However, "the notion of generally applicable norms" is still "inevitably undeveloped" (698). The development of this notion was the historical task of natural law, for it is based on the idea that legal principles can be deduced by ratiocination and are therefore universalist. It is true that natural law, like traditional law, tends to assume that principles are given. But the idea that norms can be deduced by reasoning transcends concrete formalism. However, logical formalism can flourish only when natural law, with its contradictory substantive principles, is secularized. When this happens, objective law is considered not only to be created but also to be reversible and thus fully subject to logical treatment. Law is based no longer on substantive and necessary principles but on formal and hypothetical ones. The philosophically oriented logic of natural law is transformed into the juristically oriented logic of positive law. A theoretical reflection of this transformation is provided by Hans Kelsen's "doctrine of pure law." He founds legal logic on a genetic hypothesis or norm, which identifies the highest authority entitled to establish a norm. Legal norms are valid *because* they have been established by a legislative which is entitled to do that. This genetic norm or hypothesis justifies the autonomy of the legal order and of jurisprudence. It demonstrates that "the legal order has an existence different, separate and independent from morality, religion or any other order" and that jurisprudence is "a discipline independent from theology, politics or ethics."[11]

Weber, then, distinguished not only between concrete and logical formalism, but also between the different justifications of law—whether or not law is objective, and if it is, whether it has a particularist or a universalist foundation. The validity of law in turn can be based on necessary or hypothetical principles, it can be meta-juristic or juristic. From the viewpoint of internal development, the substantive rationalization of law follows the same lines that we identified in ethical development: action, norm, principle, and reflexive principle. At the primitive level there is no objective law which would be independent of action; norm and action remain intertwined. Usage, custom and interest constellation account for the regularities of social action (29). Action is not yet oriented to legal obligations that are viewed as binding for their own sake by a circle of persons. This change happens only when primitive law is replaced by traditional law, which treats action in the light of given legal norms. Norms remain particularist and do not yet approach universalist principles. This latter stage is accomplished by natural law, which postulates that such principles can be deduced by reasoning. Then law is founded not only on principles but also on a meta-juristic basis. Each extant law must be legitimated in terms of such principles, and it can and must be changed when it conflicts with them. At this point the idea of enactment receives its decisive impulse. It is true that natural law retains the notion that legal principles are given. But when this view is un-

---

11. Hans Kelsen, *Der soziologische und der juristische Staatsbegriff* (Tübingen: Mohr, 1922), p. 86. See also Wolfgang Schluchter, *Entscheidung für den sozialen Rechtsstaat. Hermann Heller und die staatstheoretische Diskussion in der Weimarer Republik* (Cologne: Kiepenheuer und Witsch, 1968), p. 40f.

dermined and the principles themselves become reflexive, law can become positive in the strict sense. This has been accomplished in modern law, in which almost all law is considered to be enacted and thus also to be revisable. Its foundation is changed from meta-juristic to juristic principles. The later have only a hypothetical character, and this indicates that law has become autonomous, although it is not completely free from external entanglements.

The Differentiation of the Substantive Fields of Law

There is a third aspect of legal development: the differentiation of the substantive fields of law. In primitive law there is practically no differentiation between form and substance. There are the first traces of a separation between criminal and civil law, but the predominance of the principle of expiation prevents a lasting separation of delict and contractual obligation. By and large, procedural and substantive norms are not yet differentiated: the form is the content of the law. Under traditional law the distinction between criminal and civil law and, more generally, between repressive and restitutive law is stabilized and the separation between procedural norms and substantive law is advanced. There is the beginning of the separation of sacred and profane law and of private and public law. However, the boundaries remain fluid, and there are frequent shifts between sacred and secular law and between personal rights and the objective laws of the political community. Neither is the transition to natural law complete, since at first natural law complements rather than displaces traditional law. Yet when natural law explicitly appeals to reason, the tendency to differentiate sacred and profane law grows stronger. However, this is not true of every kind of philosophically oriented natural law. In Weber's view, Stoic natural law bridged sacred and profane law (828). They were definitively separated only with the transition to modern law, as is true also of the separation of private and public law. A precondition for this development was "the general transformation and mediatization of the legally autonomous organizations of the age of personal law into the state's monopoly of law creation" (705).

These consequences of legal development can be identified, for example, with regard to the institution of the contract. Contracts are already familiar in traditional law. However, they are primarily status contracts, which "involve a change in what may be called the total legal situation (the universal position) and the social status of the persons concerned" (672). They are found especially in family and inheritance law and in the rudiments of public law. They are distinguished from instrumental contracts, which safeguard especially monetary transactions. The latter kind of contract is a "specific quantitatively delimited, qualityless, abstract, and usually economically conditioned agreement" which has a "non-ethical" character (674). The instrumental contract, too, is found under traditional law, but as modern law arises, the relation of status and instrumental contracts changes. The latter come to prevail and with them a law that prefers enabling instruments to command or prohibition. Under modern law as well status contracts persist. It is even possible to say that civil rights are status contracts. But it remains a fact that in the course of legal development the realm regulated by instrumental contracts steadily expands. At the same time ethical regulations recede behind nonethical ones.

We can now summarize the analysis of internal legal development. We proceeded from Weber's distinction between revealed, traditional, deduced or natural and enacted (positive) law, on the one hand, and between formal and substantive legal rationalization on the other. Our thesis was that Weber distinguished between the procedural and the substantive aspects of law and treated the rationalization of law from both viewpoints, although he did not give equal weight to them. Therefore, there must be a rationalization of legal procedure as well as of the foundation of law; they are historically related, but must be separated analytically. Whereas legal procedure becomes more logical, the foundation of law becomes more abstract and universal. At the same time the foundation of law shifts from transcendental to inherent principles; that is, it is secularized. Indeed, in the sociology of law Weber is concerned with the "secularization of law and the growth of a strictly formal mode of juridical thought" (810). The sociology of law can be systematized from these two viewpoints and linked to his discussion of the ways in which the various areas of law have been differentiated historically. (Cf. Scheme XII.)

Scheme XII
Legal Configurations of Law

Characteristics / Type of law	Form of law	Content of law	Differentiation of legal spheres
Revealed law (charismatic)	empirical and concrete	action	--------
Traditional law	empirical and concrete	norm	criminal and civil law
Deduced law (natural)	logical and abstract	philosophical principle	sacred and secular law
Enacted law (positive)	logical and abstract	juristic principle	private and public law

We have not yet clarified how Weber can assert that law has either a more formal or a more substantive character and that its opposition to substantive rationalty increases with logical rationalization. To discuss these two claims we must include a viewpoint that transcends the internal development of law. We are no longer concerned primarily with the relation between form and content but with the relation of law to nonlegal phenomena, especially ethical norms and domination. Weber treated the problems of formal and substantive rationalization of law primarily from an external perspective, in connection with the character of religion and its relation to law and state and with the structure of political domination. Where sacred and secular law were not separated and political domination became theocracy, "there arose an indistinct conglomeration of ethical and legal duties, moral exhortations and legal commandments without formalized explicitness, and the result was a specifically *non-formal* type of law" (810).

The Relation of Ethics and Law

Before we discuss the relation of law and ethics, it will be useful to look back briefly at our analysis up to this point. The explication of Weber's sociology of religion and of law has yielded four ethical and four legal types: magic "ethic," law ethic, ethic of conviction and ethic of responsibility, on the one hand, and revealed law, traditional law, deduced law and positive law on the other. These types of ethics and law are obviously related to one another because the basis of evaluation determines both the type of ethic and the type of law. The two developmental lines approach one another not in form but in content. The underlying criteria inform us about the way in which ethics and law are inherently related, but also about the manner in which their claims can be separated from one another. The basis of evaluation has been spelled out in terms of action, norm, principle and reflexive principle. With the help of these distinctions we can coordinate the ethical and legal types and relate them to the shifts in emphasis. (Cf. Scheme XIII).

If we follow the logic of this scheme, ethic and law constitute a "unity" at the stage of action. There is no distinction between legality and morality, external and internal guarantees of the rules. As a matter of principle, this distinction is not possible at the stage of the mythological world view with its magic "ethic" and revealed law. It can arise only at the stage of the religious-metaphysical world view. But at first the distinction remains slight at this stage, since the operative rule consists mostly of ethical and legal mixtures. This is true to some extent even when ethics have been sublimated into an ethic of conviction. Weber pursues the consequences of such mixtures with regard to sacred and secular law and refers to the cases of India, Islam and Judaism. In India

Scheme XIII
Relationship of Ethics and Law

Basis of evaluation	Ethic	Law	Emphasis
Action	magic 'ethic'	revealed law	} nature v. society
Norm	law ethic	traditional law	legality v. morality
Principle	ethic of conviction	deduced law	} collectivist v. individualist morality
Reflexive principle	ethic of responsibility	positive law	

sacred and secular law were "practically undivided" (817). Under Islam all law was influenced by the Quaran and the prophetic tradition. Judaism did not distinguish between "juristically binding and ethical norms" (826). In this respect, too, Christianity has a special position. In comparison with others, its own sacred law is not only "more rational and more developed in formal-juridical terms," there is also a dualist tension with secular law, which had to be bridged by a rational construct, Stoic natural law (828). However, the religious-metaphysical world view in general can potentially overcome not only sacred and secular, but also ethical and legal mixtures. This becomes likely the more religions are sublimated in the direction of an ethic of conviction and the more traditional law is developed in the direction of natural law. When this happens, the operative rules can split up into two components that remain linked but also develop a certain autonomy. Now the way is clear for law to become "externalized" and for ethics to become "internalized." Law can be rationalized into a "pure form," ethics can be sublimated into "pure content." When this happens in a consistent manner, procedural and substantive rationality become irreconcilable opposites. The dialectic of formal and substantive rationalization reaches its high point. Weber's analysis of the relation between ethics and law is not free from this exaggerated conclusion. Our explication shows that this conclusion is systematically unsatisfactory, and we are not compelled to accept it. Weber is right insofar as he shows that the dialectic of ethics and law begins with the transition from action to norm and that it gains momentum with the transition from norm to principle and even more to reflexive principle. He is right in believing that today all theories that assert the ultimate reconcilability of ethical and legal rules for modernity have become obsolete. But he is wrong insofar as he assumes that ethics and law have no longer any connection today and insofar as he does not specify the mediating principles that still exist between the two components.

In order to clarify the connection, it must be formulated in a more abstract fashion. We can proceed from Kant's distinction between duties of virtue and duties of law as well as duties owed to oneself and duties owed to others. I propose to remove these distinctions from Kant's context and to combine them with Weber's considerations. The first distinction refers to internal and external rules, the second to rules that refer to either persons or associations. I assert that both dimensions vary independently. They represent paths along which the relation of law and ethics can develop in systematic terms. (Cf. Scheme XIV.)

With the help of this scheme we can identify three theoretical cases: (1) Ethics and law are differentiated but not yet unrelated to one another. Ethical decrees harmonize with legal injunctions and both are guaranteed primarily externally. (2) Ethics and law develop tensions with one another. The ethical decrees become autonomous. Internal sanctions appear beside external ones, the dictates of conscience beside the compulsions of law and convention. Yet the ethical decrees remain also sanctioned from the outside. Conventional compulsion however advances at the expense of legal enforcement. (3) Tension arises not only between ethics and law but also between rules referring to persons and to associations. Individual ethics become separate from social ethics and private law from public law. At the least, ethical rules referring to persons are sanctioned exclusively by the dictates of conscience. External sanctions fall away. In the first case, the distinction between nature and society applies, in the second the distinction between legality and morality, and in the third the distinction between collectivist and individualist morality.

Scheme XIV
Typology of Ethical and Legal Rules

Reference of rule / Kind of guarantee	Rules related to persons	Rules related to associations
Internal	individual ethics	social ethics
External	'acquired' subjective rights ('private law')	'imposed' objective law ('public law')

These three cases represent instances of differentiation that can be characterized not only by the degree of the relative autonomy of their components, but also by their relationship with one another. In order to clarify this point, we can fall back on our previous distinction between segmental, stratified and functional differentiation. It also applies to the relation of ethics and law, which has not only an evaluative but also an institutional component. The first case is that of segmental differentiation, in which ethics and law are similar and treat one another as equals. The second is that of stratified differentiation. Ethics and law are different, but ethics gains primacy. The third case is that of functional differentiation. Ethics and law treat one another as equals. There is no permanent hierarchy between them, but they are also not fully isolated from one another. Rather, ethics and law remain in tension: they represent an opposition that can be productive only if there is no relapse into stratified differentiation.

Against the background of these theoretical considerations we can recognize a new dimension in Weber's statements on the relation of ethics and law under the conditions of Western modernity. Weber emphasizes that the erosion of natural law, which was once the foundation of modern law, is irreversible. Law has no longer any transcendental dignity and has been reduced to a technical means for arriving at compromises between competing interests (875). But he also remarks that it is "a gross self-deception to believe that without the achievements of the age of the Rights of Man any one of us, including the most conservative, can go on living his life."[12] And in 1905/6, when he witnessed the outbreak and course of the bourgeois revolution in Russia, he advocated the struggle for "inalienable civil rights." He concedes that the Rights of Man and of Citizens do not provide "unambiguous guidelines" for social and economic progress, but if we abandon them, we will end up in the "prison of the new servitude," which the rationalism of world mastery has prepared.[13] From a systematic perspective, such statements make sense only if ethics and law have become autonomous in Western modernity but continue to be mutually dependent. We can maintain with Hermann Heller that positive law must be related not only to basic logical rules of law but also to basic ethical rules of law that constitute a *ius naturale* for a given civilization.[14] These basic rules cannot give unambiguous directives for social and economic programs, as Weber correctly

12. Weber, "Parliament and Government in a Reconstructed Germany," Appendix II, *ES*, p. 1403.

13. Weber, "Zur Lage der bügerlichen Demokratie in Russland," *Gesammelte politische Schriften* (Tübingen: Mohr, 1971), pp. 62ff., partially translated as "Prospects of Democracy in Tsarist Russia," in W. G. Runciman ed., E. Matthews tr., *Weber: Selections in Translation* (Cambridge University Press, 1978), esp. p. 281.

14. Cf. Hermann Heller, *Gesammelte Schriften* (Leiden: Sijthoff, 1971), II, 141ff., III, 305ff. I am here following up my previous interpretation of Heller's theory. Cf. Schluchter, *Entscheidung für den sozialen Rechtsstaat, op. cit.*, pp. 182ff., and "Hermann Heller 1891-1933," in P. Glotz and W. R. Langenbucher, eds., *Vorbilder für Deutsche* (Munich: Piper, 1974), pp. 217ff.

pointed out. If they are to serve this purpose, they must be transformed into positive law.

It is my thesis that basic rules of law of this kind establish a link between the ethic of responsibility and positive law. They belong to the realms of ethics as well as of law. From the ethical perspective they appear legal and from the legal perspective ethical. They are legal insofar as they provide an institutional sanction, ethical insofar as they are inalienable and thus have transcendental dignity. In Weber's terms, we can view them as part of a basic status contract. They define the "total legal situation" and "universal position" (672) of the members of a social order. "Acquired" subjective rights of this kind, subjective Rights of Man and of Citizens, which advance universalist claims, cannot be viewed as the result of nonethical instrumental contracts. These rights impart to the legal order that epigrammatic and dramatic quality *(epigrammatische Theatralik)* that Weber illustrated with the *code civil*. This dramatic quality reflects the fact that two kinds of norms of divergent qualitative dignity are related to one another.

Now we can give a first answer to the question of why Weber says that law is either more formal or more substantive and that its opposition to substantive rationality grows to the extent that logical rationalization increases. A given law is substantive if law and ethics can be directly translated into one another or if ethics retains primacy. This situation can be found mainly in the cases of traditional and deduced law, but not in those of revealed and positive law. Law is formal if its procedure constitutes its content or if law and ethics are functionally differentiated. The first is true of revealed law, the second of positive law. These two forms represent extreme alternatives. It is true that modern law, just like primitive law, is legitimated through its procedure, but it differs from it by the use of abstract and logical procedures that remain tied to content and have no legitimating power without it. However, the functional differentiation of ethics and law presupposes that both have a structure of their own which permits them to choose their mutual dependence freely, at least to some degree. This is possible only if an ethic has become an ethic of responsibility and law has become positive. Such a relationship is not possible between an ethic of conviction and positive law. An ethic of conviction polarizes ethical substance and legal formality and creates a hierarchy. Weber's diagnosis of our time is faulty to the extent that he tends at least partially to treat the two constellations as identical. This creates the following dilemma: either we have substantive ethical postulates or procedurally positive law, either value rationality or instrumental rationality, either legitimation based on natural law or legality based on positive law. Almost the whole secondary literature on Weber, whether apologetic or critical, has been caught in the trap of this false alternative. Without breaking out of it, one cannot arrive at a systematically satisfactory conclusion and cannot benefit sufficiently from the full range of Weber's diagnosis of our time.

3. The Sociology of Domination

Traditional Domination: The Guiding Principle of Personal Loyalty

A further look at the sociology of law will be useful so that we can discuss the relation of law and domination. Weber not only offers us pointers for an historical theory of constitutional development of public law but also establishes an explicit connection between the formal and substantive rationalization of law and the structural forms of domination (809ff.). Patriarchal domination is at first linked to primitive law, although it is not limited to it. However, not until the rise of the authority of princes and magistrates are "the older forms of popular justice" with their "primitive formalistic irrationality" (809) overcome and the road opened for the rationalization of law in form *and* content. This leads to the establishment of traditional law with objective norms. The interest of the political authorities and of the subjects, however, remains focused on the content of the norms; their basic orientation is substantive, not formal. Yet there can be considerable differences within this basic orientation, depending on whether a ruler tends more toward an arbitrary or a stereotyped form of traditional order. If he tends toward the former, he tries to minimize traditional limitations in favor of his discretionary powers. He can be successful with the help of two policies: (a) he does not delegate any authority to the administrative staff and (b) governs with administrative decrees that do not bind him beyond an individual case but express his will to further the welfare of his subjects. The result is a patriarchal practice that dissolves law largely into administration *(Verwaltung als Regierung)*. This inhibits a formal rationalization of traditional law. Of course, this tendency toward *khadi* justice is opposed by the interest in centralization, in the unity of the rulership. Centralization requires not only unification but also generalization, and both presuppose formal rationalization. If the rulership tends toward the sterotyped variant, this will favor traditional limitations. This is feasible if the administrative staff acquires some of the rights of rulership, and this in turn increases the inclination to limit the ruler's discretion through legal regulation. Administration is then largely reduced to law enforcement. The result is a corporate *(ständisch)* law that strengthens the formal as against the substantive rationalization of traditional law. However, this "legalization" leads not to a system of general norms but to a hierarchy of privileges. Here too we find an opposing tendency: special rights favor not the centralization, but the decentralization of rulership. Political association tends to dissolve into "a system of purely personal loyalty between the lord and his vassals and between these in turn and their own sub-vassals and so on" (256). Certain variants of "feudatory" feudalism came close to this situation. Such tendencies weaken the very affinity of corporate law and formal rationalization. The dissolution of political association into special rights radically reduces the possibility of a systematic codification which would benefit formal rationalization.

Thus, the processes of traditional law are subject to a dialectic of substantive and formal rationalization. Which tendency is followed depends not only on legal thought but also on the structure of domination. However, this dialectic unfolds on the basis of concrete and largely particularist norms. Adjudication and administration follow the maxim of "personal consideration." Both rest on the belief in personal loyalty *(Pietätsglauben)*. Therefore, Weber can write that in the case of traditional rule "obedience is owed, by virtue of filial piety *(Pietät)*, to the person of the chief who occupies the traditionally sanctioned position of authority and who is (within its sphere) bound by tradition" (216). Adjudication and administration remain committed to the notion of substantive inequality. In this sense traditional law and traditional government are elements of *personal* rule, irrespective of whether the dialectic of formal and substantive rationalization favors either the substantive or the formal component.

Nevertheless, there is an opportunity, in the context of personal rule, to further formal rationalization permanently at the cost of substantive rationalization—if the ruler's interest in abolishing corporate privileges coincides with the interests especially of the bourgeois strata in a calculable law and administration. In Weber's eyes, this interest constellation even belongs to "the most important forces promoting formal legal rationalization" (847). However, a direct political coalition of ruler and bourgeoisie is not necessary and even unlikely. For the ruler is also opposed to a general regulation of law and administration, and the bourgeoisie can satisfy its economic interests well enough under the protection of corporate privileges. This is true of politically oriented capitalism in general and even of "early mercantilist capitalism" (848). And yet this indirect interest constellation is one of the constitutive conditions for abstracting and universalizing the concrete norms of personal rulership and thus for transforming substantive legal inequality into formal legal equality, perhaps by way of natural law demands for substantive legal equality. Such constellations existed in Rome, the late Middle Ages and modernity. Where they were absent, "the secularization of the law and the growth of a strictly formal mode of juridical thought either remained in an incipient stage or was even positively counteracted" (810).

Rational Domination: The Guiding Principle of Legality

Under certain conditions, then, the dialectic of formal and substantive legal rationalization leads to an undermining of the world of legal and administrative particularity. Modern law can result therefrom. Partly because of the influence of natural law, modern law rests no longer on concrete and particularist norms but is "a consistent system of abstract rules which have normally been intentionally established" (217). However, for this to come about the ruler's *imperium* had to be transformed into "the modern state with its distribution of competence among its various organs" (652). The interest of the political authorities and of the ruled is oriented toward calculable law and administration; the content is secondary. The basic orientation is not substantive but formal. The basic maxim is "without consideration of the person." Only the abstract, general rule is valid, whether it is instrumentally rational, value-rational or both. The principle of personal loyalty has been replaced by the principle of legality, and the concrete tradition and concrete ruler by abstract rules, which may be agreed upon or imposed. Hence, Weber can say that the modern state, in contrast to the *imperium*, represents a "constitutional domination" whereby "obedience is owed to the legally established impersonal order. It extends to the persons exercising the authority of office under it by virtue of the formal legality of their commands and only within the scope of authority of the office" (215). This scope is no longer determined by the private rights of a person, but by the delimited jurisdiction of a public organ.

Weber is primarily interested in exploring this basic difference between personal and impersonal, traditional and rational domination. Only the modern legal and administrative process breaks down the personalist barrier that contained all traditional political authority, theocracy no less than the patrimonial ruler and the personal magistrate. These are "the authoritarian powers resting on loyalty" (811). They can be viewed as variants of one basic social configuration, that of personal loyalty. With the development from the *imperium* to the modern state this configuration is replaced by that of legality. A developmental stage has been reached that is based on abstract and universalist "principles" and provides a new frame for the dialectic of formal and substantive rationalization. In line with our strategy of exposition, we shall now look for historical variants of basic configurations of legality and for the manner in which they may favor the formal or the substantive rationalization of law and administration.

In order to be able to do this, however, we must interpose another consideration. Weber tends to identify legality with formal rationalization for the reasons outlined above, so that substantive rationalization appears not as a component of the guiding principle of legality but as its counter principle. Substantive rationalization means the intrusion of ethical imperatives, utilitarian pragmatism or political maxims into the autonomy of the legal and administrative apparatus, which functions as a "rational machine" and thereby provides to the citizens "a relative maximum of freedom, and greatly increases for them the possibilities of predicting the legal consequences of their actions" (811). Substantive rationalization appears to disable this machine. Compared to the developmental level achieved, it produces lack of calculability and ultimately "regression." This is the impression conveyed by Weber's description of the dialectic of formal and substantive rationalization under the conditions of legal domination. And this impression is reinforced by the fact that, in contrast to traditional domination, he analyzes here mainly one variant, the bureaucratic, and largely identifies basic configuration and variant. For instance, he tends to use the concepts rational, legal and bureaucratic synonymously, although in the newer part of *Economy and Society* he introduces a gradation: the legitimacy of all legal domination is rational and domination with the help of a bureaucractic administration is only the purest type of legal domination (215f.). This foreshortening of Weber's perspective can be explained in part by the accident that he did not live to write his chapter on the development of the modern state and the modern parties, but there are also systematic reasons.

If we want to remedy Weber's shortcoming, we must extend our analysis of the relation between ethic of responsibility and enacted law. We asserted that they are dependent on one another. Their relationship is established through functional differentiation, which is mediated in Hermann Heller's sense, by basic logical and ethical rules of law. The latter point to "durable or epochal forms of life, to institutions which have a substantive foundation."[15] A constitution deemed "believable" must give legal expression to such basic rules: it is founded on substantive as well as formal legality. The opposite of formal legality is not the concept of legitimacy but that of the substantive legality of the state.[16] If we follow classical constitutional theory, we find this double aspect in the idea of the formally and substantively constitutional state. The formal aspect comprises the constitutional constraint of legislation, the legislative constraint of administration, the general character of the law, and the constitutional division of powers. The substantive aspect includes, among other postulates, the freedom of self-determination of the people and equality as "the equal, not the arbitrary interest representation of all citizens."[17] The formal aspect refers especially to legal stability, the substantive to equity. However modified, these components remain constitutive of the *rational* state, which is "a consociation of bearers of certain defined *imperia*; these bearers are selected according to established rules; their *imperia* are delimited from each other by general rules of separation of powers; and internally each of them finds the legitimacy of its power of command defined by set rules of limitation of powers" (652).[18] These internal limits are rooted not solely in the legal fixation of the powers of command, but also in the basic rules underlying the constitution. Only a constitution founded on such basic rules can create a belief in legality that creates durable legitimacy.

Two further considerations can be added here: (1) I do not think it feasible to distinguish between a value-rational and an instrumentally rational constitu-

15. Hermann Heller, *op cit.*, II, p. 70.

16. *Op. cit.*, p. 225.   17. *Op. cit.*, p. 224.

18. Johannes Winckelmann has particularly emphasized the internal limits of legitimacy in Weber's sociology of domination. See his *Legitimität und Legalität in Max Webers Herrschaftssoziologie* (Tübingen: Mohr, 1952), pp. 39ff.

tion on the level of basic configurations, especially if this is meant to justify an opposition of legitimacy and legality. Proposals of this kind not only confuse basic configuration and historical variant; they also do not sufficiently take into account the development and differentiation of ethics and law. (2) The thesis that a constitution must be founded on basic rules of law is not a plea for the revitalization of natural law. Basic rules of law in our sense are neither revealed, given nor natural—the latter is not possible in the wake of the destruction of the natural law of reason through the "skepticism of modern intellectualism" (874). Rather, the basic rules of law are a culturally relative *ius naturale*, which has been agreed upon in complicated ways. Only if we do not interpret the basic configuration of constitutionalism one-sidedly in terms of positive law or of natural law can we keep in sight the dialectic of ethics, law and political authority. Only then can we do justice to Weber's insight that modern law is not primarily revealed, given or natural but intentionally set down; that is it not primarily a mixture of ethics and law but is based on their functional differentiation and a secularization of law as positive law.

Another elaboration is desirable here concerning Weber's statement that a constitution can have legitimacy irrespective of whether it was agreed upon or imposed in a formally correct way. This statement can be read first of all as a rejection of all exaggerated contractual theories of the state. It is no accident that Weber set off positive enactment from transcendental anchorage, the belief in legality from the belief in what "has been deduced as an absolute" (36). Weber wants to point out that in historical reality imposition is more likely than consensus and that there are not only democratic but also autocratic variants of rational domination (894). It is true that there are grounds for the distinction between consensus and imposition, but this is not an either-or proposition. In a specific sense, a rational constitution is agreed upon and imposed.

The reason for this situation lies in the relationship between basic rules of law and positive enactment discussed earlier. A basic rule of law provides a legal possibility that must be enacted in order to become real. In general, enactment implies an element of arbitrariness. Its result is valid for all and therefore is an imposition as long as there is no "unanimous consensus" (36). An enactment supported by the majority is still an imposition: the will of the majority is imposed on the minority. However, once religious revelation and sacred tradition and also the charisma of reason have disappeared, the basic rules of law, which reflect the culturally relative ideas of justice, must be viewed as agreed upon in some sense—they appear under the regulative idea of unanimous consent. Therefore, every enactment can be discussed from the viewpoint of the ethic of responsibility. In Emil Lask's sense, this dialogue reflects upon "the supra-empirical meaning of the empirical law" and upon its ethical obligatoriness. In such a critical value analysis, which must not confuse the reality of law with the normative idea of law, the significance of the values underlying the positive order is established. This presupposes, of course, that we can understand empirical reality "as the *only* kind of reality, but also as the location of supra-empirical values."[19]

However, this assertion about the relationship between agreement and imposition in the case of rational domination must be qualified further. The difference between legal value and legal reality is found not only in enacted but also in traditional law. Whenever we talk of legal values, we think of legal possibilities that must be "intentionally individualized" in order to become reality.[20] Hence, if we want to distinguish traditional from rational domination, the guiding principle of personal loyalty from that of legality, we must clearly establish the type of legal values in the two cases and the type of discretion which helps bridge the difference between legal value and positive law.

Weber described the situation rather precisely in the case of traditional domination. A command is considered legitimate "in part because of the tradition which determines its content . . . in part because of the ruler's discretion, which also derives from tradition." Weber calls this traditional discretion; it rests on the "unlimited obedience required by the demands of personal loyalty." Insofar as traditional discretion accepts any criteria, they are substantive in character, "considerations of ethical common sense, of equity or of utilitarian expediency, but not formal principles, as in the case of legal domination" (227). Thus, in the traditional realm the law consists of norms that are directly valid. They are believed to be given and to determine the content of directives with relative clarity. Therefore, the belief can arise not only that a decision applies law that has always been valid, but that its content is largely predetermined, so much so, in fact, that the norm needs merely to be followed. However, a realm "free of specific rules" is juxtaposed to the tradition-bound realm. In this sphere persons act according to their privileges. Here "the master is free to do good turns on the basis of his personal pleasure and likes, particularly in return for gifts—the historical sources of dues" (227). Weber speaks of the dual realm of traditional domination. It consists of the sacredness of given norms and the ruler's discretion, of a concretely regulated and a "free" sphere.

The comparable situation in the case of rational domination must be extrapolated to some degree. We can begin with the fact that for Weber commands are legitimate if they are oriented to intentionally established abstract rules and general principles. The legal and administrative process is subject to them: "Administration of law is held to consist in the application of these rules to particular cases; the administrative process in the rational pursuit of the interests which are specified in the order governing the organization, within the limits laid down by legal precepts and following principles which are capable of generalized formulation and are approved in the order governing the group, or at least not disapproved in it" (217). Contrary to the case of traditional domina-

---

19. Emil Lask, *Gesammelte Schriften* (Tübingen: Mohr, 1923), I, p. 279f.
20. Hermann Heller, *op. cit.*, II, p. 72.

tion, Weber does not juxtapose a realm of discretion with this abstractly regulated sphere. It appears that in the case of legality there is regulated discretion *within* the sphere of abstract norms. In analogy with traditional domination, we might call it a realm of rational discretion. Here we encounter the jurisdiction of an agency, not the personal right of a master. Subjective privilege is replaced by an objective rule, a constitutional or enacted norm. The juxtaposition of tradition and arbitrariness is replaced by the integration of enactment and jurisdiction. This results in a complex hierarchy of law and legislation, which in the last analysis is based on the character of rational legal values. They are not given, but must be agreed upon; they are not concrete but abstract. They must be enacted in order to receive a positive content. But even then they remain relatively abstract, so that every decision requires discretion and can be understood as a conscious selection. The range of discretion depends on the kind of enacted decisions as well as on their complex relationships. Therefore, in the case of rational domination too we encounter a dual realm, the sphere of abstract principle and of discretion. These two elements are bound together through legislation, which in turn is rule-bound. We might say that the arbitrary will of the ruler has been transformed into the general application of law. Thus, discretion does not disappear under rational domination, but arbitrary discretion has become rule-bound discretion. Rational domination is *regulated* discretion. This is demonstrated by the realization that every enactment could have taken a different turn. In my view, this is what Weber has in mind when he writes that under legal domination "any law" (217) or legal norm can be passed. This is true because law has here become contingent. It can no longer be anchored in a religious revelation, in the sacredness of a tradition or in a natural law.

Just as is true of the guiding principle of personal loyalty, the principle of legality overarches two different spheres and must satisfy the claims of both. Under both principles problems of legitimation are defined which must be confronted by the given social order. Rational domination, too, may solve problems at the expense of one or the other sphere. However, at this point we cannot push our analogy any further. In contrast to traditional domination, the relationship of the two realms under rational domination is ultimately not one of substitution but of mutual orientation. Here too either the "supra-positive" or the positive law may be favored. In the first case this leads to an order of natural law, in the second to an order of positive law. However, even an order of natural law that still upholds the belief in the charisma of reason could not rely exclusively on the directly obligatory character of its basic principles. It would have to transform their reasonableness into external obligatoriness and their postulates into somber legal rules. A system of natural law that does not institutionalize its postulates for all persons would remain empty. This would be true especially once the belief in the charisma of reason and the direct obligatoriness of its principles has decayed. However, just as a system of natural law would be empty without positive enactment, so a system of positive law would be blind, so to speak, without being based on legal principles. Although a positive order can consist of "any legal norm," this arbitrariness is limited not only formally but also substantively. In our view, the range for enactment is defined by the basic rules of law which are recognized as fundamental in the *ius naturale* of a given civilization. They formulate the constitutive principles with which a positive legal system that claims legitimacy must not be in conflict. The decisive question in the case of positive law concerns the way in which these legal principles and legal rules are related to one another.

We have argued that basic rules of law provide major building blocks for constructing the content of law by establishing a linkage with ethics. This is indicated by Heller's concept of the basic ethical rules. From the viewpoint of the philosophy of law, basic principles are exposed to two crosscutting demands—reasonableness and external obligatoriness. Through enactment the reasonableness inherent in the basic principles must be made externally obligatory. But this involves a transformation. The two extremes are important here: enactment can guarantee the "ethical minimum" or the "ethical maximum." In sociological terms, this means that enactment can follow two strategies: the range of interpretation between legal norms and other norms may be small or large. Weber illustrates this situation, albeit in a different context, with the example of contractual law, which consists of enabling rules in contrast to the prescriptive or proscriptive rules of basic civil rights. Contractual law grants "to individuals autonomy to regulate, within certain limits, their relations with others by their own transactions" (668). These relationships depend, among other things, upon the degree to which extralegal norms are legally recognized. Contractual law may be limited to acknowledging only a few maxims of business morality. Then the influence of extralegal norms is restricted. However, contractual law can also recognize the moral postulates of human dignity and justice. Then the impact of extralegal norms is great and legal formalism is weakened: "Such a concept as economic duress, or the attempt to treat as immoral, and thus as invalid, a contract because of a gross disproportion between promise and consideration, are derived from norms which, from the legal standpoint, are entirely amorphous and which are neither juristic nor conventional nor traditional in character but ethical and which claim as their legitimation substantive justice rather that formal legality" (886).

There seems to be an elective affinity between these two strategies and the mode of legal reasoning. If the strategy aims at the ethical minimum, this favors legal positivism. In this case the autonomy of legal norms from other norms is stressed. Positivist legal thought centers on the idea that "what the jurist cannot conceive has no legal existence" (855) and that he has the task to develop law into "a logically consistent and gapless complex of norms waiting to be applied" (855). If the legal strategy aims at the ethical maximum, this promotes anti-positivist reasoning by relativizing the autonomy of legal norms.

This solution denies that legal thought can be without presuppositions (889) and that law can be gapless. Weber not only gave attention to these two basic currents of modern legal thought, he also considered both equally feasible. However, he related the advance of anti-positivism in general with the lessening of "juristic precision" and viewed it as a " characteristic backlash against the dominance of 'the experts' " (894) and of their rationalism on the basis of this rationalism itself.

At the extremes, then, a positive enactment can guarantee either an ethical minimum or an ethical maximum. What can be said about the relationship of ethics and law also applies to the relation of law to other kinds of norms. Therefore, these extremes must not be identified with an order of enacted (constitutional) law and an order of natural law. Rather, they constitute an alternative within legal domination *(Satzungsherrschaft)*, which is characterized by the development of ethics into an ethic of responsibility and of law into positive law and by their functional differentiation. However, if enacted law tends toward the ethical minimum, it faces the danger of losing its principled basis and of severing the connection between ethics and law, so that an empty legalism results. If an enacted law tends toward the ethical maximum, it is in danger of putting ethics above law, so that there is a return to the ethic of conviction and of natural law, a revitalization of the charisma of reason. A legitimate rational order should not go to the one or the other extreme: if it carries the heterogeneity between the norms and the corresponding institutional spheres too far, it loses its substantive rationality, and if it pushes the homogeneity between the norms and the corresponding spheres too far, it loses its formal rationality.

Thus, modern law and administration, too, face the dialectic of formal and substantive rationalization. However, the context in which this dialectic unfolds is formal, not substantive as in the case of traditional law and administration. The procedural and substantive rationalization of law constitutes two modes of applying the law within this formal context: one aimed at the ethical minimum and one aimed at the ethical maximum. Both pursue different strategies. The strategy of the ethical minimum serves the continuity and predictability of legal and administrative processes; that of the ethical maximum their justness. Interest in predictability is evinced especially by "those in charge of rational economic and political enterprises" (813). Justice is championed particularly by segments of the negatively privileged strata and the intellectuals. When predictability is emphasized, there is also a tendency to reinforce professionalism in law and administration, to enlarge the difference between experts and laymen and to rely on the experts' self-control. When justice is paramount, there is a tendency to view professionalism, and especially the lack of external oversight, as the reason for the failure of law and administration to satisfy the expectations of those affected by them. The notion may arise that law and administration should be more than mere "means of non-violent interest conflicts" (894) and that they should be not only immediately intelligible but also of direct service. This may lead to the demand for administration by dilettantes, for instance, by jurors and lay judges, on the one hand, and by "direct democracy" (289) on the other.[21] These claims are sometimes advanced by the experts themselves. Weber explains them in terms of "ideologically rooted power claims" (894) on the part of some groups of experts.

Now we can move on to the historical variants of domination. We have already mentioned that Weber did not live to finish his chapter on the rational state, which very likely would have encompassed the modern autocratic and democratic forms of domination.[22] But there are enough references in the work to link some variants of rational domination with procedural and substantive rationalization, similar to our analysis of traditional domination. These references concern the opposition of expertise and dilettantism, professionalism and humanism. This opposition can be translated into that of professionalization and democratization. The former tends to be associated with procedural rationalization, the later with substantive rationalization.[23]

In order to clarify the connection between variants of rational domination and rationalization, it appears useful to sketch briefly Weber's theory of the rational state *(Anstaltsstaat)*. His views on imperative and free representation, on the one hand, and on collegial and monocratic rulership in modern political associations on the other, make suitable starting points. Appropriated representation, as it was known under traditional domination, was destroyed in the transition to rational domination: "It is not representation as such but free representation in conjunction with the presence of parliamentary bodies which is peculiar to the modern West" (295). Free representation means that the representative, who can be selected by election, rotation or some other means, remains free from mandatory instruction; he is "obligated only to express his own genuine *(sachliche)* conviction, not to promote the interests of those who have elected him" (293). Free representation contrasts with instructed representation. In this case the powers of representation are "strictly limited by an imperative mandate and a right of recall" (293).[24] However, the representatives,

21. Weber uses the phrase "administration of an association free from domination" *(herrschaftsfremde Verbandsverwaltung)*, which in English appears awkward and therefore has been rendered as "direct democracy."

22. Johannes Winckelmann has attempted to reconstruct, through the combination of published passages, the unwritten part of the sociology of domination. This compilation has been included under the title "The Rational State and the Modern Political Parties and Parliaments (Sociology of the State)" in the fifth edition of *Wirtschaft und Gesellschaft* (Tübingen: Mohr, 1976), pp. 815-868. It was not included in *ES* but instead replaced by "Parliament and Government in a Reconstructed Germany" (Appendix II). Modern forms of domination are mentioned in *ES*, e.g., p. 894, p. 226, pp. 812ff., pp. 266ff.

23. Here I am taking up points more fully developed in *Aspekte bürokratischer Herrschaft*, *op. cit.*, pp. 145ff.

24. Cf. Karl Loewenstein, *Max Weber's Political Ideas in the Perspective of Our Time* (Amherst: University of Massachusetts Press, 1966), Ch. IV.

whether free or instructed, must exercise authority together with other persons. This raises the question of the division of powers, which must be constitutional under rational domination, and of their coordination. We can distinguish two modes of rulership, the monocratic and the collegial. The former uses single officials and primarily vertical coordination, the latter uses bodies and primarily horizontal coordination. The modes can be combined, but we are here interested only in the pure case. However, the modes of representation and of rulership vary independently of one another. We can derive from them four rational forms of domination, identified in terms of who has the central position of authority. (Cf. Scheme XV.)

These four variants of rational domination can be discussed in terms of their relation to efficiency within the legal and administrative apparatus. When free representation and monocratic administration are linked, a high degree of efficiency can be achieved. In this case jurisdiction is not concrete but general, and responsibility is not diffuse but clearly visible. By contrast, instructed representation and collegial rulership can help avoid "the predominance of expertise and of secret administrative information" (289) and can contribute to a more thorough consideration of policies. However, this creates "obstacles to precise, clear, and above all, rapid decision-making" (277) and sometimes to expertise in general. Only when administration is in the hands of professional administrators, who have been appointed and have only relative discretion, can administrative actions be precise, continuous, disciplined and reliable—in short, calculable. Where these conditions are not met, efficiency will be reduced and administration will fall into the hands of dilettantes. Therefore, Weber asserts that today we have only the choice between bureaucratization and dilettantism (223). Modern technology and the modern economy clearly favor bureaucratization.

Scheme XV
Variants of Rational Domination

Modes of rulership Modes of representation	Monocratic	Collegial
Free	bureaucratic domination	parliamentary domination (rule by notables and professional politicians)
Imperative	plebiscitary domination by a leader	council rule (soviets)

Insofar as this happens, procedural and substantive rationalization are polarized. The former is equated with bureaucratization, the latter with dilettantism. The two forms of rationalization appear linked with two polar variants of rational domination, bureaucratic domination and domination by councils (soviets), which is the usual version of direct democracy in mass associations (293, 948f.). In this manner the bureaucratic modern state becomes the prototype of procedural rationality. It guarantees predictability, but is in danger of creating a technologically perfected "iron cage." For this very reason it cannot do without some elements of substantive rationality. The bureaucratic modern state must at least try to satisfy the citizens in utilitarian respects, "but this utilitarian tendency is generally expressed in the enactment of corresponding regulatory measures which themselves have a formal character and tend to be treated in a formalistic spirit" (226). In turn, domination by soviets can become the prototype of substantive rationality by guaranteeing a maximum of justice. Yet it is in danger of dissolving the rational association altogether and of ending in anarchy. Therefore, it cannot do without some elements of procedural rationality. However, domination by soviets remains committed to *khadi* justice and administration by comrades, and in case of doubt it will sacrifice all formal rules to the dominance of "ethical or political sentiments" or of welfare aims. On this score domination by soviets tends to be similar to bureaucratic neopatriarchalism, and popular democracy, with its substantive standards of rationality, similar to "the authoritarian powers of theocracy or of patrimonial monarchs" (813).

Thus, bureaucratic domination increases procedural rationalization, but it cannot abandon all elements of substantive rationality. Domination by councils increases substantive rationalization, but it must include elements of procedural rationality, if it is to master the quantitative and qualitative tasks of large-scale association and to avoid anarchy. Here, too, we recognize the dialectic of procedural and substantive rationalization. Here, too, the structure of domination, not alone the nature of legal thought, determines which component prevails. But in contrast to traditional domination, the dialectic unfolds now in the context of a formal, not a substantive orientation. This follows from the fact that personal domination has changed into impersonal domination.

The manner in which Weber relates the dialectic of procedural and substantive rationalization to the variants of rational domination also reveals a shortcoming. He seems to hold out an alternative. If we want predictability and calculability of law and administration, we must affirm bureaucratic domination. If we want justice, then we can only affirm rule by soviets, but this rule is not efficient and probably not even viable under the conditions of modern technology and economy and in view of the quantitative and qualitative tasks of modern large-scale associations. There is either domination by experts or domination without expertise. There does not seem to be domination with the help of expertise, which can balance procedural and substantive rationalization. This foreshortening of Weber's perspective corresponds to that observed in his treatment of ethic and law. It is true that today professionalization and democratization can no longer be identified with one another, but the fact that they are contradictory at a certain point does not mean that there is no relationship between them and that their opposition cannot be maintained productively. Our scheme of the forms of rational domination shows that there are alternatives. Even Weber himself does not limit them to plebiscitary domination. Here, too, our explication reveals that there is no need to follow Weber's foreshortening of perspective. It is quite possible to believe that rule by soviets is indeed unacceptable because it does not provide sufficient procedural rationality. But this is not tantamount to discounting the demand for embedding substantively rational elements in the rational association according to the legal strategy of the ethical maximum.

Traditional and Rational Domination Compared

Traditional and legal (rational) domination,then, constitute basic configurations of social order that stand in a sequence. They define the historical problems of legitimation and organization. The historical variants of traditional and rational domination emerge under contingent conditions. They must solve all the problems posed by the basic configurations. The legitimation problems concern the internal, the organizational problems the external limits of political authority. In Weber's view, no traditional and no rational political authority that successfully claims legitimation is without internal and external limits. However, the location of these limits is not a matter of "bookish wisdom."[25] This is an historical question which can only be answered by the historian. Sociological analysis can only identify the framework within which these processes take place, and it can assign the historical variants of domination to the basic configurations of a social order only after the fact.

We can now systematically summarize the comparison of traditional and rational domination. Traditional domination recognizes the dual realm of sacred tradition and ruler's discretion, of centralization and decentralization. Rational domination recognizes the dual realm of sacred legal principles and positive enactment, of professionalization and democratization. Both can be distinguished not only in terms of their guiding principle of legitimation but

25. Cf. "Introduction," p. 291: "The most varied transitions and combinations are found between the polar opposites. Neither religions nor men are like tightly reasoned books. They are historical phenomena rather than logical or even psychological constructions without contradictions. Often they have borne within themselves a series of motives, each of which, if separately and consistently followed through, would have stood in the way of the others or run against them head-on. In religious matters consistency has been the exception and not the rule." This passage accurately reflects Weber's pragmatic perspective.

also of their principle of organization. Next to the division of powers, the latter comprises especially the manner in which the relation of master, staff and ruled is regulated. Moreover, traditional and rational domination can be compared in terms of the relation between the political order and the other orders of society and in terms of the economic organization.[26] (Cf. Scheme XVI.)

In the context of traditional domination we can distinguish four variants, depending on whether they favor procedural or substantive rationalization and centralization or decentralization. The four forms are not identical with Weber's types of patriarchal domination, patrimonial domination, feudalism and *Ständestaat*. Patriarchal domination is traditional, but the political function has not yet become independent or organized on a territorial basis. Its point of reference is the kin group, not the *imperium*. Its organizational problem is the continuity of action, not the centralization of political power. Weber uses the concept of patrimonialism for all those forms of traditional domination that are based on the differentiation of the political function and on territorial organization. In contrast to patriarchal domination, patrimonial domination operates with a personal administrative and military staff. Patrimonialism can be bound more or less by tradition. Feudalism and *Ständestaat* are typical of the former tendency, sultanism of the latter, under which the ruler's discretion has been developed to an extreme extent. Sultanism achieves centralization but only a low degree of procedural rationalization. This distinguishes it from the absolutist state, for example, as it developed in the seventeenth and eighteenth century in western Europe.[27]

I would like to distinguish, therefore, between traditional-patriarchal and traditional-patrimonial domination and, within the latter, between sultanism, feudalism, *Ständestaat* and absolutist state. Sultanism favors substantive rationalization and centralization, feudalism substantive rationalization and decentralization, the *Ständestaat* procedural rationalization and decentralization, and the absolutist state procedural rationalization and centralization. Of course, this scheme indicates only the basic features of possible variants under traditional domination. On an abstract level, these features describe the range of possibilities provided by the basic configuration of traditional domination. This space can be filled by "type switch."[28]

Within the realm of rational domination, too, we can distinguish four historical variants, depending on whether they favor procedural or substantive rationalization and the professionalization or democratization of the modern state. These variants are plebiscitary domination, rule by councils (or soviets), parliamentarism and bureaucracy. Domination by a plebiscitary leader favors

26. Cf. the proposal by Wolfgang J. Mommsen, *The Age of Bureaucracy, op. cit.,* p. 76f., which I do not consider systematically satisfactory.

27. Cf. Gianfranco Poggi, *The Development of the Modern State* (Stanford University Press, 1978), esp. Ch. IV.

28. Cf. *op. cit.,* p. 60.

Scheme XVI
Criteria of Traditional and Rational Domination

Type Criteria	Traditional	Rational
1. Legitimation	personal loyalty	legality
2. Organization		
A. Division of powers	*"ständisch"* division of privileges	*constitutional* division of jurisdiction
B. Top position	*holders of privileges* hereditary, "elected" or "appointed" kings, princes, lords, patricians, notables	*organs*, elected or appt. political leaders, notables or professional politicians
C. Administrative staff	"servants"	"officials" (civil servants)
a. structure	*hierarchy of privileges* of persons	*hierarchy of jurisdiction* of "agencies"
b. definition of "office"	*"office" as personal right* tendency toward appropria- tion of means of administra- tion in the form of benefices or fiefs, "unity" of official and private sphere	*"office as impersonal right"* tendency toward expropria- tion of means of administra- tion, fixed remuneration, separation of official and private sphere
c. criteria of recruit- ment	*birth, "honor," property*	*expertise*
d. type of stratifica- tion	*hereditary estates and prop- erty classes*	*commercial classes and status groups*
D. The ruled	*traditional "members" and subjects*	*citizens*
3. Relation of the partial orders	*stratified differentiation* conflict between religious and political sphere for per- manent predominance. Theocracy, caesaropapism, dualism of political and hierocratic domination	*functional differentiation* Struggle between political and economic sphere for rel- ative autonomy. State administration
4. Economic basis	*organized want satisfaction* (self-sufficient) oikos	*market economy*

substantive rationalization and professionalization, council rule substantive rationalization and democratization, parliamentarism procedural rationalization and democratization, and bureaucracy procedural rationalization and professionalization. Here, too, we only point to basic features of possible variants under rational domination. They spell out the range of possibilities within this basic configuration.

Charismatic Domination: The Mission as Guiding Principle

Our explication has omitted up until now Weber's famous third type, charismatic domination, which rests "on extraordinary devotion to the sanctity, heroism or exemplary character of an individual person, and to the normative order revealed or ordained by him" (215). This omission has systematic reasons, for this type is not part of the developmental dimension treated up to this point. Weber describes charismatic domination not in terms of the concepts personal and impersonal but in terms of the ordinary versus the extraordinary. In contrast to traditional and rational domination, which are phenomena of everyday life, charismatic domination is out of the ordinary. It is based not on traditional and enacted law but on revealed and possibly deduced law. It does not follow either of the two other forms; rather, it offers an alternative. It appears to be a structural possibility within the framework of traditional or rational domination.

These features of charismatic domination are linked to its guiding principle of legitimation, which is based on a mission, not on personal loyalty or legality. In general, this mission is a response to distress and expectations which cannot be handled within the ordinary forms of domination. It destroys the routines of everyday life by reversing the rank order of values and places all persons who accept the mission outside the ordinary worldly attachments. The mission tends to be tied to persons who consider themselves its instrument. In contrast to traditional and rational domination, charismatic rule knows only internal limits. This is not tantamount to unlimited discretion. On the contrary, the charismatic leader is under greater pressure to live up to his promises than the traditional or rational ruler. He must prove not only that God sent him, but that God will remain on his side. He must work miracles or perform heroic deeds in order to justify his claims, and do it in such a way that the well-being of the ruled is furthered. Only if he proves himself can he hope to be recognized. Thus, he is responsible not only to his God but also to the ruled. However, at first recognition by the ruled is not the ground of legitimation. Rather, legitimation follows from the mission which the public to which it is addressed is obliged to accept. Later a reinterpretation of the missionary principle can occur and lead to the anti-authoritarian or democratic understanding of charisma. Now recognition is no longer the consequence but the basis of charismatic domination.

Herein Weber perceives one of the origins of democratic legitimation.[29] This interpretation becomes possible the more associational life is rationalized and the mythological and theocentric or cosmocentric world views are transformed into an anthropocentric world view.

The fact that external limits are absent does not imply that charismatic domination lacks a structure; rather, it has "a definite structure with a staff and an apparatus of services and material means that is adapted to the mission of the leader" (1119). This structure serves to protect the extraordinary nature of the rule. For only if it is not enmeshed in daily routine can "the call in the most emphatic sense of mission or spiritual duty" be central (244). This requires two presuppositions: (1) the personal organs must not become an officialdom. They must consist of persons who have given up their economic positions and family life and who are willing to sacrifice themselves and to fulfill their tasks freely; (2) the charismatic leader and his charismatic following must not satisfy their wants through routine economic activities. Rather, they must rely on discontinuous acquisition through booty and spoils, as in the case of warlike charismatic communities, or through begging, gifts and endowments, as in the case of peaceful charismatic communities. Moreover, these goods must be consumed communally, in the form of "the spoils communism of the military camp or the monastery's communism of love" (1119). Charismatic domination, then, has a structure, but it is highly unstable. It is viable only if it can exploit traditional or rational structures of everyday life. Therefore, it continually faces the danger either of collapsing or of becoming routinized, that is traditional or rational. There are three reasons for this: (1) the introduction of external limits of legitimation in connection with the successor problem, (2) the emergence of family ties among staff members, (3) the utilization of charismatic grace as a source of income and therefore the transition to routine economics. (Cf. Scheme XVII.)

We can recognize a dual realm also in the case of charismatic domination—the contrast between grace and proof, discontinuity and continuity. Here, too, we can read Weber as having distinguished several variants within this basic configuration. As long as the mission is interpreted in authoritarian fashion, there are the variants of hereditary charisma. When charisma is interpreted in an anti-authoritarian manner, there are the variants of plebiscitary democracy (267, 1125ff.). These forms, however, come close to those of traditional and rational domination. In fact, they can be transformed into them, depending on how far routinization goes. This reveals the instability of charismatic rule in comparison with traditional and rational domination. It does not have the potential for legitimation *and* organization that could create a durable structure of domination.

29. Cf. the section on "The Transformation of Charisma in a Democratic Direction" (*Herrschaftsfremde Umdeutung des Charisma*) in *ES*, pp. 266ff., which follows the section on feudalism. In the newer part of *ES*, Weber embedded the section on feudalism in his discussion of charisma, contrary to the old part.

However, Weber described charismatic domination not only as extraordinary but also as personal rule. Charisma is a personal quality for the sake of which a person is treated as a leader. This quality refers to powers that not everybody can have and that therefore are considered supernatural or superhuman. They cannot be separated from the person nor can they be acquired. However, the relation between the mission and the carrier is such that charisma comprises subjective qualities that must have an objective correlate. What is considered superhuman and supernatural changes with the mission and the situation. Therefore, charisma can be interpreted not only in structural terms, through the contrast of the ordinary and the extraordinary, but also in terms of developmental history, with the help of the concepts personal and impersonal. The quality of grace depends, for instance, on whether a mission was formu-

Scheme XVII
Characteristics of Charismatic Domination

1. Legitimation	mission
2. Organization	
A. Division of powers	none
B. Top position	*usurpers* neither elected nor appointed, at best chosen military heroes, prophets and demagogues
C. Administrative staff	*disciples, thanes, political trustees*
a) structure	ad hoc *concrete competences* of disciples etc.
b) definition of office	*office as vocation* no appropriation of the means of administration as benefices or fiefs, no fixed salary, unity of official and private spheres
c) criteria of recruitment	*charismatic inspiration*
d) type of stratification	*elites* brotherhoods of virtuosi
D. The ruled	*followers*
3. Relation of the partial social orders	*indifference* political order struggles against economic dependence
4. Economic basis	*spoils communism, communism of love* booty or gifts extracted from self-sufficient economic units or market economy

lated within a mythological, a theocentric or an anthropocentric world view and whether the proving gound is otherworldly or inner-worldly.

On this score, Weber has provided us with three pointers. First, he distinguishes between magical and religious charisma and the charisma of reason, second, between routinization and depersonalization, and third between exemplary and ethical prophecy. In my view, he has not sufficiently elaborated the first two distinctions, and the third appears in the chapter on the sociology of religion where it has no obvious relationship to the theory of charismatic domination. I propose to follow these three references briefly and to combine them. I would like to make it systematically intelligible that there is a developmental history of charisma and that Weber can say with justification that the "charismatic glorification of 'Reason,' which found a characteristic expression in its apotheosis by Robespierre, is the last form that charisma has adopted in its fateful historical course" (1209).

Weber distinguished clearly between magical and religious charisma, but did not emphasize the developmental significance of this distinction. In my view, the significance lies in the fact that the mission can be fully conceptualized only when the idea of god has arisen.[30] Only within the framework of a dualist world view, in which actions and norms are differentiated, can charisma be anchored in the mission, on the one hand, and in the welfare of the missionary targets on the other. As long as a mythological world view prevails, the carrier of charisma *is* the mission. When theocentric dualism has emerged, the mission can be separated from the carrier. If the carrier fails to prove himself, this does not necessarily affect the mission. In other words,the mission is stabilized against the carrier. Thus, religious charisma is a new stage compared with magical charisma. I believe that this is also true of the transition from religious charisma to the charisma of reason. In turn, reason can be charismatically glorified only as long as it is plausible to attribute to it powers which appear supernatural and superhuman. As soon as this belief fades away, because the mission of reason fails, as in the case of Robespierre, or because reason turns into critical thought, the fateful course of charisma has come to an end. What is left is either the anti-authoritarian reinterpretation of charisma or the charismatic pretension, which refers to the inscrutable decision of "private" gods primarily in order to evade critical reason (1114).

Weber also distinguished the routinization and depersonalization of charisma without clarifying their significance for developmental history. He pointed out that the routinization of charisma can have two consequences: either the charismatic qualities remain strictly personal or they are severed from the person (1135). In the latter case these qualities appear as transferable or

30. Cf. *ES*, p. 1112, where Weber says of the charismatics: "They practiced their arts and exercised their authority by virtue of this gift ('charisma') and, where the idea of God had already been clearly established, by virtue of the divine mission inherent in their ability." In my view this clearly distinguishes religious from magical charisma.

they are attributed to an institution. This happens with office charisma, when charisma takes a definite institutional turn. Weber has called this second variant of routinization a case of depersonalization (*Versachlichung*, 1113). But we should recognize that this depersonalization in the direction of institutionalization differs from the 'impersonalization' of charisma itself in the course of its historical development. An institutional turn of charisma is also possible within the framework of personal rulership. This is shown by Weber's own examples, the Chinese monarch and the Roman bishop in the early church (1114, 1140). By contrast, impersonalization as a form of development means that the charismatic mission is more and more controlled intellectually, that it is no longer simply revealed but is deduced. Weber must implicitly assume such an impersonalization if he wants to avoid confusing the difference between magic charisma and the charisma of reason and between the charisma of revealed law and that of natural law. Such a blurring of lines would make no sense systematically and would contradict his own analyses.

Therefore, I would like to distinguish between depersonalization and impersonalization of charisma in the sense that the former refers to structural changes, the latter to developmental ones. Routinization of charisma means that every charismatic domination tends to become either traditional or rational, that the charismatic quality remains either strictly personal or is transferred to an institution. Impersonalization means that the character of the mission changes in the course of development, that the magic mission changes into the religious one and the latter finally into the mission of reason. Impersonalization is thus not simply a variant of routinization. Rather, it points to the internal development of charisma itself. Impersonalization, however, remains tied to the development of the world views, affecting them in turn. Moreover, the impersonalization of charisma does not lead to the disappearance of charismatics. Rather, it befits the character of the missionary ideal that charisma must be represented by virtuosi with extraordinary powers and qualities. In this regard we can differentiate between two modes of representation that become possible with the end of the mythological world view. This leads us to the third distinction, that between ethical and exemplary prophecy. Weber illustrated these two types of prophecy in his sociology of religion with Zoroaster and Muhammad, on the one hand, and Buddha on the other, and described the difference as follows: "The prophet may be primarily . . . an instrument for the proclamation of a god and his will, be this a concrete command or an abstract norm. Preaching as one who has received a commission from god, he demands obedience as an ethical duty. This type we shall term the 'ethical prophet.' On the other hand, the prophet may be an exemplary man who, by his personal example, demonstrates to others the way to religious salvation, as in the case of Buddha. The preaching of this type of prophet says nothing about a divine mission or an ethical duty of obedience, but rather directs itself to the self-interest of those who crave salvation, recommending to them the same path as he himself traversed. Our designation for this second type is that of the 'exemplary prophet' " (447). This distinction can be translated into the theory of charisma proposed here. Then we have ethical and exemplary charisma, which parallel one another, as soon as magical charisma has been replaced by religious charisma.

The Sociology of Domination Reconstructed

We can now summarize our analysis of the sociology of law and of domination. Legal development is tied to the development of ethics and of political domination. In law both realms are combined. Political power gives the law its external force, and ethics provides its justification. Therefore, domination can be interpreted as the "legalization" of ethics and power; it has an evaluative and institutional dimension. A structure of domination combines ideas *and* interests, world views *and* associations, and it gives them duration. For this to happen, domination must become an everday phenomenon which can continuously solve problems of external want and of internal distress. This requires, first of all, a certain kind of institutionalization: the problems of legitimation and organization are considered settled, the world is declared to be the best of all possible worlds, and the missionary idea, which inheres in every legitimate domination, is pushed into the background. These powerful trends toward routinization are fought by extraordinary domination. It addresses the hopes repressed in every routinized domination by dramatizing the existing missionary idea or by creating a new one. However, it can persist only if it avoids too much institutionalization. For this reason extraordinary domination remains limited to an elite, a small circle of virtuosi. If it yields to the pressures of institutionalization, it becomes an everyday phenomenon. Then it succumbs to the dialectic of routinization and revolution, from which in the long run no everyday domination can escape.

The dialectic of routinization and revolution, which has a structural basis, is paralleled by the dialectic of procedural and substantive rationalization, which has a developmental basis. Both are related in complex ways. Only the dialectic of rationalization provides direction to revolution and routinization. This direction is indicated by the opposition of personal and impersonal domination. (Cf. Scheme XVIII.)

In Weber's sociology of domination. then, we have identified three basic configurations, two of everyday life and one out of the ordinary but structurally related to the other two. In this interpretation there are two independent and one dependent type of domination: the continuous everyday structures of traditional and rational domination, which are founded on the guiding principle of personal loyalty or legality, and the discontinuous extraordinary structure of charismatic domination, which is based on the missionary principle. These

Scheme XVIII

Systematic Representation of the Sociology of Law and Domination

personal		*impersonal*
traditional domination traditional law (substantive-nonrational)		*rational domination* enacted law (formal-rational)

rationalization

"traditionalization"

charismatic domination

revolution

revolution

revealed law (formal-nonrational)	natural law (substantive-rational)

ordinary

extraordinary

Structural
dimension

Developmental dimension

three types can have several variants. These are not simply a consequence of the mixture of the three basic configurations; rather, they are predominantly variants within one configuration. Only charismatic domination, as a rule, combines with other configurations. It either recognizes another principle for the sake of preserving the purity of its own, or it transforms itself into another configuration. Thus, the question of whether there are two types of domination within the frame of rational authority is either a question about the relationship between the guiding principles of mission and legality or a question about alternative forms made possible by the latter. Whichever way the question is posed, the answer should not lead in my view to the contrast, so popular in the literature, between value-rational and instrumentally rational legitimate domination. I would like to suggest that my explication necessitates a reformulation of these concepts and of their relationship.

4. Sociology of Domination and Typology of Action

This brings me to Weber's typology of action and the question of its relationship to the types of domination. I shall not go here into the fundamental problems of action theory and shall not ask whether Weber's approach may show weaknesses by proceeding from action rather than interaction and from the individual act rather than the action system.[31] Instead, I shall only draw some tentative conclusions from my presentation.

31. See Jürgen Habermas, *Handlungsrationalität und gesellschaftliche Rationalisierung* (Ms.). Habermas perceives difficulties with Weber's theory of action in two respects: (1) there is a discrepancy between the concepts of action and the analyses of rationalism, especially in the sociology of religion; (2) there are shortcomings in the diagnosis of the present. Habermas argues that in spite of all modifications Weber ultimately retained the teleological model of action, the basis of which is the monologic and purposive actor who is oriented toward success. He contrasts this model with the model of communicative action, which proceeds from an actor who is oriented toward dialogue and accommodation *(Verständigung)*. According to Habermas, Weber interprets the rationality of action primarily in terms of instrumental rationality because he adheres to the teleological model of action. However, this is only one aspect of rational action. Only by accepting the model of communicative action is it possible to classify instrumental action correctly, only then does it become clear that it represents only one class of rational action and that other kinds have equal rank. Habermas goes even further: ultimately he wants to demonstrate that instrumental social action can also be viewed as strategic action, a borderline case of communicative action, and hence that communicative action is superior to teleological action. I must leave it open whether this interpretation is tenable. My present concern is to strengthen Weber's position. However, I am following Habermas' thesis that instrumental rationality must be understood as merely one aspect of rational action.

Johannes Berger, too, has attempted a critique of Weber's theory of action. It differs from Habermas' in that he contrasts both the monologic and the dialogical theory of

It appears that Weber's four types of action, instrumentally rational, value-rational, affectual and traditional, are arranged along a scale of rationality. This scale seems to be constructed with the help of the criteria of means, concrete ends, abstract value and consequence. A fully controlled rational act is one in which the actor selects ends on the basis of value analysis; this also "involves rational consideration of alternative means to the end, of the relations of the end to the secondary consequences, and finally of the relative importance of different ends" (26).[32] Action that is fully controlled in this sense appears to be instrumentally rational. The other kinds of action neglect at least one criterion of rational control. In the case of value-rational action the consequence is disregarded; in the case of affectual action the consequence and the value, and in the case of traditional action consequence, value and end.

This typology reveals above all three weaknesses: (1) it tempts us to identify instrumental rationality with the ethic of responsibility and value-rationality with the ethic of conviction; (2) it suggests that the traditional and the rational do not constitute a sequence but an alternative; (3) it is incompatible with the value theory that underlies Weber's historical theory of rationalization. This value theory is based on the distinction between the true, the good and the beautiful, between cognitive, evaluative and expressive symbolism. In order to remedy these weaknesses, we must reconstruct the typology in a direction suggested by the distinction of the three value spheres.

To begin with, the distinction of the cognitive, evaluative and expressive spheres motivates us to reduce the four types of action to three: instrumentally rational, value-rational and affectual. Only these orientations of action, not traditional action, can be linked to these value spheres. Instrumentally rational action, in which the success of an action is primary, can be assigned to the cognitive sphere; value-rational action, for which the value of an action is dominant, to the evaluative sphere; and affectual action, in which affects and sentiments predominate, to the expressive sphere. A concrete act is always embedded in all three value spheres. Thus, the three types tell us at first only which of these relationships are predominant. A fully developed theory of action would have to demonstrate that these relationships are constitutive of all actions and therefore represent formal possibilities. Action theories of this kind are found in the work of Talcott Parsons and Jürgen Habermas.

The differentiation into the three fundamental value spheres also suggests the separation of the structural from the developmental perspective. Weber's

---

action with a structural theory derived from the Marxian tradition. However, this leads him to the very dichotomization of action and structure which can be overcome, in my view, with Weber's help. Cf. Johannes Berger, "Die Grenzen des handlungstheoretischen Paradigmas am Beispiel der 'soziologischen Grundbegriffe' Max Webers," in K. M. Bolte, ed., *Materialien aus der soziologischen Forschung* (Darmstadt: Luchterhand, 1978), pp. 1081ff.

32. Cf. *ES*, p. 26. I owe the suggestion for this systematization to Enno Schwanenberg.

treatment of instrumentally rational, value-rational and traditional action shows that he blurred the difference between these two perspectives. If we want to avoid this problem, we must terminologically distinguish the structurally possible orientations from their development. Success-oriented action is not in itself instrumentally rational, just as value-oriented action is not in itself value-rational. Therefore, following Weber very closely, I would like to propose labeling the structurally possible orientations success-oriented action, value-oriented action and affectual action. This proposal approximates that of Jürgen Habermas, who distinguishes between success-oriented, consensus-oriented and expressive action.[33] These structurally possible orientations are subject to development, which leads to a general rationalization of action. However, this is apparently fully true only of success-oriented and value-oriented action. As Weber's terminology suggests, affectual action does not seem to be amenable to rationalization in the same way. In the "Theory of the Stages and Directions of Religious Rejections of the World" we find a passage that clearly expresses this condition. There Weber contrasts the ethic of religious brotherhood not only with the "autonomous dynamics of instrumentally rational action," but also with the dynamics of affectual action, not only with the economic, political and scientific spheres, but also with the esthetic and erotic spheres "whose character is essentially non-rational and anti-rational."[34]

In order to determine the degree of rationalization of actions we can use the scale that we attributed to Weber. Action is more rational, the more action aspects it controls. The more aspects it controls, the greater is the degree of freedom. In moving from means to ends, the means are freed for selection; in the transition from concrete ends to abstract value, the ends are freed, and from value to consequence the values themselves become subject to rational choice. This scale can serve to further specify the distinction between nonrational-formal, nonrational-substantive, rational-substantive and rational-formal, which we extracted from Weber's sociology of law. If action is oriented exclusively to the means, it is nonrational-formal to the extent that it cannot weigh means in relation to ends and cannot choose rationally among different possible means. This is the case with magically conditioned action, which is for this reason ritualist. If action is oriented toward means and ends, it is nonrational-substantive insofar as it cannot weigh concrete ends against abstract values and rationally decide among possible ends. This is the case with traditional action, which for that reason is conventional. If action is oriented toward means, ends and values, it is rational insofar as it permits this very particular decision. It is at the same time substantive insofar as it is oriented toward absolute values. Only if action is also oriented toward the consequences is this absolute position of values undermined. Action then remains rational, but it becomes formal inso-

33. Cf. J. Habermas, *op. cit.* He combines the three kinds of action with the three models of action, the teleological, the communicative and the dramaturgical.
34. "Theory," p. 341.

far as it must weigh not only the means against the ends and the ends against the values, but also the values against the consequences and other possible values. Now there is no longer an Archimedian point for making choices between conflicting and colliding values; there is no longer a safe foundation from which an adequate ground can be established as is true of conflicting and colliding concrete ends. Decisions are no longer absolutely but only relatively rational, for they are the consequence of critical examination and can always take a different course.[35]

If we link these four levels of rationality with the two types of action that are amenable to rationalization, we should expect to find two variants of instrumentally and value-rational action, substantively instrumental and formally instrumental action, on the one hand, and substantively value-rational and formally value-rational action on the other, in addition to ritual action for which success and value-orientation coincide, and instrumentally traditional and value-traditional action. Our analysis has tried to show that this distinction makes sense for value-oriented action. Substantive value rationality is the action correlate of the ethic of conviction, and formal value rationality for the ethic of responsibility. However, the distinction may also be useful in the case of success-oriented action, as is indicated by Weber himself, if only ambivalently. He distinguished between subjectively instrumental and objectively correct *(richtigkeitsrational)* action, between "action that is oriented to fully understood ends and to means which are consciously selected as being adequate" and action "oriented to what is objectively correct."[36] In the history of science there was a parallel development. With its switch from dogmatic to critical rationalism the Kantian revolution probably had a significance similar to that which we suggested for ethical development.[37] Only through the transition from dogmatic to critical rationalism could success-oriented action base itself increasingly on scientifically correct experience, so that the choice between competing and colliding values no longer required resorting to "the value-rational orientation toward decrees and commandments" (26). Only under the conditions of a formal instrumental rationality in this sense could interest constellations freely develop. Of course, this also increased the danger that the necessary relation between success-oriented and value-oriented action would disintegrate and be replaced by mere interest orientation.

Thus, if we want to coordinate types of legitimate domination with types of action, we must not relate the four types of action directly with the three types of legitimate domination, as has frequently been done in the literature, nor

35. On the practical significance of the principle of critical examination see especially Hans Albert, *Traktat über rationale Praxis* (Tübingen: Mohr, 1978).

36. Weber, "Über einige Kategorien der verstehenden Soziologie," *Gesammelte Schriften zur Wissenschaftslehre* (Tübingen: Mohr, 1951), p. 433f. For an English version see Edith Graber, tr., "On Some Categories of Interpretive Sociology," unpubl. ms., 8f.

37. Cf. Emil Lask, *op. cit.*, I, pp. 32ff.

must we draw the conclusion that Weber ultimately had in mind not only three but four types of legitimate domination. Instead, we must clearly distinguish the structural from the developmental perspective and recognize that under the former there are only three types of action. However, insofar as a structure of domination is a living reality, it always combines all three types of action.

From the structural perspective there is a conceptual correspondence between the three types of action and three types of domination. It is indicated by two distinctions: (1) domination by virtue of interest constellation and by virtue of authority; (2) the latter's division into ordinary and extraordinary authority, that means, an authority on an evaluative and an expressive basis—by virtue of ethics and by virtue of charisma. However, Weber views the distinction between domination by virtue of interest constellation and domination by virtue of authority not only in structural but also in developmental terms. He contrasts a power which "has its source in a formally free interplay of interested parties such as occurs particularly in the market" (946) with domination by virtue of authority especially because it rests historically on the separation of the economy from the household, on the transition from the *oikos* economy to the market economy and thus on the differentation of two ways of controlling social relationships, through the market and through command.[38] Similarly, Weber uses the distinction between ordinary and extra-ordinary domination, domination by virtue of ethics and by virtue of charisma, not only structurally but also developmentally. Charismatic domination is contrasted with traditional and rational domination especially because it "is indeed the specifically creative revolutionary force in history" (1117). However, these distinctions also retain a structural significance: every stable structure of domination combines market and command, ordinary and extraordinary control mechanisms, and it endeavors to solve at the same time the material and ideal, the social and the nonsocial problems. Yet insofar as a structure of domination is always also an historical phenomenon, it represents specific articulations of these three types of action. The types are characterized by levels of rationality, more generally, of depersonalization. These levels involve above all success-oriented and value-oriented action, but we noted a tendency toward depersonalization also for affectual action, for charisma. However, this does not mean that affectual action

---

38. On this distinction see also Hans Albert, "Individuelles Handeln und soziale Steuerung, " in Hans Lenk, ed., *Handlungstheorien interdisziplinär IV* (Munich: Fink, 1977), pp. 177ff. Weber's distinction between domination by virtue of authority and domination on the basis of interest seems to follow the transition from the theory of the household to the theory of the market economy, from Aristotle to Adam Smith. The Aristotelian tradition analyzed the connection between household and domination, the classical theory studied the market as a social control mechanism without authority. This does not mean that the market is a power vacuum. On the contrary, Weber analyzes it form the viewpoint of the unequal distribution of power among the participants. However, domination through monopolistic control of the market must be distinguished from the authoritarian power of command.

loses its fundamentally nonrational and anti-rational character—it remains a specifically irrational force. (Cf. Scheme XIX.)[39]

5. Preliminary Conclusion

This concludes the explication of Max Weber's sociology as a developmental history of the West. I have tried to elaborate the theoretical framework that Weber had to use in order to "comprehend the distinctiveness of Western and especially modern Western rationalism and to explain it genetically."[40] The explication focused on Weber's limited program in evolutionary theory and in value and institutional theory. I presented both together. My starting point was a distinction between basic social configurations and historical variants. A variant can be subsumed under a basic configuration, which is realized by it under historically contingent conditions. Configurations follow one another. They define a range of possibilities that changes in the course of historical development. Thus, basic social configurations define at the same time *historical* problems of social order. Such problems are "solved" by variants in alternative ways. These solutions refer primarily to two dimensions of basic configurations: the world view and its institutionalization. Therefore, variants must solve above all two historical problems: the problem of legitimacy and the problem of organization. World views, in turn, have several dimensions. They comprise—in neo-Kantian terms—claims of truth, correctness and truthfulness in the spheres of evaluation, cognition and expression. These claims must be institutionalized. The result is always several institutional realms which are related to these value spheres. Four of them are particularly important because they address problems of basic inner and external needs and wants: the political order, the cultural order, the economic order and the educational order. The developmental levels to which this theoretical framework applies can be labelled "primitive civilization," "archaic and historical civilization," and "modern civilization."[41] The first distinction, in particular, is relative. The main difference results from the fact that on the second stage the political function is organized in terms of

39. This scheme has been elaborated further in Schluchter, "Gesellschaft und Kultur. Überlegungen zu einer Theorie institutioneller Differenzierung," in id., ed., *Verhalten, Handeln und System* (Frankfurt: Suhrkamp, 1980), pp. 122ff. Other contributors are Carl Graumann, Niklas Luhmann, Jürgen Habermas and Talcott Parsons. These are the lectures presented on the occasion of the fiftieth anniversary of Talcott Parsons' doctorate at the University of Heidelberg, May 2-4, 1979, shortly before his death.

40. "Author's Introduction," p. 26.

41. In the recent literature a number of proposals have been made to classify the different levels of cultures and societies. Robert Bellah, for one, distinguishes between primitive, archaic, historical, early modern and modern religions, Talcott Parsons, partly following him, between primitive and archaic societies, historical empires and the sys-

Scheme XIX

Relationship Between Typology of Action and of Domination

Prevailing action aspect / Level of rationality	Success-oriented action	Value-oriented action	Affectual action	Stages of Domination — ordinary	extraordinary
non-rational-formal	ritual	ritual	(magic-charismatic)	traditional-patriarchal	
non-rational-substantive	traditional	traditional	religious-charismatic	traditional-patrimonial	
rational-substantive	instrumentally rational	ethic of conviction	charisma of reason		charismatic
rational-formal	objectively rational	ethic of responsibility	anti-authoritarian charisma	rational	
Prevailing aspect of domination	domination by virtue of interest constellation	domination by virtue of everyday authority	domination by virtue of extraordinary authority		

territorial claims and the cultural function in terms of world religions, that is religions "that have succeeded in mobilizing very large numbers of believers."[42] (Cf. Schemes XX and XXI.)

Weber's interest was primarily directed toward the second stage, especially the question of the conditions under which a theocentric or cosmocentric world view is transformed into an anthropocentric world view and stratified into functional differentiation. By comparison, his analysis of the primitive and modern levels remains rather sketchy. This distinguishes Weber from Emile Durkheim, who was much more concerned with the analysis of the primitive level. It also distinguishes him from Karl Marx, whose attention was much more riveted on the "developmental laws" of modern Western capitalism. However, Weber's interest in the archaic and historical level and its developmental potential was ultimately an interest in modern Western rationalism. Its roots lay in the world of theocentric dualism and stratified differentiation. This raises the question of how this modern Western rationalism, which is a rationalism of world mastery, could arise on the historical level and transform it in turn. And why did this happen only in the West? In trying to answer this question, Weber used a sociological frame of reference, the framework which I have elaborated here. Weber developed it primarily for the sake of answering this question. However, the framework does not serve this purpose alone. What Weber said about the relation of sociology and history in general applies here too: sociology creates types and looks for general rules, whereas history is concerned with the "causal analysis and attribution of individual, culturally significant actions, structures and personalities." Nevertheless, generalizing sociology is not only a *Kulturwissenschaft* in the sense of a theory of action, it also "creates types and searches for rules from the viewpoint of serving the historical, causal attribution of culturally important phenomena" (19). One of these phenomena is the modern Western rationalism of world mastery. We must now ask whether this frame of reference can facilitate its causal explanation. The explication of Weber's developmental theory of the West should not be limited to the clarification of the philosophical status and the substantive content of its theoretical framework; it should also try to apply this frame to the limited causal program with which Weber attempts to explain the transition to Western modernity.

---

tem of modern societies. He tends to reduce this scheme to the three concepts primitive, imtermediate and modern. Jürgen Habermas distinguishes neolithic societies, early and developed civilizations and modernity, whereas Niklas Luhmann seems to prefer a global typology of archaic, developed culture (*hochkulturell*) and modern. I adopt a version of Bellah's scheme.

42. "Introduction," p. 267. This is Weber's pragmatic definition of world religion; it emphasizes the aspect of historical impact. However, in my view, the definition also implies something else: a world religion must have reached the level of metaphysical dualism.

Scheme XX
Development of Basic Social Configurations

Developmental level	Basic social order	World views	Basis of association	Problems of order
Primitive civilization	traditional-patriarchal	mythological with pre-ethical evaluations (magic)	blood groups (sibs)	discontinuity versus continuity
From archaic to historical civilization	traditional-patrimonial	religious metaphysics with law ethics / from religious to secular metaphysics with ethic of conviction	city-states and patrimonial empires	double realm of sacred tradition and free discretion; centralization versus decentralization
Modern civilization	rational	secular metaphysics, science, ethic of responsibility	rational state	double realm of legal principles and legal rules; democratization versus professionalization

Scheme XXI

Basic Social Configurations and Institutional Realms

Developmental levels Institutional realm	Primitive civilization	Archaic and historical civilization	Modern civilization
Political order	*patriarchal domination* primary patriarchalism and gerontocracy, early forms of rule by notables patriarch and elder rule directly over group members and subjects	*patrimonial domination* Sultanism, feudalism *Ständestaat*, absolute state prince, landlord, patrician rule indirectly over group members and subjects	*legal domination* plebiscitary domination, councils (soviets), parliamentarism and bureaucracy professional politicians rule indirectly over citizens
Cultural order	*sociocentric monism* mythological thought, pre-ethical evaluations, early law ethics, "natural" unity of cognitive, evaluative and expressive symbolism, segmental differentiation of symbolism myth sorcerers and magicians	*theocentric or cosmocentric dualism* metaphysical thought, law ethics as well as ethics of conviction, beginnings of empirical science and of autonomous development of cognitive, expressive and evaluative symbolism, world views primarily produced by religious elites, stratified symbolism theodicy priests and prophets, philosophers	*anthropocentric dualism* from metaphysical to empirical thought, ethics of conviction and of responsibility, autonomy of cognitive, evaluative and expressive symbolism, world views primarily produced by secular elites, functional differentiation of symbolism anthropodicy "intellectuals"

Scheme XXI (Cont.)
Basic Social Configurations and Institutional Realms

Developmental levels / Institutional realm	Primitive civilization	Archaic and historical civilization	Modern civilization
Economic order	*household* (small-scale, self-sufficient) from no exchange to exchange in kind household communism	*oikos and city* (large-scale self-sufficiency) from "natural" economy to market economy extraction of rent, political capitalism	*market economy* profit orientation of economic units economically and politically oriented capitalism
Educational order	*heteronomy* concrete relations of personal loyalty in primeval groups, esp. household, neighborhood and sib "the good son and servant" heteronomous types of conscience	*religious autonomy* abstract relations of personal loyalty in the *oikos* and in extra-familial educational organizations (churches, universities) "the obedient subject" heteronomous and autonomous types of conscience	*secular autonomy* legal relationships learned primarily in organizations of public education "the good citizen" "world citizen" autonomous types of conscience

VI

THE ROLE OF THE
REFORMATION
IN THE TRANSITION
TO MODERNITY

Methodological Aspects of the Sociology of Religion

As is well known, Weber first attempted to explain the genesis of modern
Western civilization in *The Protestant Ethic and the Spirit of Capitalism* in
1904/5. He tried to trace the religious origins of modern vocational ethics, which
are part of modern civilization.[1] From the beginning (and ever since) this study
has been interpreted as a plea for an idealist interpretation of history and as an
attack on historical materialism. This is not fortuitous. Some of Weber's remarks point into this direction. Thus, he wrote to Heinrich Rickert on April 2,
1905: "In June or July you will receive an essay on cultural history that may be of
interest to you: Protestant asceticism as the foundation of modern vocational
civilization *(Berufskultur)*—a sort of 'spiritualist' construction of the modern

---

1. There are two versions of this study, as Friedrich H. Tenbruck has repeatedly
pointed out. Weber revised the study, which had triggered a lively controversy, for the
first volume of *The Collected Essays in the Sociology of Religion*, presumably in 1919/20.
He made numerous insertions in the text and in the notes dealt extensively with the
literature published in the meantime, especially with Werner Sombart and Lujo Brentano. The notes also contain some hints about Weber's plans in the field of the sociology
of religion. Thus, they help us understand the sequence of Weber's writings. I notice
three new accents in the text: (1) The difference between an ethically controlled and an
ethically uncontrolled capitalism is brought out more sharply; (2) the concept of disenchantment is added and related to ascetic Protestantism; (3) the distinction between
asceticism and mysticism is introduced and applied to religious currents after the Reformation. However, none of these new accents changes the original thesis. This is true even

economy."[2] In the tentative table of contents for the *Handbook of Political Economy* (later *Outline of Social Economics*), which Weber probably drafted in 1909 and which was sent to the anticipated collaborators in May 1910, he reserved the following entry for himself: "a) Economy and Law. 1) Their Relationship in Principle; 2) Epochs of the Development of the Present State of Affairs; b) Economy and Social Groups (Family, Community, Status Groups and Classes, State); c) Economy and Culture (Critique of Historical Materialism)."[3]

In Weber's own view, then, the study on the Protestant ethic and the essay on "The Protestant Sects and the Spirit of Capitalism" as well as the comparative analyses of religion and economy have a "spiritualist" and antimaterialist thrust. But we must spell out what that means. These studies point to the limitations of the materialist interpretation of history. However, they do not "substitute for a one-sided materialistic an equally one-sided spiritualistic causal interpretation of culture and of history."[4] Weber conceded "a trivial justification" to the materialist interpretation of history.[5] Ideas are always embedded in interest constellations. In discussing the methodological foundations of a *Kulturwissenschaft* as an historically oriented social science, Weber emphasizes "that the analysis of the social phenomena and cultural processes from the viewpoint of their economic presuppositions and consequences has been a fruitful scientific principle and will remain so if it is applied sensibly and free from dogmatic blinders."[6] But recognizing the importance of this scientific principle must not lead us to ignore the fact that interest constellations always comprise material as well as ideal interests and that ideas are not simply a mere function or even only a mere reflection of such interest constellations. Ideas always have a significance that transcends an interest constellation, even if they are its ideology. They contain a surplus of meaning, a utopian element. In the case of a religious ethic, for example, this surplus derives from "the content of its annunciation

---

for the notion of disenchantment (cf. *PE*, pp. 105, 117, 147, where Parsons translates "disenchantment" as "elimination of magic" and "rationalization"). As early as 1904/5 Weber clearly described the substance of disenchantment: it was the cultural achievement of ascetic Protestantism to have devalued salvation through the sacraments of the church. It seems true that at the time Weber did not yet perceive ascetic Protestantism in the context of a long-range process of religious development. However, he had identified the distinctiveness of ascetic Protestantism. Thus, his introductory remarks about the revised version were not unduly defensive: "I invite anyone who may be interested to convince himself by comparison that I have not in revision left out, changed the meaning of, weakened, or added materially different statements to, a single sentence of my essay which contained any essential point. There was no occasion to do so, and the development of my exposition will convince anyone who still doubts" (*PE*, p. 187).

2. Marianne Weber, *op. cit.*, p. 356.

3. Cf. *Handbuch der politischen Oekonomie* (introduction to planned table of contents), undated, but with the handwritten remark: "Relates to Max Weber's letter of May 24, 1910." Archive of publishing house J. C. B. Mohr (Paul Siebeck), p. 2. Marianne Weber writes that the plan was drafted in the summer of 1909. Cf. *op. cit.*, p. 440.

4. *PE*, p. 183.   5. *PE II*, p. 169.   6. "Objectivity," p. 68.

and its promise," that is, "from religious sources."[7] The surplus enables a religious ethic to influence not only the conduct of its immediate "carriers," but also "very heterogeneous strata."[8] As a rule, therefore, a religious ethic that has attained the level of a religious-metaphysical world view has economic presuppositions but is also "economically relevant."[9] This dual position of an economic ethic points to the existence of two classes of causes, interest constellations and idea constellations. We cannot attribute a priori primacy to either class of causes. We must assume that both originated at the same time. When human beings began to interpret their interests, they postulated the possible autonomy of interests and ideas. This assumption of the simultaneous genesis of interests and ideas permits Weber to state at the end of *The Protestant Ethic* that the materialist and spiritualist interpretations of history are "equally possible." However, for the same reason, he also says that each interpretation, "if it serves not as the preparation, but as the conclusion of an investigation, accomplishes equally little in the interest of historical truth."[10]

The Analysis of the Breakthrough in the Study of Ascetic Protestantism

Weber asserts that the vocational ethics of modern Western civilization must be treated under two one-sided viewpoints which cannot be reduced to one another: determination by idea constellations and by interest constellations. His study of Protestantism does not claim to follow both viewpoints, and he declared it to be incomplete.[11] He wanted to explain primarily the manner in which the "capitalist spirit" and the modern vocational ethic were shaped by the religious ethic of ascetic Protestantism. As he put it later, he tried to tackle "the aspect of the problem that most of the time is the hardest to grasp."[12] Unlike the determination of ideas by interests, the reverse is not as obvious, especially if the ideas belong to different spheres of the social order. Like Georg Jellinek in his earlier study on the origins of the rights of man, Weber wants to demonstrate, in his study of the origins of the modern vocational ethic, the impact of the religious factor in spheres in which it is unlikely to be sought.[13] For pragmatic reasons he is willing to exclude for the time being the effects of interests. Weber first wants to establish a single causal relationship, but even this purpose is very limited. His demonstration of religious strands in the modern vocational ethic is not meant to explain the impact of all ideas on it, nor does he

7. "Introduction," p. 270.   8. *Loc. cit.*.
9. On this distinction, see "Objectivity," p. 64f.   10. *PE*, p. 183.
11. *Loc. cit.*, and *PE II*, p. 183f.   12. "Author's Introduction," p. 27.
13. Cf. Weber's remarks quoted by Marianne Weber, *op. cit.*, p. 476. Georg Jellinek published his brilliant study on the rights of man in 1895. See *The Declaration of the Rights of Man and of Citizens*, tr. Max Farrand (New York: Holt, 1901). Cf. Bendix and Roth, *op. cit.*, pp. 308ff.

claim to have a sufficient or even a quantitative explanation. He views the religious ethics of ascetic Protestantism as only one constitutive component of modern conduct. He merely tries to establish the "general direction" of this causal relationship, the "elective affinities" that can be observed "between certain forms of religious beliefs and vocational ethics."[14] Therefore, Weber's study states three reservations: (1) It analyzes not the economic conditions but the economic consequences of ascetic Protestantism. (2) It establishes the relationship between the ethic of ascetic Protestantism and important aspects of modern vocational culture, but not the relationship between this ethic and modern conduct as a whole or even the relationship between this ethic and modern science.[15] (3) It is concerned not with a measurement of the cultural significance of ascetic Protestantism for modern vocational culture, but only with a general elective affinity between the two phenomena. It is true that Weber's analysis can illustrate the general manner "in which ideas become effective in history."[16] For this purpose he deals not only with the doctrines but also with their practical consequences. But this does not turn his analysis into a plea for a spiritualist or idealist interpretation of history. Rather, on this score too he wants to show the limits of this perspective. Thus, he can oppose two views that derive from "foolish and doctrinaire" theses: the view that "economic shifts made the Reformation a developmental necessity," and the view "that the 'spirit of capitalism' . . . could only have arisen as the result of certain effects of the Reformation, or even that capitalism as an economic system is a creation of the Reformation."[17] Weber was not moved to make these unambiguous declarations against a materialist *and* idealist interpretation of history under the pressure of his critics. Rather, from the very beginning these formulations shaped the tone and the methodological status of his study. Weber is convinced that not only the 'capitalist spirit' but all culturally significant phenomena are subject to a dual determination. Whoever is interested not in ideology but in historical truth must, in the context of an historically oriented social science, recognize "both causal relationships" and must not elevate one or the other to the level of a "general formula for the causal explanation of historical reality."[18]

Thus, Weber's study of ascetic Protestantism and modern vocational culture is neither an investigation of the genesis of the modern capitalist economic *system* or, more generally, of modern social organization, nor does it intend to explain the origin of modern theoretical rationalism, of modern science. Rather,

14. *PE*, p. 91. Parsons translates 'elective affinity' as 'correlation.' For an alternative translation, see R. Bendix, *Max Weber, op. cit.*, p. 63f. On the philosophical and literary history of the concept of elective affinity, see Richard H. Howe, "Max Weber's Elective Affinities. Sociology Within the Bounds of Pure Reason," *American J. of Sociology*, 84 (1978): 366-85.

15. Weber, "Anticritical Last Word on 'The Spirit of Capitalism,' " tr. Wallace Davis, *American J. of Sociology*, 83:5 (1978): 1129.

16. *PE*, p. 90.   17. *PE*, p. 91.

18. "Author's Introduction," p. 27 and "Objectivity," p. 68.

his study deals exclusively with one factor causally relevant for the genesis of modern practical rationalism and for the resulting capacity of human beings to engage in "practical rational conduct" of a certain kind, a lifestyle of inner-worldly asceticism that combines active self-control with world mastery.[19] In the economic realm this combination did not originally lead to a release of the acquisitive or consumptive "drives," but to their rational moderation; it led not to a compromise between economic and moral action but to a radical subordination of economic conduct to morality and to the historically unlikely congruence between the striving for inner and external goods, salvation and happiness. This congruence was the work of the Reformation, which added new strands to Western development.[20] Not only can these strands be traced up to the present, they also impart to Western development a unique quality which has helped to shape the distinctiveness of modern rationalism. This factor alone cannot possibly explain the genesis of this rationalism. But there can be no satisfactory causal explanation which ignores it. As early as in his reply to H. Karl Fischer (in 1908) Weber once more specified his thesis precisely: (1) Independently of the various political, economic, geographic and ethnic conditions, but also of the "extent of capitalist development as an economic system," ascetic Protestantism promoted the transformation of vocation in the direction of rational economic conduct. (2) In the areas of the "highest development of capitalism before the Reformation, in Italy (but also in Flanders)" this methodical conduct was absent in the economic realm; there was no capitalist spirit in the sense of a restraint of the propensities for acquisition and consumption.[21]

In Weber's eyes, then, the religious ethic of ascetic Protestantism, which did not reach its full development until the "great religious epoch of the seventeenth century," had constitutive significance for the ethical development of Western modernity.[22] For this reason it is a "turning point of the whole cultural development of the West."[23] The religious ethic of ascetic Protestantism reenforced rather than obstructed other developments that pointed in the same direction. This reenforcement had two sides. The new ethic dismantled resistance to ongoing developments, but it also directed them into new channels. First it removed the resistance of the older Christian ethic against the commercial profit motive, which flourished as early as the sixteenth century, by overcoming the injunction of the *deo placere vix potest*. Through this injunction the religious ideal of the "serious Catholic believer" and also of Luther's followers had imposed traditionalist limitations on acquisition.[24] The new ethic helped transcend the deep anguish from which the Catholic and Lutheran believer suffered when they juxtaposed the religious injunction with the imperatives of capitalism. It gave the following periods, especially the age of utilitarianism, that "amazingly good, we may even say a pharisaically good, conscience in the acquisition of money, so long as it took place legally."[25] In this manner the new

19. "Author's Introduction," p. 26.   20. Cf. *PE II*, p. 170.   21. *PE II*, p. 47f.
22. *PE*, p. 176.   23. *AJ*, p. 5.   24. *PE II*, p. 168f.   25. *PE*, p. 176.

ethic created a spirit highly compatible with a capitalist economy, a spirit that permitted an elective affinity with this economic form. The result was an historical "development of great internal consistency."[26] Furthermore, the new ethic opened up new opportunities for this economic form through the methodical and rational moderation of the acquisitive and consumption propensities and the way in which it combined both. It curtailed consumption, especially luxury consumption, and rewarded acquisition for religious reasons. The "ascetic compulsion to save" facilitated capital accumulation.[27] Once this happened, the dynamics of economic interests became oriented toward the capitalist enterprise and capitalist system. This was one of the preconditions that helped economic capitalism gain control over the whole economy. In his dispute with Felix Rachfahl Weber summarized the process in terms of a "development from the romanticism of the economic adventurer to rational economic conduct . . . from occasional profit to an economic system."[28]

Thus, the rational capitalist enterprise and capitalism as an economic system have not only material but also ethical preconditions; they encounter beliefs that either obstruct or promote them. As an economic form capitalism cannot produce of its own accord an "appropriate ethical lifestyle."[29] In Weber's view, this is shown by the history of capitalism before the Reformation. The ethical conditions of capitalism cannot be reduced to the material ones. They have a history of their own in two respects: on the one hand, the genesis of the religious ethic of ascetic Protestantism is dependent on the broader history of the Western ethic, and on the other hand this religious ethic and the related vocational ethic did not intentionally produce the spirit of capitalism. Rather, this particular effect of the Reformation was "to a great extent, perhaps in the particular aspects with which we are dealing predominantly, an unforeseen and even unwished-for result of the labors of the reformers."[30] We have here a process that reveals "the principle of the irrationality and value incongruence of cause and effect."[31]

We can now sketch the outlines of the explanatory model that Weber uses in his study of Protestantism. The distinction between internal and external factors, between the spirit of capitalism and the form of capitalism, is basic to Weber's model. The two are related but also have a separate history which must be traced at first in relative isolation so that we can identify the gradations of elective affinity that obtain between spirit and form. At the same time this relative isolation takes into account that the history of modern economic rational-

26. *PE II*, p. 171.   27. *PE*, p. 172.
28. Weber, "Anticritical Last Word," *op. cit.*, p. 1128.
29. *PE II*, p. 286.   30. *PE*, p. 90.
31. From Weber's comments on Troeltsch's speech on Stoic and Christian natural law at the first meeting of the German Sociological Association in 1910; published in English under the title "Max Weber on Church, Sect and Mysticism," *Sociological Analysis*, 34 (1973): 140–49.

ism—like that of modern rationalism in general—"shows a development which by no means follows parallel lines in the various spheres of life."[32] There may be capitalist form without capitalist spirit and vice versa. Therefore, the spirit of capitalism cannot be a mere reflection of the form of capitalism. First of all, ideas are conditioned by other ideas. However, we also cannot interpret the spirit of capitalism as a mere reflection of the religious ethic of ascetic Protestantism. After all, ideas are also determined by interests. A culturally significant phenomenon like the capitalist economic ethic must not be attributed to a single factor but in principle to several. It must not be viewed as the consequence of a unidimensional and unilinear development. In principle, it must be conceived as the consequence of a multidimensional and multilinear development. Moreover, the lines of this development do not run parallel and straight. They follow the principle of uneven development, the paradox of effect in relation to intent, and the principle of irrationality and value incongruence, which as a rule applies to the relation between intention and consequence.

Weber's study of Protestantism, then, is one-sided. It presents only a partial view of "concrete historical reality." However, this partiality is not just pragmatic; it also has an epistemological foundation. For Weber historical knowledge is always knowledge from "particular and one-sided viewpoints," with the help of which social phenomena "are selected, analyzed and portrayed by the researcher, whether implicitly or explicitly, consciously or unconsciously."[33] This one-sidedness makes for a certain unreality. The partial picture drawn by the study on Protestantism originates not in a *reproduction* but a *reconstruction* of some aspects of "concrete historical reality." One-sidedness and unreality are characteristics of historical knowledge. No progress in our knowledge can change this fact. Weber's methodological writings on *Kulturwissenschaft* as an historically oriented social science are the elaboration of this idea. There he is primarily concerned with the "logical bases" and the "general methodological consequences" of this state of affairs.[34] Thus, we can also read the study on Protestantism as an attempt to translate this view into the practice of research. The study affirms the necessity of *one-sided reconstruction* without propagating monism.[35]

This is also true of the question of causality. In the final analysis, Weber wants to know whether the religious ethic of ascetic Protestantism was causally important for the genesis of modern vocational culture. For this purpose he proposes a causal hypothesis in several steps and concludes that the causal relevance can be maintained.[36] Logically, this conclusion rests on judgments of objective possibility. Such judgments are reasoned answers to a certain type of question. In the present case the question is: If we exclude or modify the factor of ascetic Protestantism, could Western development, "according to general

32. *PE*, p. 77.   33. "Objectivity," p. 72.   34. *Loc. cit.*
35. Cf. "Objectivity," p. 68f.
36. Cf. *PE*, p. 39 and "Anticritical Last Word," *op. cit.*, p. 1112.

rules of experience, have taken a different direction with regard to the points that are decisive for our interests?"[37] In other words, could this mentally changed constellation of factors have led to another development?[38] If we can answer this in the affirmative, we can conclude that ascetic Protestantism was causally relevant for the genesis of modern vocational culture. Of course, in view of the complexity of the matter, it is extraordinarily difficult to give a clear answer. It is even more difficult to indicate the *degree* of effectiveness that must be attibuted to this factor. But such answers are possible *in principle.* In fact, we give such answers whenever we make causal attributions. Judgments of objective possibility require not only experience and the knowledge of facts, nomological and ontological knowledge, they also rest upon isolating and generalizing abstractions. We must "take phenomena apart until each component fits a rule of experience."[39] When this process of abstraction leads to a reasonable judgment of objective possibility, we are justified in classifying a factor as causally significant. But we can only speak of adequate not of necessary causation. When we say that history could have taken a different turn if we exclude or modify a factor, we must not be understood to imply that things would necessarily have been different. For Weber such a judgment is "simply impossible."[40] Moreover, asserting an adequate causation does not mean that other adequate causes cannot exist beside it. On the contrary, the positive critique of an established causal relationship presupposes the search for other causally relevant factors. In his controversy with H. Karl Fischer, Weber touched upon this aspect and once more underlined his methodological position. When Fischer objected that Weber had not excluded *every* other possibility with regard to the causal relationship asserted by him, he answered that no historian can "accept the burden of proof for such a negative fact as a general maxim of his mode of operation." Rather, a historian will "do the opposite and investigate the other causal components with regard to their effects and thus pursue a lengthening (but never complete) causal regress—just as I had declared it to be by my intention in my articles."[41]

Thus, historical knowledge aims at causal attribution on the basis of judgments of objective possibility. With them we can distinguish favorable and unfavorable factors and assess the degree of facilitation and obstruction, by relating the isolated factors in changing combinations and estimating the possible outcomes on the basis of nomological knowledge. But we must be aware that through this procedure we achieve only a mental reconstruction of our subject and not a portrayal of the actual course of events. Strictly speaking, the distinction between facilitation and obstruction is not appropriate to the actual course,

37. Weber "Objective Possibility and Adequate Causation in Historical Explanation," in E. Shils and H. Finch, trs. and eds., *The Methodology of the Social Sciences* (New York: The Free Press, 1949), p. 180.

38. Cf. *op. cit.,* p. 174.   39. *Op. cit.,* p. 173.   40. *Op. cit.,* p. 185.

41. *PE II,* p. 48f.

the totality of effective condition. A concrete event happens exactly because all antecedent factors coalesce in a certain constellation; all of them are "favorable." Facilitation and obstruction of an effect can mean only "that certain elements of the initial situation, if we isolate them mentally, in general tend to favor an effect of a certain kind according to rules of experience, that is, in the great majority of possible combinations of factors, whereas other elements tend to lead to other results."[42]

For Weber the constellation of factors to which he attributed the modern vocational culture was never exhausted by ascetic Protestantism. There were other internal and external factors which were also causally relevant. Therefore, at the end of his study he sketched a research program that was supposed to widen the range of attribution. He listed five areas of concentration: (1) the history of ascetic Protestantism "from the beginnings of inner-worldly asceticism to its dissolution in utilitarianism"; (2) the history of humanist rationalism and its relation to this kind of ethic; (3) the history of modern science and technology and its relationship to this ethic; (4) the analysis of the impact of ascetic Protestantism on noneconomic spheres; (5) the analysis of the "manner in which the genesis and character of Protestant asceticism were influenced by the totality of cultural conditions, especially the economic ones."[43]

As is well known, Weber did not immediately take up this program. Instead, he turned to another program, with which it was only indirectly connected. He began a sociology of the ethics of the salvation religions and of their relation to social and economic structures. The results of this program were written down in the chapter on the sociology of religion in *Economy and Society* and in the essays on the economic ethics of the world religions. Both manuscripts remained incomplete. However, Weber stated explicitly that they were meant to complement and interpret one another.[44] Therefore, they should be read together. The essays dealt with Confucianism, Taoism, Hinduism and Buddhism. They also contained some remarks on Islam and Eastern and Western Christianity, but especially an investigation of the roots of the Western Christian ethic in ancient Judaism. In the revised version of *The Protestant Ethic* (1920) Weber listed two reasons for the shift and enlargement of his interests: the desire to take the study out of its isolation and to put it in the context of cultural development, and the fact that Ernst Troeltsch had begun, shortly after the appearance of the study, to publish *The Social Teaching of the Christian Churches.* Weber called this enterprise a "universal history of the ethics of western Chris-

42. "Objective Possibility," *op. cit.*, p. 187.   43. *PE*, p. 182f.

44. Apart from the references cited above, see also a letter by Weber to Siebeck, June 22, 1915: "I would be willing to give to the *Archiv* a series of essays on "The Economic Ethics of the World Religions," which have been lying here since the beginning of the war and which only need stylistic revisions. They are preliminary studies to, and commentaries on, the systematic sociology of religion in the *Outline of Social Economics*." Archive of J. C. B. Mohr (Siebeck), Tübingen.

tianity," which executed part of his earlier program "in the most satisfactory manner," at least with regard to the doctrines. He believed that the planned continuation of his project on ascetic Protestantism would in part have been a "useless duplication."[45]

The Analysis of the Breakthrough in the Comparative Studies of Religion and Economy

It is a moot point whether Weber in fact sacrificed the earlier to the later program or whether he retained the former, perhaps in modified form because of Ernst Troeltsch. Whatever our conclusion may be in this very difficult biographical matter, in my view one point cannot be denied. Until the end of his life Weber meant to continue his study of the history of Western ethics beyond ascetic Protestantism and ancient Judaism. This is shown not only by the insertions in the 1920 version of *The Protestant Ethic*, but also by documents about his later intentions, especially by Marianne Weber's preface of October 1920 to the third volume of the collected essays in the sociology of religion and by a letter Weber wrote to his publisher in the fall of 1919. In this letter he explained the planned sequence of his collected essays.[46] The beginning would be made by two volumes, which would contain the revised essays on the economic ethics of the world religions first published in his *Archiv für Sozialwissenschaft und Sozialpolitik* and *The Protestant Ethic* as well as the essay on the sects. To this would be added "a brief treatment of the Egyptian, Mesopotamian and Zoroastrian ethics, but also a sketch of the development of the Western *Bürgertum* in Antiquity and the Middle Ages." These two volumes were to be followed by a "third volume" of previously unpublished essays, comprising early Christianity, Talmudic Judaism, Islam and Oriental Christianity. Weber wanted to conclude the series with a volume on "Western Christianity," that is a fourth volume, in which presumably not merely the "religious distinctiveness of Christianity in general" would have been analyzed but also the stages of its development, such as the Christian ethic of the Middle Ages and the post-Reformation ethics, "insofar as Troeltsch's writings had left any room."[47] Troeltsch had done so by dealing primarily with the doctrines, not the practical effects of the ethics of West-

45. *PE*, p. 188. See also Weber's comments on Troeltsch in *PE II*, pp. 54, 151, 322. Whoever wants to understand the reasons which motivated Weber to discontinue his more narrow program for the time being must take into account Troeltsch's research program.

46. Archive of J. C. B. Mohr (Siebeck), Tübigen.

47. "Anticritical Last Word," *op. cit.*, p. 1127. Cf. *PE*, p. 258. This note was added in 1920 and reads: "That the difference of dogmatic basis was compatible with the adoption of the crucial interest in proof is to be explained in the last analysis by the historical peculiarities of Christianity in general which we cannot yet discuss." Weber used this formulation in 1910 when he referred to his research program for the Protestant ethic.

ern Christianity and had barely touched upon the other causal relationship—the manner in which the religious ethic was influenced by social structure.

We can say, therefore, that Weber planned to continue his studies of Western development beyond the published works. This is the reason for the reference in the "Author's Introduction" to "the further investigation of Western development."[48] Weber's interest, recognizable from 1909 on, in the world religions and civilizations genetically unrelated to Western development did not become an independent concern in the course of his later studies. Rather, these studies remained tied to the earlier interest. Indeed, Weber pointed out afterwards that he had "quite deliberately emphasized the elements in which other cultures differed from Western civilization."[49] Weber's new interest does not focus on a comprehensive theory of culture or even a universal theory of evolution, in spite of ambiguous phrases such as "the whole of cultural development."[50] Rather, he wants to overcome the isolation of *The Protestant Ethic* by studying not only the distinctiveness of modern vocational culture but also that of Western, and especially of modern Western, rationalism. Thus, his later program aimed at enlarging the developmental history of modernity which he had begun with his study of Protestantism and at embedding it in the developmental history of the whole West. In this respect Weber had only a limited interest in the developmental history of other civilizations, and therefore his later analysis had asymmetric features which were accentuated by the later program. We must not misinterpret this asymmetry as an instance of ethnocentrism. Weber no longer identifies the universal history of the West with the history of the human species. When he speaks of universal history, he has in mind a kind of cultural horizon for the identification of Western culture. This horizon is supposed to help identify its distinctiveness and to establish analytical criteria. However, we must separate the problem of identification from that of explanation. The latter requires not only that we identify this tradition in terms of historically important phases but that we explain the manner in which one emerged from the other.

If we accept this interpretation, we have not only biographical but also systematic reasons for asserting that Weber intended to analyze the history of Western ethics beyond ancient Judaism and ascetic Protestantism. It is true that both are "turning points" of the "whole cultural development of the West" and, in the case of ancient Judaism, also of the Near East.[51] It is also true that both preconditioned the direction in which the dynamics of interests would move. Ancient Judaism became in this way important for Western rationalism and ascetic Protestantism for *modern* Western rationalism. But the rational ethics of inner-worldly action, as we find them in ancient Judaism, ascetic Protestantism

48. "Author's Introduction," p. 27. Parsons omitted this phrase after "points of comparison with the Occidental development."

49. *Loc. cit.,*   50. *PE*, p. 284.   51. *AJ*, p. 5.

and finally in the Enlightment and utilitarianism, are not only worlds apart, but are also separated by ethical innovations. Without grasping these innovations, we cannot understand the whole development. Therefore, we must attribute to them an "independent significance."[52] In my view, Weber intended until the end also to study the phases and processes linking ancient Judaism and ascetic Protestantism as well as those linking the latter and "mechanical" capitalism, more generally, scientific and technological civilization. Only with the Protestant contributions to technology were the "capitalist developments," which had remained "highly unstable in the late Middle Ages," permanently stabilized.[53] Only then were modern conduct and the modern ethos of vocation irreversibly established. This is the history of an ideal which articulates itself more and more sharply in various doctrines and becomes more and more effective through various institutionalizations. This is the ideal of the "active individual who is oriented toward a transcendental or inner-worldly center" and who endeavors "to master the world by discovering its impersonal laws."[54] It is true that this ideal was conceived as early as ancient Judaism, where it remained within a law ethic. Ancient and medieval Christianity sublimated the ideal by turning it into an ethic of conviction. It was institutionalized by ascetic Protestantism, under which it remained purely religious. But with mechanical capitalism the ideal became secularized. This sequence provides us with the historically significant phases, into which we must differentiate the whole development. After Judaic prophecy, crucial phases appear to have been Paul's mission, the Gregorian reform, the Reformation and the scientific-technological revolution. The causal significance of the Reformation, which Weber maintained from the beginning, can be properly evaluated only within the sequence of these phases. The Reformation was one of the decisive turns in the direction of the modern ethic and modern conduct. In the array of internal factors only the Renaissance has a comparable importance. Just as the spirit of Western rationalism was created by ancient Judaism and "Hellenic intellectual culture,"[55] so modern rationalism was created by the Renaissance and the Reformation.[56]

In sum, we can say that from the first Weber considered the Reformation causally important for explaining the transition to modernity, but that his further program lifted this factor out of its isolation, located it in relation to other internal factors and also showed the complexity of its prehistory. This is true not only with regard to the role of ideas but also with regard to interests, and it is especially true of the combination with external factors, that is, the constellation of factors that alone can explain the transition to modernity. As Weber's replies to his critics show, he did not want to limit himself to the lower capital-

52. *PE*, p. 283. Weber speaks of humanist rationalism in the context of modern Western rationalism.
53. "Anticritical Last Word," *op. cit.*, p. 1129.
54. *India*, pp. 339 and 342.   55. *AJ*, p. 5.
56. "Anticritical Last Word," *op. cit.*, p. 1129.

ist strata of the Reformation in identifying the interests that shaped the religious ethic of inner-worldly asceticism. Rather, the analysis of this factor was supposed to be embedded in the history of the Western citizenry and the Western city.[57] As early as his study of the social structure of antiquity in 1909, Weber pointed to the distinctiveness of the medieval inland culture and of the medieval producers' city in comparison with the coastal culture and polis of antiquity. When he drafted the outline for his studies in the sociology of religion in 1919, he was consistent in wanting to supplement his study of Protestantism with a sketch of the development of the Western citizen in antiquity and the Middle Ages. Parts of this program were realized in the "large manuscript," which Marianne Weber found among Weber's literary remains, apparently under the title "Forms of the City," and which was incorporated into *Economy and Society*.[58] The study of Protestantism must be supplemented by this text if we want to free it from its isolation not only within the history of Western ethics but also of Western stratification. We must go further: Weber's rejoinders indicate the importance which he attributed to the commercial, political and religious organizations, in short, to the history of the Western configurations of social order. The texts are contained in *Economy and Society*. They too must be drawn upon, especially the analysis of Western feudalism and its tranformation into the *Ständestaat* and the analysis of the relations between the political, hierocratic and urban powers. It is not accidental that Weber listed internal as well as external factors at the beginning of *Ancient Judaism*, with which he embarked on his enlarged study of the history of Western ethics. Ancient Judaism, Hellenic intellectual culture and Protestantism were internal factors, Roman law, the Roman church and the *Ständestaat* external ones.[59]

If we accept Talcott Parsons' terminology, we can call these factors "bridge structures," which mediate between the ancient, medieval and modern world. But in order to become such structures the most important innovations of ancient Judaism and Hellenic intellectual culture had to be received in a specific way, to be combined with one another and to be institutionalized. This hap-

---

57. *Op. cit.*, p. 1128.

58. Cf. Marianne Weber's letter to Siebeck, June 30, 1920, in which she refers to the posthumous manuscripts: "Would you please return the galleys to the Sociology once more [i.e., Part I of *ES*] . . . so that Dr. Palyi can check how much of the extant manuscripts has been worked into the basic concepts. It appears that the following sections are ready for the printer: sociology of religion, sociology of law, forms of society (ethnic groups, kin groups, nation, state and hierocracy etc.); furthermore, forms of domination (charisma, patrimonialism, feudalism, bureaucracy) and a large manuscript: forms of the city, and finally a highly interesting section on the sociology of music." If we link this statement with Weber's remarks in the fall of 1919, we cannot preclude that he would have published "The City" in the context of the collected essays in the sociology of religion. A major topic in these essays is the development of the European *Bürgertum* in antiquity and the Middle Ages.

59. Cf. *AJ*, p. 5.

pened first in the Hellenized, then in the Christianized Roman empire. However, the decisive innovation of ancient Judaism was the idea of a transcendent creator god, who had established a good order to which human beings must submit. On the basis of this ethical monotheism social action could be oriented toward the notion of a political and social revolution willed by God, and the world could be comprehended as an historical phenomenon which was destined to be replaced by the divine order. However, the transformation of the Judaic oath-bound community into the Jewish pariah people removed the universalist dynamic from this idea. It became part of a morality distinguishing the in-group from the out-group and was believed to be addressed primarily to an ascriptive "chosen people." By contrast, the crucial discovery of Hellenic intellectual culture was the idea of an intelligible "natural" order, to which gods and human beings must submit equally. This cognitive universalism permitted the orientation of action toward the idea of a general just order. However, the polis realized this idea of political and social life only in a very limited manner, and religious life remained shaped by the polytheist religiosity of the mysteries in spite of the rise of "universal" gods. Against this background Paul's mission gains its decisive importance. It broke through the ascriptive confines of Jewish ethical monotheism by suspending the Law with the help of the Christian savior, and it provided a new basis for Hellenic mystery religion by placing the suffering, death and resurrection of the savior in the context of ethical monotheism. For this reason Weber considered Paul's achievement of tremendous historical importance. Without it the Christian world mission would have been impossible (623). Without his selective use of the Old Testament and his combination of norms from the Old and New Testament as well as of Hellenist norms, "gnostic sects and mysteries of the cult of Kyrios Christos would have existed on the soil of Hellenism, but never a Christian church and a Christian ethic of workaday life. Without emancipation from the ritual prescriptions of the Torah, which were the underpinning for the caste-like segregation of the Jews, the Christian congregation would have remained a small sect of the Jewish pariah people comparable to the Essenes and the Therapeutics."[60] However, for Paul's mission to grow into a Christian world mission, it was necessary for the Christian congregation to change from a sect into a church, from heterodoxy into orthodoxy. The Roman empire provided not only the political framework but also a crucial institutional innovation, the rational corporation, which developed in the Imperial period (715). The rational corporation facilitated the consolidation of the western Church under "a 'universal' episcopal system under the see of Rome."[61] After the downfall of the western Roman empire the church, which had at first rejected the new secular power and then tolerated it under

60. *AJ*, p. 4.
61. Talcott Parsons, *The System of Modern Societies*, op. cit., p. 34. On the classification of Israel and Greece, see id., *Societies*, op. cit., pp. 95ff. I am here combining Weber and Parsons.

Augustine's influence, elaborated this innovation. This became one of the reasons for a relationship between sacred and secular law as it is found nowhere else in the world: "Canon law became indeed one of the guides for secular law on the road to rationality" (829). Thus, the development of Western culture is unthinkable without the independent significance of the Christian and Roman components. Not until the rise of ancient Christianity was the ethical symbolism fully elaborated which is constitutive of Western culture and partly fused with its cognitive symbolism; and only the Roman empire provided Western culture with institutions viable in the long run. Therefore, for Talcott Parsons, Israel and Greece are seedbed societies of the Western development, but only the Christianized Roman empire functioned as "the 'historic' intermediate empire" that linked and promoted the developmental innovations on the level of the world view and the institutions. As for Weber, for Parsons bridge structures are "the basic orientation of Western Christianity, the relative functional specificity of the Church's organizational structure, the territorial principle of political allegiance, the high status of the Roman legal system, and the associational structure of the urban community."[62]

If we combine these considerations with the analytical scheme explicated in our study, we can say that the Reformation's turn toward ascetic Protestantism occurred within a traditionalist and patrimonial variant which had a number of peculiarities within its own cultural tradition, but especially in comparison with other cultural traditions. The ethical component of this tradition, the Judeo-Christian religious ethic and its interpretation in medieval ascetic monasticism and the medieval sects, had a relatively high potential for inner-worldly action. Its legal component, the Stoic-Roman law and its interpretation in medieval canon law, had a relatively high potential for an inherent legal formalization. Its institutional component, the Roman church as it was completed by the Gregorian reform, and feudalism as it was transformed by the legalism of the *Ständestaat,* had a relatively high potential for corporate organization. Only because there existed this general developmental potential for a rationalism of world mastery—more generally, for depersonalization—could ascetic Protestantism shape so much of the direction of modern ethical conduct. Only because of this developmental potential could this particular course of events have such a transformative effect. However, it was necessary that ascetic Protestantism not be limited to the religious order and purely religious dynamics. Rather, it had to diffuse into other spheres and meet other segmental developments which moved in the same general *direction* but were not necessarily related to it in a functional or merely contemporaneous manner. We must go even further. The solution which ascetic Protestantism found for the problems of inner need (that is, of salvation) must be viewed at first as traditional. The solution remains within the horizon of possibilities fixed by the basic social configuration

---

62. Parsons, *The System of Modern Societies, op. cit.,* p. 37.

of traditionalism with its theocentric world view and stratified differentiation. It was, strictly speaking, accidental that the selective elaboration of this developmental level by ascetic Protestantism not only changed the religious order but had more far-reaching effects, that it met environmental conditions compatible with it, and that it became a constitutive factor in the transition to Western modernity. This was an unintended consequence in the light of the religious problem to which ascetic Protestantism offered a solution. What is true of the religious development is also true of other segmental developments. At first they too offered traditional solutions that had unintended consequences. Their combination with other consequences led to the transformative effects that were decisive for the transition to modernity. We can now formulate in general the logic of the transition from one basic social configuration to another. It is the logic of the paradox of effect as compared to intent. More accurately, it is the paradox of combined inner and external effects in relation to internal and external intentions. The new must arise in a paradoxical fashion because the replacement of one basic configuration by another cannot have been programmed as a possibility.

The transition to Western modernity presupposes not only that several unintended developments, which are not necessarily contemporaneous and cannot be reduced to one another, point in the same general direction, but also that there are "carriers" who can compete with one another and infuse an historical variant with a high degree of developmental dynamics. In this regard too Weber attributed a special position to the patrimonial structure of the medieval West. In contrast to other patrimonial structures, "there were strong and independent powers" in the Holy Roman Empire, with which "princely power could ally itself in order to shatter traditional fetters, or, under very special conditions, these forces could use their own military power to throw off the bonds of patrimonial power."[63] In the Western Middle Ages there was a comparatively high degree of internal competition within the structure of traditional domination. The central power competed "with the great vassals and the hierocratic power of the church" (1352), but also with the cities, whose opportunities for political autonomy grew as the most important territorial powers struggled openly with one another. As a rule, in the Middle Ages "authority was set against authority, legitimacy against legitimacy, one office charisma against the other" (1193). In spite of continuous efforts to impose a matrix of superordination, the juxtaposition and opposition of powers ultimately prevailed. The relation between political and hierocratic power is prototypical. Of course, there are similarities with other patrimonial configurations outside the West, either in the direction of caesaropapism or theocracy. Weber points to two sets of examples: "The first time in the Carolingian empire and during certain periods in which the Holy Roman empire attained the height of its power; the second time in the few cases of

63. *China*, p. 62.

Calvinist theocracy and, in strongly caesaropapist form, in the states of the Lutheran and Anglican Reformation and in the great unified states of the Counter-Reformation: Spain and Bossuet's France" (1193). Yet these solutions, which we expect to find in traditional configurations because they conform to the principle of stratified differentiation, are more the exception than the rule. The rule followed from the resolution of the Investiture Conflict. The "equalitarian," not the hierarchical, institutionalization of conflicting ideas and interests became the rule, but without the abandonment of procedural mediation.[64] In the context of traditional domination this solution was an innovation of the greatest historical consequence, and it gave an enormous impetus to the Western developmental dynamic. All historical variants of the traditionalist configuration face typical problems, but in the medieval West such institutional solutions brought the tensions to a head: in the religious realm the tension between "office charisma and monasticism," and in the relation between the religious and the political realm the tension between "the contractual character of feudalism and *Ständestaat* and the autonomous, bureaucratic hierocracy" (1192). In addition, there was the tension between want satisfaction and profit orientation, and between the use of economic units for rent and for profit. Profit orientation found its institutional support in the production-oriented inland city of the Middle Ages (1353). Moreover, the city became the focal point for an alternative principle of legitimation, one based on enactment not on patriarchal subordination, for a republican not a feudal or *ständisch* model of domination. The Holy Roman Empire had enough political and cultural unity to provide these tensions with a setting and to perpetuate them, but not enough to escape their revolutionary consequences. In Weber's view, the great revolutions that shaped the fate of the West arose out of these tensions and the resulting power struggles: "the Italian revolution of the twelfth and thirteenth century, the Dutch of the sixteenth, the English of the seventeenth, and the American and French of the eighteenth century."[65] If we add to these political revolutions the Reformation and the two other intellectual revolutions, the Renaissance and the Englightenment, we have before us the most important events in which the developmental dynamics of the West expressed themselves from the eleventh century on. Through these events the theocentric world view was gradually transformed into an anthropocentric world view and stratified differentiation transformed into functional differentiation.

Thus, the Reformation and its turn to ascetic Protestantism was only one of several fateful revolutions. However, it was the one which initiated the ethical lifestyle adequate to modernity. How was this possible? Why did Weber not attribute this achievement to other manifestations of Western Christianity? In order to answer this question we must reconsider and systematize Weber's analy-

---

64. Cf. M. Rainer Lepsius, "Modernisierungspolitik als Institutionenbildung: Kriterien institutioneller Differenzierung," *op. cit.*, p. 25.

65. *China*, p. 62.

sis of the distinctiveness of Western Christianity and especially of ascetic Protestantism. In part we must fall back on conjectures, but also on a combination of his earlier and later research program. I would like to propose that Weber convincingly demonstrated the distinctiveness of ascetic Protestantism both through inter- and intra-cultural comparison, but that we can accentuate its causal significance for modernity differently from the way Weber did in *The Protestant Ethic*. In my view, the cultural significance of ascetic Protestantism lies more in having favored the spirit of depersonalization *(Versachlichung)* than the spirit of capitalism. The ethic of ascetic Protestantism stands at the beginning of the "world domination of unbrotherliness."[66] This has to do with the manner in which ascetic Protestantism treated the guiding principle of patriarchal subordination and filial piety: for religious reasons it was made extremely one-sided and abstract. This gave a decisive developmental impulse for the transition to legality. This treatment of the guiding principle of patriarchal subordination benefited a patrimonial order which, for the reasons indicated above, modified stratified differentiation through the equalitarian institutionalization of antagonistic values in the direction of functional differentiation. Hence, the ethical development represented by ascetic Protestantism has a logical affinity to a series of institutional developments. This is true even though Calvinism continued to adhere to the stratified differentiation and indeed revitalized it on the institutional level in theocratic form *against* the general direction of development. This suggests that Calvinism facilitated the transition to modernity on the ethical level but probably obstructed it on the institutional level, not only with regard to the relation among the different partial orders, but also with regard to the religious order itself.[67]

The Cultural Significance of Christianity: A Comparison of the World Religions

Weber demonstrated the distinctiveness of Western Christianity through a comparison with the Asian salvation religions, especially through a comparison with the Indian orthodox and heterodox salvation doctrines. He thought that the latter had unsuccessfully tried to play a role in Asia that Christianity in fact played "for us in the Middle Ages and until after the Westphalian peace" of 1648.[68] This comparison leads to an ideal-typical accentuation of the contrast between two dualist world views. These two interpretations of the relation between the deity and human beings are conceptualized in such a general fashion

66. "Theory," p. 357.
67. Rainer Döbert has called attention to the regressive character of the Reformation. Apart from the writings cited above, see "Die evolutionäre Bedeutung der Reformation" in C. Seyfarth and W. M. Sprondel, eds., *Seminar: Religion und gesellschaftliche Entwicklung* (Frankfurt: Suhrkamp, 1973), pp. 303ff.
68. *India*, p. 329 (corrected).

that they can comprise the most diverse currents in the Near East, the West and Asia. Following Habermas, I shall call the world views theocentric and cosmocentric.[69] The world view of the Near East and the West is based on the concept of a transcendental personal god, that of the Asian tradition on the concept of an immanent impersonal divine power.[70] These two views of the divine also contain different conceptions of the human being. In the Near East and the West human beings are viewed as instruments of God, in Asia as the vessel of the divine. In both cases there is a hiatus between deity and human being: the divine is the permanent and eternal, whereas human beings and the world are impermanent and contingent. In one case the perfect and eternal is an ethical god, in the other an intelligible and intuitable order; in one case the impermanent and contingent is a sinful creature, in the other a mortal one. Correspondingly, the objects of salvation are different—to gain God's favor or to incorporate and possess the divine. In one case human beings fear nothing more than to violate God's commandments and to be disowned by him; in the other they fear most their inability to escape the impermanence of life on earth and the cycle of death and rebirth. In both cases the hiatus between deity and human being must be overcome—either through action pleasing to the deity or through emptying the soul of everything worldly and through union with the One and All. The two diametrically opposed strategies for transcending dualism are proving oneself in this world and proving oneself through nonaction. The two strategies explain why the active personality ultimately became the Western ideal, whereas the Eastern ideal is the wise man who withdraws from the turmoil of life and quiets his instinctual drive for existence with contemplative knowledge. The highest forms of Asian religiosity are based on saving oneself through contemplation, not on faith in God and hope for his grace. Saving oneself not only frees the self, but is also understood as one's own achievement. The believer strives not for a state of grace which will be realized in a future life in heaven, but for a this-worldly state of illumination.

The idea of saving oneself through literary or gnostic knowledge imparts to the Asian salvation religions an intellectualist and aristocratic character. Salvation results from acquired knowledge and thus is in principle not accessible to everybody. Of course, there has been intellectualism and religious aristocracy in the Near East and the West. Indeed, the opposition between intellectual and nonintellectual, between the religiosity of the virtuosi and the masses, between the particularism and the universalism of grace, has been the decisive developmental factor especially in Western Christianity and partly in ancient Judaism. But from the beginning this Western tradition was not so much cognitive as ethical, and it tends more toward a universalism than a particularism of grace.

69. Here I am following a proposal by Jürgen Habermas. Cf. Handlungsrationalität und gesellschaftliche Rationalisierung, II, p. 4. (Ms.)

70. Cf. "Theory," p. 325.

The pre-Exilic prophets are primarily nonintellectuals from different social strata, and their message is addressed to the whole people.[71] "The Christian gospel arose . . . as a nonintellectual's proclamation directed to nonintellectuals, to the 'poor in spirit,' " that is, it was conceived in opposition to Rabbinical and Hellenist wisdom (631). Finally, the Gregorian reform institutionalized the gospel as the "constitution of a universal framework for the salvation of all human beings," as a kind of spiritual entailed estate, out of which arose the unified culture *(Einheitskultur)* of the church.[72] In Asia such a unity of *religious* culture was never achieved. In contrast to the West, Asian salvation religion did not develop beyond a juxtaposition of the religiosity of the virtuosi and the masses, of salvation ethic and everyday ethic: "An inner connection of performance in the world with the otherworldly soteriology was not possible."[73] The only doctrine and institutional invention which mediated between the virtuosi and the masses was the caste soteriology of Vedanta Brahmanism in India. It translated the *samsara* and *karma* teachings into a systematic doctrine of the transmigration of the soul and of compensation, and combined it with the caste order.[74] However, the consequence was that the extant traditionalist social order was justified in the face of every change and its principle of stratified differentiation was pushed to an extreme.

The Near-Eastern and Western tradition and the Asian religious and metaphysical tradition have dealt with dualism differently not only in the realm of action but also in thought, that is, in their metaphysics and their formally most complete theodicies. The rise of a metaphysics of history was promoted by the idea that the world is not only governed by a transcendental god but was also created by him and will one day be revolutionized by him. World history could be viewed as the history of salvation, which had a beginning and will have an end. By contrast, the elaboration of ontological metaphysics was supported by the idea that the divine is immanent in a world that has not been created. Hence, there is an elective affinity between the philosophy of history and the Near Eastern and Western tradition and between the Asian tradition and ontology. The theodicies, too, which try to settle once and for all the problem of the world's imperfection, the problem of the discrepancy of fate and merit, show characteristic differences (524). The doctrine of predestination and of *karma* are the formally most complete solutions. The former interprets the fate of human beings as a consequence of God's decision which cannot be influenced by human deeds, the latter as a consequence of a universal mechanism of retribu-

71. Cf. *AJ*, p. 277.

72. Cf. Ernst Troeltsch, *The Social Teaching of the Christian Churches*, tr. Olive Wyon (New York: Macmillan, 1931), p. 369. On the church as a kind of entailed estate of eternal goods, see *ES*, p. 1193. The ecclesiastic unified culture *(Einheitskultur)* implied neither the absence of internal differentiation nor the unitary character of the culture-at-large. The latter was, in Weber's view, relatively weak because of the opposition of hierocratic and political authority.

73. *India*, p. 333.   74. *India*, p. 118.

tion that takes into account all human actions. According to the world view of the Near East and the West, omnipotent God grants his grace to the sinful human being; according to the Asian world view, the good and evil deeds are weighted against one another and the result determines life in a future incarnation. In Asia, therefore, there is no need for an omnipotent god who intervenes in the historical process in the interest of compensatory justice: "The eternal world process solves the ethical tasks of such a god through its own automatic functioning" (525). The idea that an omnipotent and free god created the world and will bring it to an end contrasts with the idea that the world was not created but is subject to an imperishable universal mechanism of retribution, the idea of the "supra-divine character of the eternal order of the world" (525).

We can now systematize the two world views in an ideal-typical articulation. Our criteria are their content, the manner in which they deal with dualism in thought and action, their most important components and relationships. (Cf. Scheme XXII.)

The theocentric and cosmocentric constructs, then, define two basic relationships between the divine and human beings, which imply at the same time fundamental relationships to the world. In one case the religious postulate affirms the effort to change the imperfect and contingent world, in the other it denies any such effort. But this opposition must not be identified with the difference between mythological monism and religious and metaphysical dualism. Rather, it is an opposition within the framework of religious and metaphysical dualism itself. Both theocentrism and cosmocentrism reject the world in the sense that they judge it to be imperfect and contingent in the light of a religious postulate and therefore want either to change it or to be indifferent to it. Not only the Near Eastern and Western and the Indian tradition, but also the Chinese one must be considered world-rejecting in this sense. However, as I pointed out already, Weber classified the Chinese tradition as tending toward monism, a wrong classification in my view. But it would be an inadmissible simplification to attribute the tendency toward action in the world exclusively to the Near Eastern and Western tradition and the tendency to indifference solely to the Asian tradition. Confucianism, too, aimed at transforming the world politically and socially. This was one of the reasons for the remarkable development of science in China. Conversely, ancient Christianity in particular showed "absolute indifference to the world and its concerns" (633). In its negation of the world it is quite similar to most Asian salvation religions. However, these two cases are not typical of the two traditions. Confucianism remained marginal to the Asian salvation religions. Ancient Christianity was transfused with the eschatological exultation of its earliest phase, which was a major reason for its indifference to the world. After Paul's conversion, two attitudes about the world became decisive: "One was the expectation of the Second Coming, and the other was the recognition of the tremendous importance of charismatic gifts of the spirit. The world would remain as it was until the master came" (634).

Scheme XXII
Religious-Metaphysical World Views

Type / Characteristics	Theocentric	Cosmocentric
Content of world view	transcendental personal creator god, human beings as God's instruments	supra-divine, impersonal and eternal order, human beings as vessels of the divine
Theoretical solution of dualism	doctrine of predestination	*karma* teaching
Practical solution of dualism	acting in this world to realize God's will	rejecting action by emptying one's mind and attaining a state of illumination
Cognitive component	historical metaphysics	ontological metaphysics
Evaluative component	faith-oriented ethics	intellectualist ethics
Expressive component	ethically conditioned charisma—ethical prophecy	gnostic charisma—exemplary charisma
Relation of cognitive and evaluative component	evaluative component has precedence over cognitive component—tendency toward practical rationalism and anti-intellectualism	cognitive component has precedence over evaluative component—tendency toward theoretical rationalism and intellectualism
Representative	Near Eastern and Western tradition: Judaism, Christianity and Islam	Asian tradition: Confucianism, Taoism, Hinduism and Buddhism

Weber linked this basic elective affinity between the believer's world view and relationship to the world not only with the dogmatic foundations but also with the methods of salvation—asceticism and mysticism. He modified his usage in the course of his investigations, and even in the late formuations there are ambiguities. Contrary to his own intentions, he sometimes identifies dogma and method, world view and action.[75] But it is undeniable—and he himself em-

75. Compare "Theory," p. 325, where Weber emphasizes that the connection between the basic conception and the methodology of salvation is not absolute and that the "transcendental god has not, as such, determined the direction of Western asceticism."

phasizes it time and again—that the Near Eastern and Western tradition has known mysticism in spite of its tendency to asceticism, and the Asian tradition asceticism in spite of its tendency to mysticism. In India ascetic methods have been incredibly refined. Weber says of Indian asceticism that technically it "was the most rationally developed in the world."[76] Thus, we must treat doctrinal basis and method of salvation as two independent dimensions. This does not preclude inner affinities. Despite its technical perfection Indian asceticism remained bound by its context: it is an "intellectualist technique of salvation" for methodically emptying the soul of all worldly relations and cares.[77] It is not a praxis-oriented technique for this-worldly conduct. Only in the West is the latter consistently developed. This helps account for the distinctiveness of ascetic Protestantism, which became the primary agent for perfecting a method of this-worldly conduct in the context of the Christian tradition, although it had some medieval antecedents.

The distinction of salvation methods into asceticism and mysticism and the linkage with the theocentric and cosmocentric doctrinal foundation makes it possible to differentiate the currents of salvation. It provides us with a broad scheme for identifying Western Christianity and ascetic Protestantism in comparison with the Asian tradition. However, Weber is not content with such a scheme. He goes on to distinguish inner-worldly from world-fleeing asceticims and inner-worldly from world-fleeing mysticism. The believers can either remain within the orders of the world or try to evade them; they can either try to master the world's sinfulness or merely their own spiritual depravity; their methods can be oriented either to the world or to the realm beyond. Ascetic Protestantism is characterized not only by the anti-intellectualist but especially the inner-worldly turn of asceticism, the methodical control not only of one's own depraved nature but also of the corrupt world. In the framework of the religious-metaphysical world view and of the developmental level of "historical civilization," ascetic Protestantism brought about a particular combination of theocentrism, asceticism and this-worldliness.

We have now uncovered a part of the conceptual structure with which Weber organizes the comparison of salvation religions in his sociology of religion: the basis (or goal) of salvation, the method (or path) of salvation, and the sphere of religious effort (or the religious proving ground). These three dimensions are independent of one another. The juxtaposition of their historical manifestations provides us with a rough scheme, with the help of which we can classify salvation religions. Of course, Weber did not mean to force the complexities of religious life into a simple scheme. His substantive analyses deliberately re-

---

Nevertheless, active asceticism and contemplative mysticism represent two different conceptions of salvation, one based on the idea of a personal god and the other based on the idea of an impersonal divine. This ambiguity can be resolved by translating the differences into the categories of active and passive.

76. *India*, p. 149.   77. *India*, p. 165.

veal time and again the one-sidedness of his own conceptual attributions. But the classification is there, and it is particularly important in the comparisons. With this caveat we can now present the scheme and illustrate it with major currents of salvation religions in the East and West. (Cf. Scheme XXIII.)

Scheme XXIII

Comparison of Select Salvation Movements in East and West

Goal and path of salvation / Direction of religious effort	Theocentric		Cosmocentric	
	ascetic	mystical	ascetic	mystical
Inner-worldly	Calvinism Anabaptism			Confucianism
Otherworldly	Medieval Christian monasticism	early Christianity	Jainism	early Buddhism

It is possible to differentiate this scheme further. If we want to go more deeply into internal variations of the Asian tradition, it is important to know whether the eternal order is indeed viewed as being impersonal or whether it is personalized, or whether literary or gnostic knowledge is believed to bring salvation. If we want to probe into the internal variations of the Near Eastern and Western tradition, it is important to find out whether the personal god remains in fact transcendent or whether he becomes part of the world, as in the doctrine of the Trinity, or whether the religious ethic of the Old or the New Testament is dominant. However, in our context another consideration is more important for the time being. If we follow our scheme, it appears, at least on the level of the virtuosi, as if cosmocentrism and inner-worldly asceticism as well as theocentrism and inner-worldly mysticism exclude one another. In view of Weber's problem, the first of these is the more important. If it can be shown that the Asian tradition hinders inner-worldly asceticism and that the Near Eastern and Western tradition favors it, we have gained a strong indicator for the religious distinctiveness of ascetic Protestantism. I believe that in his comparative studies Weber in fact follows this line of reasoning. It is true that the Asian tradition also knows inner-worldliness and asceticism, but not their combination in one of the culturally powerful religions of salvation. This is one of the most important conclusions which Weber draws from his survey, "which is very superficial in view of the tremendous richness of the Asian world."[78] This is made clearer by Weber's discussion of two cases which at first appear to have some similarity with ascetic Protestantism: inner-worldly Confucianism and ascetic Jainism. Both have effects which might parallel those of ascetic Protestantism. The religious ethic of Confucianism provides a motivation for rational transformation of the world; Jainism even offers incentives for capitalism, if only trade-oriented capitalism. However, Confucian inner-worldliness is not linked to asceticism, and the actively oriented asceticism of Jainism ultimately leads away from the social order. It is no accident that neither case led to a religious *mastery* of the world. Confucianism favored world adjustment, and Jainism ultimately world indifference and even world flight, as has been true of all radical Asian religions of salvation. Confucianism not only lacked the ascetic method, its inner-worldliness was also related to a considerable weakening of cosmocentric dualism: the world appears as the best of all possible worlds and man "as by nature ethically good" and therefore "perfectible without limit." Hence, the motivation for rejecting the world is greatly reduced. The road to salvation consists in "adjustment to the eternal, supra-divine order of the world, the Tao," and in "filial obedience to the constituted order of the secular power."[79] By contrast, Jainism adheres to cosmocentric dualism without qualification and even develops an activist asceticism. But its radical rejection of the world prevents any turn toward the world, for this rejection is based on the classical doctrine "that salvation consists in being liberated from the wheel of rebirth and that it is attainable only by detachment from this world of imperfection, from inner-worldly action, and from *karma* attached to action."[80] This led to a considerable degree of ambivalence. Jainist teaching "was contradictory insofar as its highest good of salvation was a mental state attainable only through contemplation, whereas its specific road of salvation was asceticism."[81] Not activist asceticism, but contemplative mysticism would have been adequate for the spiritual goal of Jainism, a combination that is found in early Buddhism. For this reason Buddhism is the polar opposite not only of Confucianism but also of ascetic Protestantism. The historical significance of Buddhism lies in the fact that it pushed world flight to an extreme. A consistent inner-worldly asceticism and, as a consequence, religiously motivated world mastery can come into being only when the basis of salvation is not a supra-divine order but a transcendent creator god, punishing and loving, and when the goal of salvation is not eternal rest but eternal grace, which can be gained through doing god's will in the world, through doing good works. In Asia crucial preconditions for this development were absent, nor could they be brought about by the personalization of the

78. *India*, p. 329 (corrected). 79. *China*, p. 228. 80. *India*, p. 194.
81. *India*, p. 204.

highest divinity and the "occasional instance of the transcendental existence of a personal god."[82] The possibility, inherent in religious-metaphysical dualism, of a religiously motivated world mastery was actualized only in the Near Eastern and Western tradition.

This does not mean, of course, that Western Christianity was characterized only by world mastery. Rather, here too the religious virtuosi were primarily indifferent to the world, but in view of the theocentric basis and goal of salvation, world indifference took on a particular meaning. This becomes clear when we compare the typical form of the Western and Asian monastic ethic. At first sight the ethics show several similarities. As a rule, they both demand poverty and chastity and especially a turning away from worldly affairs. In Asia this can take the extreme form of a classical rule of Jainism that the monk must accept "the obligation of restless wandering from place to place."[83] The monastic ethic requires contemplation *and* asceticism, but the former is predominant in Asia, the latter in the West. However, a decisive difference lies behind these similarities. In Asia the rule "ora et labora," which characterizes the basic orientation of Western monasticism, does not exist. This activist turn is distinctive of Christian asceticism. It requires continuous and hard labor, mental and physical, through which man's natural state may be overcome.[84] This emphasis imparts even to contemplation a basically rational and methodical character. This has helped save Western monasticism from "random world flight and the extremes of self-torture."[85] After its beginnings in antiquity, Christian asceticism developed into work-oriented asceticism in the Middle Ages. Of course, this asceticism remained otherworldly. By contrast, this activist turn of otherworldly asceticism did not come to prevail in Asia. There it remained basically passive. Proving oneself *against* the world and its everyday ethics, but in one case *through* action, and in the other *against* action—these are the two variants of world indifference which might be called overcoming the world (*Weltüberwindung*) and world flight. Just as we should distinguish in the case of action in the world (*Weltformung*) between world adjustment and world mastery, so in the case of world indifference between world flight and overcoming the world.

Thus, our comparison of salvation religions points to four ways of relating to the world: world adjustment, world mastery, world flight and overcoming the world. If we want to describe them formally, we can accept Weber's dimensions with some modification. He gives the basis (or the goal) of salvation a concrete content. I propose to collapse the distinction betwen theocentric and cosmocentric and ascetic and mystical and to translate it into active and passive.[86] Then it becomes decisive whether within a religious-metaphysical world view the goals and paths of salvation favor an active or a passive attitude toward

82. *India*, p. 333.   83. *India*, p. 197.   84. *PE*, p. 158.
85. *PE*, p. 118.   86. Cf. Habermas, *loc. cit.*

the world. Moreover, I propose to retain the distinction between inner-worldly and otherworldly, while adding the dimension of temporality. Then it becomes decisive whether the goals and paths of salvation are primarily related to an orientation toward the present or the future. In this manner we obtain the four relations to the world which we can extract from Weber's sociology of religion. We might want to say that Weber exemplifies the formal relation of world mastery in his study of ascetic Protestantism, of world adjustment in his study of Confucianism, of world flight in his study of Hinduism, and of overcoming the world at least implicitly in his study of ancient Judaism and his remarks on Western monasticism. Whereas in Asia the religious pursuit was for world adjustment and world flight, in the Near East and West it was for overcoming the world and especially for world mastery. This denotes the distinctiveness of Western rationalism and, as a partial consequence of it, of modern Western rationalism. (Cf. Scheme XXIV.)

Scheme XXIV
Typology of Formal Relations to the World

Mode of action Sphere of action	active	passive
inner-worldly	world mastery	world adjustment
otherworldly	overcoming the world	world flight

The religious-metaphysical world view represents a stage of development with a horizon of possibilities of which four directions were selectively used. It is in this sense that we should understand the title Weber gave to the last version of the "Zwischenbetrachtung": "Theory of the Stages and Directions of Religious Rejections of the World."[87] Unintentionally one of these directions promoted depersonalization *(Versachlichung)* in connection with other factors. It had this effect not because of its generality but because of its particularity, not because it enveloped the other directions but because of its selectivity. Therefore, world mastery cannot be considered the highest form within the religious-metaphysical world view. Its developmental success does not vitiate the "rightness" of the other alternatives. Weber's treatment shows the premises which must be respected by a developmental theory based on his research program: this theory must combine the model of stages with that of alternatives.

Up to now we have not yet dealt adequately with the question of how world mastery arose in the West and why it was first realized only in ascetic Protes-

87. "Theory," p. 323.

tantism, apart from some medieval antecedents. In order to answer this question, we must uncover further aspects of the conceptual structure which played a role in Weber's comparative studies of the salvation religions. These aspects concern the intra-cultural, not the inter-cultural comparison. We must now deal not with the distinctiveness of the Western in comparison with the Asian tradition but with that of ascetic Protestantism in comparison with Western monasticism, Catholicism and Lutheranism. According to Weber, only the Reformation, by turning to ascetic Protestantism, provided the potential for the transition to modernity on the level of evaluative symbolism.

The Cultural Significance of Ascetic Protestantism: A Comparison of Salvation Movements During the Reformation

A first indication for the dimensions Weber had in mind can be gleaned from Ernst Troeltsch's *The Social Teaching of the Christian Churches*, which Weber influenced, but which also seems to have helped him understand the history of Christian ethics. According to Troeltsch, the gospel is based on the idea of a "Holy Divine Will of Love." The gospel has two sides, what Troeltsch calls an absolute individualism and an absolute universalism. It is individualist insofar as every person is called upon to follow God and be his child and can follow this call "only through self-abnegation in unconditional obedience to the Holy Will of God." The gospel is universalist insofar as those who abnegate themselves in this manner constitute an absolute "fellowship of love among those who are united in God; from this springs an active realization of the love of God even towards strangers and enemies, because only through the revelation of absolute love can a true understanding of God be awakened and the way opened to Him."[88] This universalism of love, which is expressed in the demand for brotherhood and the love of one's neighbor, is originally understood in terms of a religious aristocracy: "Nothing was further from Jesus' mind than the notion of the universalism of divine grace" (632). This universalism is impeded by the tremendous requirements which Jesus' ethic makes upon the believer, but also by the eschatological expectations. Nevertheless, in principle all people can be part of the fellowship of God, if they only make a turnabout and unconditionally submit to the divine commandment of love. This dual character of the gospel was elaborated in two independent directions during the development of Western Christianity: the idea of universal salvation, made possible by the gospel, in the form of the Christian church; and the idea of self-sacrifice, demanded by the gospel, as a personal achievement in a "fellowship of saints," a community of religious virtuosi, a sect. Whereas the church universalizes the idea of grace and

88. Troeltsch, *op. cit.*, pp. 55ff.

treats it objectively, the sect particularized it and treats it subjectively. On the one hand, there is "the objective impartation of grace through the sacraments" to all, on the other the personal achievement of sanctification by a few.[89] Thus, the Christian church and sect appear as two equal ways of realizing the basic idea of the gospel. They have a dialectical relationship which reaches its high point in the Reformation. Troeltsch summarizes his view of the potential for church and sect formation inherent in the gospel in these words: "The Church administers the sacraments without reference to the personal worthiness of the priests; the sect distrusts the ecclesiastical sacraments, and either permits them to be administered by laymen, or makes them dependent upon the personal character of the celebrant, or even discards them altogether. The individualism of the sect urges it towards the direct intercourse of the individual with God; frequently, therefore, it replaces the ecclesiastical doctrine of the sacraments by the Primitive Christian doctrine of the Spirit and by 'enthusiasm.' The Church has its priests and its sacraments; it dominates the world and is therefore also dominated by the world. The sect is lay Christianity, independent of the world, and is therefore inclined towards asceticism and mysticism. Both these tendencies are based upon fundamental impulses of the gospel. The gospel contains the idea of an objective possession of salvation in the knowledge and revelation of God, and in developing this idea it becomes the Church. It contains, however, also the idea of an absolute personal religion and of an absolute personal fellowship, and in following out this idea it becomes a sect."[90]

In Troeltsch's view, Augustine conceived the idea of the Christian church and Gregory VII expanded it decisively. The Reformation was a reaction to the church that had emerged from the Gregorian Reform, and it also reacted by forming sects. Gregory VII aimed at a monocratic organization of the church and at subordinating political authority to hierocratic authority in all matters religious. Thus, he aimed at the monopoly of psychic coercion by combining "the unity and autonomy of the church and the penetration of humanity with sacramental grace."[91] In ideal-typical terms, the medieval church is a universalist institution of grace. Its domination over believers rests ultimately on the fact that the priests hold the power of the keys and have the authority to dispense the sacraments. The dogma of the infusion of grace through the seven sacraments is central to ecclesiastical salvation. However, this priestly sacramentalism partially undermines the tremendous tension inherent in theocentric dualism. For "the sacraments are the extension of the Incarnation, a repetition of the spiritual process through which Divine grace enters into human life."[92] The sacraments also manifest the miracle-working power of the church. An institution which mediates between the divine and the human through miracles is charismatic in Weber's sense.

89. *Op. cit.*, p. 339ff.　　90. *Op. cit.*, p. 342.　　91. *Op. cit.*, p. 234.
92. *Loc. cit.*

Thus, the sacraments perpetuate the miracle of transubstantiation; it is accomplished by priests. Therefore, Weber tends to classify the medieval Catholic priest as a magician.[93] However, this is not a sufficient description. Catholic sacramentalism must not be misinterpreted as mere magic, as Troeltsch pointed out. The Christian view of salvation imparts to the ecclesiastical sacraments a tendency toward an ethical guidance of the believer's actions. This is evident, among other things, from the fact that "the Sacrament of Penance, which is conceived in an entirely ethical spirit," becomes in practice "the main sacrament . . . together with the Mass."[94] Weber too classifies the medieval Catholic ethic as an ethic of conviction[95] and distinguishes between magic and miracle. In contrast to magic, a miracle is "always viewed as an act of some sort of rational divine guidance, as a divine dispensation of grace."[96] However, Weber also believes that the miracle of the sacraments did not further "the elimination of magic as a means of salvation,"[97] and that this was one of the reasons for the absence, on the part of the Catholic laity, of a consistent ethical systematization of conduct and of good works. Hence, with the help of the sacramental miracle, which is performed by the priests, the medieval church interposes itself in the ethical relationship between the transcendental creator god and human beings. The miracle serves as a means of compensation, especially for those who have low religious qualification. Insofar as average believers are willing to repent their sins, to do penance, to shoulder temporally limited penalties and do single good works, the miracle mitigates their anxiety about salvation. It is true that average believers, too, want to be certain of their salvation, just like the virtuosi, and have recurrent anxieties. But the church can always offer the certainty of forgiveness. This weakens the tremendous emphasis which "the soteriology of the Western doctrine of the beyond placed upon the short span of this life."[98] The transformation of the Christian idea into an office-charismatic institution, into which human beings are born and which administers equally to the just and the unjust, permits at least to the Catholic laity a tolerable religious life, with its "very human cycle of sin, repentance, atonement, release, followed by sin."[99]

The ingenious invention of medieval Catholicism, however, the church as an office-charismatic institution of grace, could not satisfy two demands: the demand of the religious virtuosi to establish an exclusive "community of saints" which visibly separates those religiously qualified from those who are not, and the individual's demand for a direct relationship to God. The first demand was opposed by the church's universalism of grace, the second by the priesthood's sacramentalism. If we accept Troeltsch's argument, both demands were founded on the gospel. The first was indeed raised and satisfied in medieval monasticism and the medieval orders. This did not undermine the church's uni-

93. *PE*, p. 117.   94. Troeltsch, *loc. cit.*   95. *PE*, p. 116.
96. *India*, p. 335.   97. *PE*, p. 117.   98. *India*, p. 332.   99. *PE*, p. 117.

tary culture *(kirchliche Einheitskultur)*, but only differentiated it. The second demand was put forth and realized ultimately in the Reformation, and this time the church's unitary culture was destroyed. The Reformation's individualism attacked the core of the office-charismatic institution, its sacramental doctrines and practices. However, both demands were consistently fused only when the Reformation turned into ascetic Protestantism. Herein lies the latter's distinctiveness, from an intra-cultural perspective. It took over the exclusiveness of medieval monasticism, but rejected at the same time the belief in the sacraments: "This, the complete elimination of salvation through the Church and the sacraments (which Lutheranism by no means developed to its final conclusions), was what formed the absolutely decisive diffence from Catholicism."[100] It is true that Calvinism, in contrast to the other movements of ascetic Protestantism, retained the church organization and thus univeralism. However, the church was no longer a "vehicle of grace but a scourge" (1199). Not only the just but the unjust must be subjected to it for the greater glory of God. With the help of the theodicy of predestination[101] the Calvinists availed themselves of the particularism of grace typical of the sect. Therefore, Weber asserts that the Calvinist church is spiritually akin to the sect. There are two features which unite the various currents of ascetic Protestantism in spite of all differences in dogma and organization— the particularism of grace and the complete devaluation of sacramental grace, more generally, of all external means of salvation. Absolute individualism with its subjectivism of grace takes the place of the absolute universalism of the medieval Catholic church with its objectivism of grace. What counts is only "conduct according to God's commandment, and this only on the basis of a sanctified attitude."[102] In ideal-typical terms, the Protestant sect is a particularist association of those religiously qualified. Members are not born into it; they can be admitted only by virtue of personal religious achievement. It is a "visible community of saints" (1204), whose domination over the faithful rests ultimately on the belief that it is "immediate to God," and on the demand for every member's self-sacrifice and unswerving obedience to God's will. What the Donatists began in the controversy with Augustine's church, ascetic Protestantism carried to its conclusion in the conflict with the post-Gregorian church. Thus, the Catholic church and the Protestant sect represent two Christian ideas with regard to both belief and organization. Not only the interpretation of the grounds and means of salvation but also of its organization—universalist versus

100. *PE*, p. 104f.

101. On the merely relative importance of the doctrine of predestination see Rainer Döbert, "Methodologische und forschungsstrategische Implikationen von evolutionstheoretischen Stadienmodellen" in U. Jaeggi and A. Honneth, eds., *Theorien des Historischen Materialismus, op. cit.*, pp. 544ff. Weber explicitly distinguishes between the Predestinarians and the Baptists, but labels both ascetic Protestants, because they devalue, for different reasons, the sacraments as means of salvation. Cf. *PE*, p. 146f.

102. *China*, p. 227.

particularist—are polar opposites. For the Protestant reformers the degree of religious regulation of life did not go far enough. Ascetic Protestantism demanded of the laity what Catholicism at most expected of the monk and, less so, of the priest: "The church never dared to demand the self-control, asceticism and ecclesiastical discipline that the great ideological opponents of the papacy, the Anabaptists and the related sects, imposed upon themselves, to a degree sheerly incomprehensible for us today" (1197).

We can now specify Weber's dimensions for comparing the most important salvation currents from the early Middle Ages to the Reformation: grounds and means of salvation, on one hand, and organization of salvation on the other. The Christian idea can be interpreted in terms either of a grant and objective sacramentalism or of a commandment and personal sanctification; it can be organized either in universalist or particularist terms. One combination results in the church, the other in the sect. However, these combinations are not exclusive. Historically, there has been a church without sacramentalism as well as a sect with the belief in sacramental grace. The first case is represented by Calvinism, the second by Western monasticism. Ecclesiastical Calvinism recognizes sacraments, but "though they have been ordained by God for the increase of His glory, and must hence be scrupulously observed, they are not a means to the attainment of grace, but only the subjective *externa subsidia* of faith."[103] Western monasticism constitutes a community of saints and an aristocracy of religious virtuosi, but ultimately it does not deny the belief in sacramental grace. It retains what is for Weber the most sublime form of magic, the institutionalized miracle. Lutheranism stands, so to speak, between the Catholic and the Calvinist church. It opposes the former's priestly sacramentalism, but does not completely abandon the idea of sacramental grace. Only in Calvinism and Baptism is sacramental grace completely devalued in favor of a spiritual attitude and personal sanctification. With this spiritual turn ascetic Protestantism carried "the religious disenchantment of the world to its ultimate conclusion."[104] (Cf. Scheme XXV.)

In Weber's view, ascetic Protestantism combines five characteristics which up to the Reformation no other salvation movement had successfully fused in Asia or the West: theocentrism, asceticism, inner-worldliness, personal sanctification and virtuosity. Only this combination produces the religious motivation for world mastery. This combination is buttressed internally by the content of salvation and externally by the particularist organization, which is instrumentalized as a "scourge." Compared to Catholic religious culture, ascetic Protestantism intensifies the religious control and regulation of life. It tolerates neither the peaceful coexistence of monastic, priestly and lay ethic nor that of religion, politics and economics. Ascetic Protestantism aims at a unified ethic

103. *PE,* p. 104.

104. *PE,* p. 147. Weber attributes this achievement not to Calvinism but to the Baptist sects. The passage was inserted in 1920.

Scheme XXV

Comparison of Selected Salvation Movements during the Reformation

Organizational criterion of salvation / Means of salvation	Ascriptive	Achieved
Priestly and sacramental	Catholic church	Catholic orders
Spiritual	Lutheran church	Ascetic Protestantism

and ultimately at the total subordination of the most important spheres of life. None of them is accorded any autonomy. The divine will alone counts. The world must comply with it; it becomes the means for a religious purpose. When Weber speaks of the disenchantment of the world, he means that it has lost any inherent value before God and thus can become the object of God's will, which is fulfilled by the religious virtuosi.

Ascetic Protestantism, then, formulates for the laity a virtuoso ethic that appears inhuman from the viewpoint of the common Catholic believer. It exacerbates the tensions rooted in theocentric dualism. Significantly, its absolute individualism does not lead back to the love community of early Christianity. In its most consistent form, it permits the idea that believers are God's children but not that they are a fellowship in god. Weber illustrates this with the Calvinist doctrine of predestination. Its basis is not "the father in heaven of the New Testament, who rejoices over the repentance of a sinner," but the harsh transcendental God of the Old Testament who shows no human understanding and is beyond human comprehension. There is an "unbridgeable gulf" between him and all human beings, who must subject themselves blindly to him and act upon his decrees for his sake, for his greater glory, without considering the consequences to themselves and others.[105] Human fate has been decided from eternity: "God's grace is, since His decrees cannot change, as impossible for those to whom He has granted it to lose as it is unattainable for those to whom He has denied it."[106]

This absolute individualism does not even permit a "community of the church based on love." Rather, it completely eradicates all elements of brotherly love which had been part of the Christian ethic from its very beginning. Not only the individual, but also the community of saints is primarily a means for God's glory, and this is true not only of religious but also of nonreligious relationships, which lose their natural or social value. Therefore, consistent Calvinism has had

105. Cf. *PE*, p. 103.   106. *PE*, p. 104.

above all two consequences: the inner loneliness of the individual and the treatment of 'brothers' as 'others.'[107]

We can say, then, that the religious ethic of ascetic Protestantism is a *monologic* ethic of conviction with *unbrotherly* consequences. Exactly herein lies its developmental potential. This ethic not only places the relationship of human beings to God above their relations to one another—as does all consistent Christian religion—it also provides a new meaning to this relationship by no longer interpreting it in terms of filial piety. Thus, it creates a motivation for depersonalizing first religious and then nonreligious human relationships. This reenforces the tendency of the patrimonial order toward the formalization of law, bureaucratization and the extension of the market principle.

We can clarify this thesis by referring to a study by Robert Bellah. He has compared the symbolism of father and son in Christianity and Confucianism,[108] and found a paradox: In Christianity this symbolism, and not the natural family, plays a central role in the religion, whereas the matter is reversed in Confucianism. Bellah relates this difference to the two notions of the divine, the personal god versus the impersonal deity. Yahwe is a personal god, who can be appropriately described in terms of paternal symbolism. However, he is not a familial god, but the god of a political association. When Christianity dramatized Jesus as the son of God, it gave a great impetus to the father-son symbolism, but in a setting in which the religious and the family order had already been differentiated to a significant extent. By contrast, the Tao refers to the cosmic harmony of heaven, earth and man, and here the father-son symbolism is not suitable. Instead, an organic symbolism appears appropriate. At the same time, however, the religious and the family sphere largely coincide within the institutional order. The natural family is a "holy family"; the basis of religious life is the family and ancestor cult. Hence, whereas in the Near Eastern and Western tradition religion and family are represented by the same kind of symbolism but are institutionally differentiated, in China they overlap institutionally but are symbolically differentiated. This explains why the Christian ethic tends to devalue the actual (familial) relation of personal subordination in spite of its symbolism, whereas the Confucian ethic tends to glorify this relation in spite of its organic symbolism. The Christian ethic recognizes the injunction that we must obey God more than man, the heavenly father more than the natural father, and in addition it has supported the maxim institutionally by separating the religious sphere first from the family and then from the other institutional realms.

This differentiation occurred in the context of a traditionalist and patrimonial configuration, the guiding principle of which was filial piety and personal loyalty. I suspect that this differentiation was facilitated by the filial symbolism

107. *Loc. cit.*

108. See Robert Bellah, "Father and Son in Christianity and Confucianism," *Beyond Belief* (New York: Basic Books, 1970), pp. 76-97.

of the religious order. As long as it coincided with the symbolic universe which was defined by the same guiding principle, the institutional autonomy of the religious order could be greatly advanced. This seems to have happened in the medieval West. Here a high degree of symbolic integration was combined with a high degree of institutional differentiation. But once the symbolic unity was shattered, a developmental dynamic was bound to be set free. This break seems to have occurred with the Reformation's turn to ascetic Protestantism. The result was a radicalization of the view that God must be obeyed more than man. This was directed against all extant social orders and formulated in a manner that undermined even the symbolic universe of filial piety. The God whom human beings must obey was no longer the kind father in heaven, but an abstract law imposed from eternity.

This concludes our investigation of Weber's attempt to explain historically the transition to Western modernity. We have ascertained that Weber seeks to establish the distinctiveness of ascetic Protestantism and its causal significance for the rise of modern Western rationalism. In order to identify this distinctiveness, he must compare religious salvation movements in inter- and intra-cultural terms. Five dimensions of salvation are of particular importance: its basis, method, sphere, means and organization. A salvation religion can be either theocentric or cosmocentric, ascetic or mystical, inner-worldly or otherworldly, magical or spiritual, universalist or particularist. Depending on the combination of characteristics it realizes, a salvation religion tends either to world mastery, overcoming the world, world adjustment or world flight. Ascetic Protestantism is theocentric, ascetic, inner-worldly, spiritual and particularist. In this combination it stands largely alone, and herein lies its historical peculiarity: "Only ascetic Protestantism completely eliminated magic and the supernatural quest for salvation, of which the highest form was intellectualist, contemplative illumination. It alone created the religious motivation for seeking salvation primarily through immersion in one's worldly vocation" (630). We can ascribe causal significance to this basic orientation for the rise of Western modernity, a vocational culture that is based on world mastery. This relationship to the world had to be invented, and this again was not possible, given the religious-metaphysical world view, without an input from salvation religion. This input was provided by ascetic Protestantism. It enabled a group of religious virtuosi, who originated largely in "bourgeois circles" (1197), to overcome the psychological barriers which the guiding principle of personal loyalty put in the way of depersonalizing man's relationship to the natural and social world. This contribution of ascetic Protestantism influenced at first predominantly the conduct of religious virtuosi. It affected neither the masses nor the cognitive symbolism nor the institutional principle which had to be pushed through in the transition to Western modernity. At least in institutional respects, ascetic Protestantism was even a step backward from the level reached by the West. Its ethical contribution, too, remained ultimately oriented toward the Catholic ethic of conviction.

Ascetic Protestantism arose as an historical reaction to it. Thus, if the transition to modernity would probably have taken a different course *without* ascetic Protestantism, it was not brought about by it alone. Other factors had to come into play to which we must also attribute causal significance. This is true not only of the cognitive but especially of the institutional components. Just as the cultural significance of ascetic Protestantism emerges only against the background of the ecclesiastical unitary culture, so did the institutional components arise only against the background of the medieval *Ständestaat*.

Ascetic Protestantism, then, was only one factor in a constellation of factors. Only on the basis of this constellation did the religiously motivated world mastery favored by it attain cultural significance. The formalization of law, bureaucratization and the extension of the market economy were as important as the religious disenchantment of the world. All of them were causally important partial processes. All of them had an autonomous dynamic. Only their combination could bring about—unintentionally— the great transformation. This transformation brought into being a world which soon followed its own laws. However, even in its mechanized and spiritless manifestations, the autonomous vocational culture of Western modernity reveals the remnants of the religious elements which helped bring about its birth. They continue to haunt us in the secularized attitude of world mastery and the world domination of impersonality and lack of brotherhood.

VII

CONCLUSION

My purpose has been to elucidate the philosophical background and substantive content of Max Weber's sociology as a developmental history of the West and to apply this theoretical framework to the specific historical problem of the Reformation's role in the transition to modernity. I have followed Weber's way of posing the problem, but not always his solution. I had to go beyond him to later theoretical orientations, especially to some contemporary neo-evolutionary approaches in sociology. But I wanted to improve his own approach and not leave it behind. My basic assumption has been that Weber's research program retains viability even in the face of these new kinds of evolutionary theory. I adopted his own but neglected notion of developmental history and tried to show that it amounted neither to a mere stage theory nor an inclusive typology—in part against some of his own formulations. Weber's developmental history contrasts one cultural tradition with others for the sake of identifying its distinctiveness and its specific historical course. Such a directional analysis must select a value position that is intrinsic to this cultural tradition but also points beyond it. This value position guides an ideal-typical construct of development, which involves a sequence of basic social configurations and their historical variants.

Following an observation by Guenther Roth, we can discover three kinds and levels of analysis in Weber's work: configurational analysis, which employs typological, "socio-historical" models; situational or constellation analysis, which is primarily descriptive; and historical or developmental analysis, which works with secular theories.[1] This observation can be translated into the terms of our explication. It is also linked to Weber's view that sociology treats typical action series, while history deals with fateful individual sequences of action. Configurational analysis is concerned primarily with typical actions, situational analysis with individual ones. They should be utilized together. Configurational analysis is primarily structural analysis; it investigates the range of actions a

1. Cf. Bendix and Roth, *op. cit.*, Chs. VI and XIII; Roth and Schluchter, *op. cit.*, Ch. III and Epilogue.

social order provides. Situational analysis is primarily concerned with events; it shows how this range of possibilities was actually utilized. Therefore, we can argue that sociology must be historically oriented and history sociologically, but we cannot assert a hierarchy between the two or advocate a reduction of one to the other. Both are necessary perspectives, for they are tied to the nature of historical subject matter. However, it is also in the nature of historical subject matter that it demands not only configurational and situational analysis but ultimately a directional analysis. Only from a developmental perspective can we establish which individual actions have *fateful* consequences for basic social configurations. Only in this manner can we separate events that transcend a given structure from those that preserve it, events that lead to a transformation from those that remain within the range of a given structure. Such directional analyses constitute the subject matter of developmental histories. They rest, so to speak, on the other kinds of analysis and must retain the same categorical framework—that of a realistic theory of action that concerns "itself with the interpretive understanding of social action and thereby with a causal explanation of its course and consequence" (4).

Developmental history remains rooted in a theory of action and advances only heuristic claims on the level of developmental logic. It deals primarily with ideal-typical sequences of world views and of institutional differentiation. These provide at the same time the framework for the analysis of alternatives and aid the causal attribution of culturally significant phenomena. They make possible periodizations, provide criteria for diachronic and synchronic comparisons and link configurational and situational analyses. Developmental analysis must treat order and action, structural history and history of events, as two aspects of the same historical reality. Above all, however, it must abandon all open or hidden claims for analyzing the historical totality. Thus developmental history adheres to a philosophical creed that Georg Simmel formulated in an exemplary manner: "We cannot describe the individual phenomenon as it really was, because we cannot describe the whole. A science of everything that happens is impossible not only for reasons of unmanageable quantity; it is also impossible because it would lack a point of view—a requirement for producing a construct that would satisfy our criteria for knowledge. There is no Knowledge per se. Knowledge is possible only insofar as it is produced and structured by concepts that are qualitatively determined and inevitably partial and biased. If the criterion for knowledge is that it be perfectly general, it would be impossible to identify or distinguish any element of reality. This is the deeper reason why there are only histories, but no History per se. What we call general or world history can at best be the simultaneous application of a variety of these diverse viewpoints or it may be the sort of history that throws into relief the aspects of the event that are most significant from the perspective of our sense of values."[2]

2. Georg Simmel, *The Problems of the Philosophy of History*, tr. and ed. Guy Oakes (New York: Free Press, 1977), p. 82f.

Index of Authors

Index